NEW INTERNATIONAL BIBLICAL COMMENTARY

New Testament Editor,
W. Ward Gasque

REVELATION

New Testament Series

NEW INTERNATIONAL BIBLICAL COMMENTARY

REVELATION

ROBERT W. WALL

Based on the New International Version

paternoster press

Revelation
© 1991 Hendrickson Publishers, Inc.
P. O. Box 3473
Peabody, Massachusetts 01961-3473
U.S.A.

Original Hendrickson Publishers edition 1991. First published jointly, 1995, in the United States by Hendrickson Publishers, and in the United Kingdom by the Paternoster Press.

Paternoster is an imprint of Authentic Media,
9 Holdom Avenue, Bletchley, Milton Keynes, MK1 1QR, UK
1820 Jet Stream Drive, Colorado Springs, CO 80921, USA
OM Authentic Media, Medchal Road, Jeedimetla Village,
Secunderabad 500 055, A.P., India
www.authenticmedia.co.uk
Authentic Media is a division of IBS-STL UK, a company limited by guarantee (registered charity no. 270162).

Printed in the United States of America

Sixth printing — December 2008

Library of Congress Cataloging-in-Publication Data

Wall, Robert W.
    Revelation   /   Robert W. Wall.
        (New International biblical commentary; 18)
        Includes bibliographical references and indexes.
        1. Bible. N.T.   Revelation — Commentaries.   I. Title.
    II. Series.
    BS2825.3.W29   1991
    228'.077 — dc20   91-32871
                                                                  CIP

ISBN 978-0-943575-49-0 (U.S. softcover)

British Library Cataloguing in Publication Data

Wall, Robert W.
    Revelation. — (New International Biblical Commentary Series;
    Vol. 18)
    I. Title.   II. Series
    228.07

ISBN 978-0-85364-672-3 (U.K. softcover)

Table of Contents

Foreword
New International Biblical Commentary

Although it does not appear on the standard best-seller lists, the Bible continues to outsell all other books. And in spite of growing secularism in the West, there are no signs that interest in its message is abating. Quite to the contrary, more and more men and women are turning to its pages for insight and guidance in the midst of the ever-increasing complexity of modern life.

This renewed interest in Scripture is found both outside and inside the church. It is found among people in Asia and Africa as well as in Europe and North America; indeed, as one moves outside of the traditionally Christian countries, interest in the Bible seems to quicken. Believers associated with the traditional Catholic and Protestant churches manifest the same eagerness for the Word that is found in the newer evangelical churches and fellowships.

We wish to encourage and, indeed, strengthen this worldwide movement of lay Bible study by offering this new commentary series. Although we hope that pastors and teachers will find these volumes helpful in both understanding and communicating the Word of God, we do not write primarily for them. Our aim is to provide for the benefit of every Bible reader reliable guides to the books of the Bible—representing the best of contemporary scholarship presented in a form that does not require formal theological education to understand.

The conviction of editor and authors alike is that the Bible belongs to the people and not merely to the academy. The message of the Bible is too important to be locked up in erudite and esoteric essays and monographs written only for the eyes of theological specialists. Although exact scholarship has its place in the service of Christ, those who share in the teaching office of the church have a responsibility to make the results of their research accessible to the Christian community at large. Thus, the Bible scholars who join in the presentation of this series write with these broader concerns in view.

A wide range of modern translations is available to the contemporary Bible student. Most of them are very good and much to be preferred—for understanding, if not always for beauty—to the older King James Version (the so-called Authorized Version of the Bible). The Revised Standard Version has become the standard English translation in many seminaries and colleges and represents the best of modern Protestant scholarship. It is also available in a slightly altered "common Bible" edition with the Catholic imprimatur, and a third revised edition is due out shortly. In addition, the New American Bible is a fresh translation that represents the best of post-Vatican II Roman Catholic biblical scholarship and is in a more contemporary idiom than that of the RSV.

The New Jerusalem Bible, based on the work of French Catholic scholars but vividly rendered into English by a team of British translators, is perhaps the most literary of the recent translations, while the New English Bible is a monument to modern British Protestant research. The Good News Bible is probably the most accessible translation for the person who has little exposure to the Christian tradition or who speaks and reads English as a second language. Each of these is, in its own way, excellent and will be consulted with profit by the serious student of Scripture. Perhaps most will wish to have several versions to read, both for variety and for clarity of understanding—though it should be pointed out that no one of them is by any means flawless or to be received as the last word on any given point. Otherwise, there would be no need for a commentary series like this one!

We have chosen to use the New International Version as the basis for this series, not because it is necessarily the best translation available but because it is becoming increasingly used by lay Bible students and pastors. It is the product of an international team of "evangelical" Bible scholars who have sought to translate the Hebrew and Greek documents of the original into "clear and natural English . . . idiomatic [and] . . . contemporary but not dated," suitable for "young and old, highly educated and less well educated, ministers and laymen [*sic*]." As the translators themselves confess in their preface, this version is not perfect. However, it is as good as any of the others mentioned above and more popular than most of them.

Each volume will contain an introductory chapter detailing the background of the book and its author, important themes, and other helpful information. Then, each section of the book will be expounded as a whole, accompanied by a series of notes on items in the text that need further clarification or more detailed explanation. Appended to the end of each volume will be a bibliographical guide for further study.

Our new series is offered with the prayer that it may be an instrument of authentic renewal and advancement in the worldwide Christian community and a means of commending the faith of the people who lived in biblical times and of those who seek to live by the Bible today.

W. WARD GASQUE

Preface

No writing of any commentary is a private project—especially writing one on John's Revelation. Not only have I depended upon the work of many other scholars, I have benefitted enormously from four conversation partners. Two of these partners are Mercer Island Presbyterian Church and First Covenant Church, both in Seattle, where I taught the book of Revelation to adult classes of mature believers during the past year. Their hard questions and perceptive comments during our study together forced me to relate Revelation's message to everyday life in practical ways. If I have succeeded at all in providing readers with a "sensible" commentary on Revelation, it is a debt I owe in part to them.

Two other conversation partners are classes of students, one graduate and the other undergraduate, whose completed assignments and class discussions were stimulating and enriching. No doubt my students will claim the best parts of this commentary for themselves, finding here the precipitates of new insights that were jointly achieved by shared research and reflection upon the biblical text. Teachers everywhere depend upon their students for those ideas that focus their scholarship, and they draw from their students the required energy and excitement to see their work to completion.

I am indebted as well to the dean of the School of Religion at Seattle Pacific University, Dr. William L. Lane, and to my other colleague in New Testament, Dr. Eugene E. Lemcio, for their help during this project. Sitting in with Gene's class in Apocalyptic Literature in the spring of 1989 provided a stimulating reintroduction to Revelation, and Bill's unfailing support both spiritually and intellectually provides a gracious setting in which to work as scholars for the church. Thanks are also due Mr. Patrick Alexander, Academic Editor of Hendrickson Publishers, for his helpful suggestions and steadfast encouragement throughout the preparation of this commentary.

I am most thankful to God for Carla, my dearest friend and spiritual mentor. Without her love and wisdom, I would certainly fail more than I do to know God's gospel and to find it in our shared life and common faith. Even though she was not directly involved in editing this commentary (as she has been in much of my other work), the maturity I absorb from her as her husband has no doubt produced a better work.

Finally, this commentary is dedicated to my beloved parents, Elizabeth E. and Robert R. Wall. Not only did they lead me as a young lad into God's salvation by their teaching, and keep me there through my youth by their example, Dad was the first to call my attention to the power and importance of Revelation's message for today. His life-long interest in the prophetic books of Scripture was passed on to me, my two sisters, and my Mom around the dining room table, and it now has born some fruit—although still too meager for its source—in this commentary.

Robert W. Wall
Lent, 1991

Abbreviations

AB	Anchor Bible
ACNT	Augsburg Commentary on the New Testament
ATR	*Anglican Theological Review*
AUMSR	Andrews University Monograph Series in Religion
AUSDDS	Andrews University Seminary Doctoral Dissertation Series
AUSS	*Andrews University Seminary Studies*
BETL	Bibliotheca ephemeridum theologicarum lovaniensium
BGBE	Beitrage zur Geschichte der biblischen Exegese
Bib	*Biblica*
BibLeb	Bibel und Leben
BibSac	*Bibliotheca Sacra*
BJRL	*Bulletin of the John Rylands University Library of Manchester*
BTB	*Biblical Theology Bulletin*
CBQ	*Catholic Biblical Quarterly*
cf.	compare
CQR	*Church Quarterly Review*
CSR	*Christian Scholars Review*
CurrTM	*Currents in Theology and Mission*
EQ	*Evangelical Quarterly*
ET	English Translation
ExpT	*Expository Times*
Gk.	Greek
GorR	Gordon Review
HNTC	Harper's New Testament Commentary Series
HorBT	Horizons in Biblical Theology
IBT	Interpreting Biblical Texts
ICC	International Critical Commentary

IDBSup	Supplementary volume to G. A. Buttrick, ed., *Interpreter's Dictionary of the Bible*
Iliff R	Iliff Reporter
Interp	*Interpretation*
ITQ	*Irish Theological Quarterly*
JB	The Jerusalem Bible
JBL	*Journal of Biblical Literature*
JETS	*Journal of the Evangelical Theological Society*
JR	*Journal of Religion*
JSNT	*Journal for the Study of the New Testament*
JSNTSup	Journal for the Study of the New Testament—Supplement series
JSOT	*Journal for the Study of the Old Testament*
JTS	*Journal of Theological Studies*
KNT	Kommentar zum Neuen Testament, ed. T. Zahn, Leipzig
KPG	Knox Preaching Guides
LXX	Septuagint (pre-Christian Gk. translation of the OT)
MeyerK	Meyer Kritisch-exegetischer Kommentar über das Neue Testament
MNTC	Moffatt New Testament Commentary
NA[26]	Nestle-Aland *Novum Testamentum*, 26th ed. (1979)
NCB	New Century Bible NFTL, New Frontiers in Theology Library
NICNT	New International Commentary on the New Testament
NIGTC	New International Greek Testament Commentary
NIV	New International Version
NovT	*Novum Testamentum*
NRT	*La nouvelle revue théologique*
NT	New Testament
NTD	Das Neue Testament Deutsch
NTM	New Testament Message (series)
NTS	*New Testament Studies*
OT	Old Testament
OTL	Old Testament Library

PC	Proclamation Commentary
RefJ	*Reformed Journal*
RevExp	*Review and Expositor*
RHPR	*Revue d'histoire et de philosophie religieuses*
RQ	*Restoration Quarterly*
RSV	Revised Standard Version
SBLSemPap	Society of Biblical Literature Seminar Papers
SBT	Studies in Biblical Theology
SJT	*Scottish Journal of Theology*
SNT	*Studien zum Neuen Testament*
SNTSMS	Society of New Testament Studies Monograph Series
TCGNT	B. Metzger, *A Textual Commentary on the Greek New Testament* (UBS, 1971)
TDNT	G. Kittel and G. Friedrich, eds., *Theological Dictionary of the New Testament*, trans. G. W. Bromiley (1964–72)
THKNT	Theologischer Handkommentar zum Neuen Testament
TNTC	Tyndale New Testament Commentary
TS	*Theological Studies*
TU	Texte und Untersuchungen (series)
TynB	*Tyndale Bulletin*
TZ	*Theologische Zeitschrift*
VT	*Vetus Testamentum*
WBC	Word Biblical Commentaries
WTJ	*Westminster Theological Journal*
ZAW	*Zeitschrift für die alttestamentliche Wissenschaft*
ZNW	*Zeitschrift für die neutestamentliche Wissenschaft*

Introduction

The purpose of this series is to produce commentaries for students and for pastors and their parishes. The technical discussions of biblical scholarship have been considered but not included in this commentary. Of primary interest is the relationship of what St. John of Patmos wrote some two millennia ago with today's church—a somewhat presumptuous interest! On the one hand, the interpreter's ability to discern fully what John intended to convey to his first readers is limited by time and place. The variety of historical and literary methods biblical scholars use to reconstruct John's world and the meaning of his Revelation issue important but imperfect results. Especially when interpreting this complex composition, one is wise to draw upon the expertise and insight of many others, past and present, for help and understanding: Charles, Caird, Beasley-Murray, Ladd, Mounce, Schüssler Fiorenza, Morris, Collins, Ford, Boring, Krodel, and still others who belong to this "cloud of witnesses." They are often mentioned in this commentary in gratitude. While this commentary presents a distinctive perspective on the meaning of Revelation for today, many other perspectives are consulted in search of the text's full meaning. The interpreter is well advised to use a number of commentaries on Revelation and to draw upon other studies that treat more specific aspects of John's composition.

On the other hand, the interpreter presumes to know something about the situation of today's church. Especially this commentary, written by a believer, is written for the church. The questions asked of Revelation address those concerns which are meaningful to God's people. Indeed, John's emphasis on worship both in heaven and on earth commends his work to the worshiping community. Further, he writes as a pastor to nurture a people-at-worship, a community-at-faith. He did not write an esoteric thesis, ciphered only by academics with proper credentials and requisite skills. The point is that Revelation was written by John for the church; the ongoing interpretation of Revelation must continue to make sense of what John wrote in ways which address the concerns of the church.

Of course, the greatest danger facing the student of Scripture is provincialism—finding only those meanings in biblical texts which justify what one already believes and values. In my case, interpretations of biblical texts can easily become too American, too middle class, too male, and too irrelevant for many believers. Therefore, my confidence must reside in the continuing community of interpreters, where one interpretation of Revelation checks and balances another. Further, insofar as these partners-in-dialogue are believers, God's Spirit points the Christian community to meanings which nurture and challenge life and faith. In fact, at the very center of Revelation the good interpreter will always find the simple (*not* simplistic!) gospel of God. In this way, any interpretation worthy of the gospel will bear witness to the slain, yet exalted, Lamb through whom the salvation of God breaks into and radically transforms those who depend upon his dependable work; it will celebrate the triumph of God's kingdom, which is already realized in the Lamb's shed blood and which will be fully realized at his return.

General Considerations

The status of Revelation within the church has always been somewhat marginal. Most believers feel threatened by this book of visions; its apocalyptic language seems strange and its language of harsh judgment too violent for a loving God. The church's natural response to Revelation is to neglect it or dismiss it as irrelevant. More conservative believers, who have always recognized the importance of Revelation, scrutinize its visions as the prediction of a declining culture and its imminent destruction. Regrettably, their interpretations are often colored by religious fanaticism or ideological rhetoric, which only heightens the suspicion of others concerning the book's usefulness in forming a people who love God and neighbor.

In recent years, perhaps stimulated by the popularity of books like Hal Lindsey's *The Late Great Planet Earth*, mainstream Christianity has become more interested in the study of Revelation. Liberation and feminist theologians have applied sociopolitical models of interpretation to Revelation to find there a timeless message of God's retribution against society's injustices. The learned societies of biblical scholars have also taken to Revelation, producing fresh insights into the historical and spiritual circumstances which first occasioned its writing. Even outside the worshiping community, artists and literati are continually fascinated with the shapes and images found in John's book of visions. The history of art and music is marked by a body of creative work that has been stimulated by Revelation. Some biblical scholars find this interest apropos, since in their view Revelation was composed as a liturgical drama. In addition, at a time when many Christians still hesitate to embrace the vitality of an apocalyptic faith, cultural critics like Christopher Lasch (*The Culture of Narcissism*) or literary critics like Walker Percy (*The Second Coming*) have pointed to Revelation as a work of uncommon power which speaks directly to the peril of societal selfishness.

While the history of the church's interpretation of Scripture may slight Revelation, especially when compared with the attention other books of the Christian Bible have received, we would suggest that there is considerable evidence both inside and outside the church that John's Apocalypse has a certain galvanizing power. In fact, the cumulative evidence is that this NT book continues to attract serious readers, rarely evoking the cynicism of the playwright, G. B. Shaw, who once called it "a curious record of a drug addict's visions," or even the verdict of Luther, who dismissed it as unedifying for the ordinary believer (Krodel, *Revelation*, pp. 14–23). We would argue that the variety of positive responses to Revelation commends its usefulness. Perhaps even the mistaken interpretations call attention to the need to build a solid structure within which to interpret and apply its meaning to the life and faith of today's church. We believe that Revelation can be studied with great profit. There are certain clues, however, to which we must be attentive, for they guide the reader to appropriate meanings for life and faith.

In particular, there are four "moments" in the history of any biblical text where the careful student finds clues to guide the interpretation of Scripture. In this introduction, these four "moments" will be described and discussed in chronological order, with an eye to those clues important for a proper interpretation of John's Revelation. Naturally, the critical point of departure is the "moment of origin," when John wrote down his visions for seven congregations of southwest Asia. A careful consideration of the historical and theological crises which occasioned this correspondence will help one discern how this book was first heard as "word of God." In this sense, the interpreter considers Revelation as a historically conditioned document; its message must be understood in light of its original historical setting, and its messenger as one whose convictions about God shaped what he wrote down. To the extent the evidence allows, then, the interpreter's first task concerns the question: what circumstances prompted this author to write this particular book for those particular congregations? In response, the interpreter functions as a historian, concerned to attend to the evidence in a neutral manner.

Of course, the neutrality of the interpreter is limited by the ultimate value of the historical task, which is to help form the believing community's understanding of God. Only when John's context of life and faith is related by the interpreter to the current context of life and faith can the Spirit of God point the believing community in a direction leading to truth and love.

Additional clues are found at the "moment of composition." The author's second decision, after receiving the commission to write down his visions for the seven congregations, was to format and frame his visions in a specific way. John writes a literary composition whose coherence is known by its form (genre) and its function. The interpreter must study Revelation in literary terms, recognizing that the author's intended meaning is conveyed by the very way in which he has put together and written down the visions he received. Literary considerations are especially essential for interpreting Revelation, since many distortions of John's intended message have resulted from the interpreter's neglect of the composition's literary apocalyptic forms and epistolary format. If the meanings interpreters properly continue to assign to biblical texts must be in continuity with the author's intended meanings, and if the author's intended meanings are clarified by his choice of genre, then the very literary structure of a composition helps to focus what a text means. Common sense tells us that we should read poetry as poetry, not prose; tragedy as tragedy, not comedy; and so on. Likewise, the Apocalypse must be studied in a manner congruent with the forms of apocalyptic literature rather than discursive or narrative works of history.

One who interprets Revelation for the church must also pause at the "moment of canonization" to consider why the early church formed a NT and included Revelation in it. To recover all the clues found at this "moment" in the history of Revelation, the interpreter must consider its status during the long process which ultimately led the church to include Revelation in the NT canon. Any interpretation of Revelation must be in continuity not only with the author's intentions but also with the church's intention in forming the Christian biblical canon: to guide the formation of the worshiping community's ongoing witness to the reigning God. More specifically, the interpreter should also pay close attention to those reasons for placing Revelation as Scripture's concluding book.

The final point in the history of Revelation which yields important information for the interpreter is the ongoing "moment of interpretation." Sharply put, today's interpretations must be informed by the ways our forefathers and foremothers used Revelation to nurture their faith. Time and time again believers have picked up Revelation to find meanings which function as the spiritual rule for this congregation or that communion of believers. Their interpretations of Revelation have reflected different theologies and different crises.

In retrospect, the "cash-value" of knowing this history of interpretation is to provide a system of checks and balances by which current interpretations are measured. The profound depth of this composition's inherent ambiguity has only extended the range of its possible meaning, which in any case should yield the requisite humility—a necessary attribute for biblical interpretation.

The Moment of Origin

The clear consensus of modern biblical scholarship is that Revelation was written during the first century to address a spiritual crisis threatening the faith and witness of Christian congregations along the coastline of southwest Asia.[1] Most still accept Irenaeus' dating (mid-90s), although a minority of historians contends that an earlier Neronic dating (late 60s) is more likely.[2] In our view, the letters to the seven churches (Rev. 2-3), together with the vision of Babylon's destruction (Rev. 17-18), reflect the *Sitz im Leben* ("life setting") of the Asian church during the Domitian period (A.D. 81-96). Whatever the interpreter finally decides about the date of Revelation's composition, however, it is neither a blueprint for future history nor one person's poetic understanding of faith written without reference to a particular point in time. In fact, we are inclined to accept the author's own statement of purpose that his book intends to relate the "word of God and the testimony of Jesus Christ" to his first readers, in an effort to call them to a more disciplined faith when challenged by real threats to it.

The exegetical task of reconstructing the basic ingredients of the first conversation between congregations and author has continuing relevance, since the church's situation is always more or less analogous to the situation Revelation first addressed and interpreted by its author. In stating the historical problem in this manner, we do not deny the importance of explaining, whenever possible, the book's symbol systems by the historical events and places known to its first-century readers. Especially the great commentaries by W. Bousset and R. H. Charles are helpful in this regard. Our sense, however, is that such efforts are of little help theologically and too often "freeze" Revelation's significance in the late first or early second century—a tacit rejection of its subsequent role as canonical literature, which intends to shape the witness of the ongoing church.

In this introduction, we will be content to concern ourselves with questions of authorship and audience, especially as they relate to what occasioned the writing and first reading of the book. Our handling of these issues, however, will be different in emphasis from their traditional formulation in modern commentaries on Revelation. In our discussion of the issues relating to the book's authorship, we are primarily interested in the book's (rather than the author's) apostolicity—a more theological than historical concern. In addition, our interest in the historical crisis which occasioned this composition will finally be more theological than historical. This orientation derives from our "canonical" perspective, which places premium on the ongoing religious function of biblical texts and their theological importance for today.

Authorship. Virtually all modern historians admit that the problems relating to Revelation's authorship are difficult to resolve. There are disagreements on particulars even among those who otherwise agree on final matters. The unsettled status of this question might seem odd at first, since the author identifies himself as John (1:4), a seer (1:1) and Christian prophet (1:3), currently living in exile on the Roman penal island of Patmos (1:9). Apparently John belongs to the Asian church (1:9), with whose situation he is familiar and to which he now writes. Because of the large number of Hebraisms in his Greek text and his familiarity with the Jewish Scriptures and their rabbinic midrashim, one might also speculate that he is a Jewish convert to Christianity. This may explain his special sensitivity to the conflict between the Asian church and Jewish synagogue, apparent in the messages to the faithful congregations in Smyrna (2:9) and Philadelphia (3:9).

Ancient tradition identifies this John as the beloved apostle of Jesus, the presumed author of the Fourth Gospel and the three Johannine letters of the NT. Indeed, only a few courageous commentators assumed otherwise until the modern period (1800 to present), when the compositional unity of Revelation came under closer scrutiny and its Johannine authorship was questioned. The early church fathers are virtually unanimous in their verdict that the Apostle John wrote Revelation, although such a strong and singular external witness may well reflect the apologist's compensation for Revelation's difficult and provocative content.[3]

In addition, one finds thematic and linguistic similarities between Revelation, the Fourth Gospel, and 1 John that would seem to justify this ancient consensus (Morris, *Revelation*, pp. 27–35). Several have also noted that this corpus of Johannine writings shares a body of common phrases and that all speak in similar and distinctive ways about Jesus as Messiah: he is the executed and exalted Lamb, and he is the word of God. To be sure, most would reasonably allow that their different literary fields (Gospel, letter, apocalyptic) highlight different dimensions of their polyvalent meaning, so that an apocalypse will always provide new meanings to old themes. Perhaps the same point can be made to explain any stylistic or grammatical difference between the Gospel and the Apocalypse, or between 1 John and the Apocalypse. Moreover, both the Gospel and Revelation contain citations, allusions, and echoes of a particular body of OT texts, comprised mostly of prophetic oracles and priestly themes. Finally, as E. Stauffer has contended, both the evangelist and the seer share common liturgical sensibilities.

On the other hand, more recent arguments against attributing Revelation's authorship to the Apostle John constitute a considerable challenge to the ancient consensus. Most scholars now agree that the John of Revelation is neither the author of the Fourth Gospel nor the Apostle John. We agree with this conclusion (although the evidence on both sides of the issue remains inconclusive). The internal reasons seem clear and persuasive: (1) the John of Revelation does not identify himself as the apostle, but as a "servant" of Jesus Christ (1:1). (2) His vocation and the authority of his composition derive more from his prophetic task (cf. 1:10; also, 22:18–19) than from an apostolic office (cf. 21:14; although see Morris, *Revelation*, p. 35). (3) Some cite stylistic differences (Charles, *Revelation*, vol. 1, pp. xxix–xxxvii), while others contend that the theological disagreements between the writings of the Johannine corpus, especially in matters of eschatology and Christology, make it impossible to think of them as coming from a single pen. And Beasley-Murray, who otherwise argues for the theological continuity between the teaching of Jesus and Revelation, seems to have in mind the teaching of the synoptic Jesus rather than John's Jesus.

The history of interpretation demonstrates that concerns about authorship are usually vested with theological or ideological commitments and apologetic interests. This seems especially true for Revelation, where the historical and grammatical evidence, which properly determines judgments of this sort, is inadequate and often leads to conjecture upon conjecture (Beasley-Murray, *Revelation*, pp. 36–37). For example, those who queue up behind the Apostle John usually link their conclusions about authorship to notions of apostolicity and authority: that is, an "apostolic" writing, which has continuing authority for the church, must be written by one of the first apostles (Johnson, "Revelation," pp. 404–5). R. H. Charles makes the opposite point in following the same premise. His influential commentary on Revelation follows the lead of Dionysius in rejecting the Apostle John's authorship on stylistic grounds and then the credibility of the book's theological vision by that conclusion (*Revelation*, vol.1, xxi–xxiii). In my opinion, Charles exemplifies the dangerous tendency of modern scholarship to confuse historical quests after apostolic authors with the church's recognition of a book's apostolicity and canonicity. The assumption that the Apostle John must have written Revelation since its inspiration and canonicity depend upon it is simply wrong. The apostolicity or trustworthiness of the content of a NT writing (many of which are anonymous or quite possibly pseudonymous) is determined by a *theological* rather than historical perspective. In applying the criterion of apostolicity, earliest Christianity was fundamentally concerned with the congruence of a book's message with its memory of the apostles' witness to Christ. In this sense, the issue at stake, whether to include Revelation in the NT canon, was not a question of authorship; rather, at issue was whether its message comported well with the theological tradition the Apostle John "founded." Each of the compositions that make up the NT Johannine corpus transmits a particular understanding of the significance of Jesus Christ that no doubt originated with the ministry of the Apostle John. Even if Revelation were not written by the apostle, its content continues to be trusted because its message is true to the witness of the Apostle John.

There is a sense in which Revelation represents the best illustration in the NT of a book whose authority derives from its revelatory content rather than from its author's status.[4] Clearly the author's self-introduction intends to subordinate the author to the visions he has received from God through Christ, who then commissions him to write them down. The authority of Revelation does not derive from an apostle who writes his visions down; rather, it derives from their source, God, and from the one who commissions their writing, the Risen Christ.

Therefore, although he follows the teaching of the Apostle John, the John who wrote Revelation is not John the beloved apostle of Jesus. Nor does the author use a pseudonym to disguise his real identity and legitimize his writing by giving credit to John the Apostle; he simply uses his real name to identify himself to his audience. Some scholars have suggested that John belongs to a "school" consisting of Christian teachers or prophets.[5] The most one can suggest in this regard is that John belongs to a school of Christian prophets which sought to preserve and transmit to others the Apostle John's unique witness to the risen Lord Jesus. Even if one concludes that the evidence does not support this particular conclusion, the ongoing authority of Revelation is not ultimately determined by the ideology which equates an apostolic writer with an apostolic writing. The church's recognition that John's Revelation belongs to the Christian biblical canon and continues to serve the "one holy catholic and *apostolic* church" stems from its confidence that this composition constitutes a normative witness to the "word of God and the testimony of Jesus Christ" (cf. Rev. 1:2).

Audience.[6] The believers for whom John of Patmos writes are members of Christian congregations located along the coastline of southwest Asia, an ancient Roman province which is now Turkey. The general experience of faithful Christians to whom John writes was one of real hardship and heartache; the costs of remaining Christian were great. Irenaeus wrote toward the end of the second century that Revelation was written late in the first century during the reign of Domitian (*Against Heresies* 5.30.3), whose official repression of Christianity as a politically and religiously deviant movement is well attested. John himself was exiled to Patmos, a Roman penal colony, as a result of his prophetic ministry (1:9).

Recent research, however, suggests that Rome did not single out Christianity for persecution; neither is there much evidence to confirm an empirewide effort to repress Christian worship (Boring, *Revelation*, pp. 13–18). In the first century, martyrdom was still exceptional. No doubt, various forms of persecution were commonplace; the suffering was therefore quite real. This persecution precipitated ideological tensions between Rome and Christianity. Rome's cultural myths and mores tended to subvert both the worship and the witness of earliest Christianity. For example, the church's conflict with the emperor cultus, an important background element for understanding parts of Revelation, does not center on the worship of the current Caesar. Supposed tensions between the Roman ruler and the Lord Jesus were those not of personal rivalry but of ideological disagreement: the Roman Caesar symbolized the imperial and secular Roman culture whose commitments and values were utterly contrary to the kingdom of God. Of course, to the extent that anyone participates in the social order—at work, at play, in school, as a member of various communities and associations—one comes under the influence of secular society's myths and ideals. This more "ordinary" reality was more central to John's pastoral purposes. For him, the experience of powerlessness and helplessness within the Roman world was the cost exacted because of Christianity's refusal to submit to Rome's secular vision.

No doubt the persecution of many believers was sponsored by local Jewish leadership (2:9; 3:9). The church should expect greater sympathy from the synagogue: Christianity began as a sectarian movement within Judaism; and Jews and Christians share a common religious history and a common experience of alienation and persecution at the hands of society's ruling elite. This shared history and experience, however, was viewed as a threat by the synagogue (A. Collins, *Crisis and Catharsis*, pp. 85–87). Especially toward the end of the first century, the church was still attracting converts from Judaism, while at the same time it was being influenced by a growing gentile majority which sometimes retained its anti-semitic sentiments. Christians both confessed Jesus from Nazareth, viewed as a "criminal" or "Antichrist" by outsiders, as Lord Messiah and thought of themselves as the "true Israel" in whose congregational life the biblical promises were being fulfilled by the God of Israel. While other themes of the emerging Christian systematic theology had antecedents in Judaism, these two foundational convictions of Christian proclamation would have been disputed, if not deplored, by "official" Judaism. Religious Jews may well have understood Christians as calling into question the very right of Judaism to exist—a perception intensified by Judaism's recent history which included expulsion from both Rome (in A.D. 49) and Palestine (in A.D. 70). Many Jews had found their way to this region from Rome and Palestine to establish the bulkhead for their Diaspora; there was no retreat for the Jews from southwest Asia too. Further, the Jewish synagogue was an affluent and politically respectable social institution in Asia. By contrast, the young church was marginal and without much political influence or economic affluence; thus, its struggle with Judaism often went in favor of its much stronger foe.

Against this sociological backdrop, the interpreter understands better that the theological crisis facing John's Christian readers was how to form their now embattled identity as the "true" Israel. The real temptation facing many new converts was to define notions of power (ethics) and truth (theology) in secular terms—by money and social status—rather than in spiritual terms. No doubt, this crisis was more keenly experienced by the Jewish converts to Christianity (like John himself), whose return to the Jewish synagogue would have guaranteed some sense of personal security and material comfort. The crisis facing John's readers is theological and spiritual: who is Lord over human and historical existence, God or Mammon? Of course, believers are paying costs for their faith; they are suffering because they are powerless and refuse to be a part of the mainstream where creature comforts are found. At least one element in John's response to his readers accords with the "deeper-logic" of biblical teaching: for the community of faith, the costs and trials of human life are tests of its devotion to God (cf. James 1:2–3).

The crisis facing John's church has confronted every generation of Christians. The costs of forming a community which bears witness to God in a secular and materialistic world are manifold; the temptation to compromise is strong, because, especially for the new believer, the gods of this world seem stronger than the God of Israel. John's advice for his first readers is sound advice for current readers too: in the executed and exalted Lamb, a sovereign God has disclosed the Lord's triumph over the idols and ruling elite of the anti-Christian kingdom.

The Moment of Composition

Specific cues are provided the readers at the beginning of the composition to signal what kind of literature they are about to read. In fact, the very first word of John's composition identifies it as a "revelation" or apocalypse (1:1). Most educated readers in the first century were familiar with the forms and conventions used in the literature of apocalypticism. Other prophets, whether Jewish or Christian, had written books based upon their visions of the "other world." Thus, when John began his composition as an apocalypse, he was in effect locating it within a familiar literary tradition known to his readers who were able to make meaning of what he wrote.

John quickly follows with a second cue: his composition consists of "the words of prophecy" (1:3). Modern biblical criticism rightly distinguishes the prophetic literature of the OT from the apocalyptic literature of the Second Temple period of Judaism.[7] This distinction between an "apocalypse" and a "prophecy" helps focus the literary analysis of Revelation: how can a single composition function as both apocalypse and prophecy? To answer this question a further distinction needs to be made between the form of a literary work and its function. In the case of Revelation, John employs many literary forms and themes found in other apocalypses, and yet his composition's overarching function is prophetic. At the very least, the second cue tells his audience that they should read this particular apocalypse in a qualified way, differently from other apocalypses with which they were familiar.

The readers are afforded a final cue when John greets them by using the familiar salutation of the "Pauline" letter: "Grace and peace to you" (1:4). This conventional letter greeting both complicates and qualifies the composition's apocalyptic forms and prophetic function.[8] J. J. Collins has documented the fluidity of format in the apocalyptic genre. The arrangement of visions within an apocalyptic composition varies greatly from one apocalypse to another. According to Collins, the interpreter should carefully distinguish forms from format. Typically ancient visionaries wrote their visions down in a variety of literary formats. For instance, John has shaped his visions into a letter, not unlike the letters written by Paul or Peter. Not only does Revelation's epistolary format provide the readers with a more definite structure, perhaps to aid its analysis or memorization, but its format also indicates that the book's prophetic function serves a pastoral aim.

Let me explain. Letters were typically written by people like Paul to give pastoral advice and theological counsel to particular congregations to help resolve problems that threatened their spiritual formation. Letters were used as literary "substitutes" for those who wrote them and "performed" the work of a pastor in their stead. John's situation-in-exile prevented him from coming to the seven congregations in person; therefore, he writes down his visions in a letter format to clarify his pastoral intentions. These intentions of the author must control any interpretation of Revelation. The interpreter should render the meaning of Revelation in ways which demonstrate the practical significance of what John has written down.

Revelation as an apocalyptic composition.[9] John is a pilgrim in a strange world—a world constructed by dramatic visions and impressive sounds. Revelation, then, is something like a travelogue; in it is a record of John's impressions of his visits to new places and introductions to new people, like the cities Babylon and the new Jerusalem, or the elder he meets in the heavenly throneroom of God. In a literal sense, John's visionary world is unlike our own—past, present, or future; in a metaphorical sense, however, John's visionary world is very much like our own—past, present, and future. For example, while John's vision of Babylon does not have an exact counterpart in human history, it does speak of the very stuff that determines the structures of human life and history: in this sense, Babylon speaks about modern America as much as about ancient Rome.

In this regard, the very first word of John's composition is the interpreter's most essential clue: the word is *apokalypsis*, "revelation," which designates the entire work as belonging to a particular classification of literature, "apocalyptic," and of thought, "apocalypticism." The primary intent of this literature is to reveal the "mysteries of God" to believers presently experiencing oppression and suffering. While the real consequence of its "other-worldly" language is often to conceal divine truth from its readers, its intended consequence is to reveal the truth of God. Some scholars incorrectly suppose that apocalyptic images of violence and divine judgment intend to hide John's criticism of his opponents. In truth, this conclusion seems quite unlikely. The vivid nature of John's images clearly indicates the nature of his criticism of the social order and identifies the church's enemies. Further, I suspect that John has an evangelistic purpose for writing Revelation: his desire is that even the non-believer respond to his message of God's triumph over the anti-Christian kingdom and be converted. To disguise his message would only undermine its missionary role. Revelation's harsh criticisms of the social order, represented in part by the total destruction of Babylon, seek to distinguish the church as an alternative to other institutions which have been shaped and therefore corrupted by secular notions of power and security. Knowing that this "sociology of conflict" is so central to the rise of apocalypticism helps the interpreter of Revelation to understand both its visionary images and its pastoral advice: to resist Babylon is to persevere and ultimately to participate in the eschatological triumph of God over Babylon.

There are four *literary "forms"* characteristic of apocalypses. First, apocalyptic compositions have structural unity. In responding to the criticism that Revelation is disjointed and fragmentary (Charles), we would agree that Revelation is a book that combines different visions that sometimes obscure its overall structure and central message. Actually, the architecture of the composition follows a deliberate plan, combining blocks of triads and septets that are then fitted together as parts of a single, coherent whole. I will argue, for instance, that John's three visions of seven judgments are integrated within the body of his composition, effecting the impression that history is moving toward God's final destruction of evil and death at Christ's return. Further, the author often repeats similar words and phrases in inverted (ABC C'B'A') or chiastic (ABCDC'B'A') order. John also employs common "catch-phrases" to relate different sections of his composition; for example, the terms of Christ's exhortations to the seven congregations (Rev. 2–3) are employed again to describe results of his glorious return (Rev. 19:11—20:6a).[10] In the case of this rhetorical device, John seeks to make a critical theological point: the consequences of following Christ's advice to either repent or endure, will be felt by all at Christ's return. In addition, extended prose episodes are typically autobiographical, providing an additional dimension of continuity to the whole work.

The literary coherence of the apocalypse, as concentrated by John's theological convictions, clarifies how his visions correspond to "the real world." In this sense, the language of Revelation is "non-objectifying" (Boring, *Revelation*, pp. 53–54); its disunity will always be insisted upon by those who think of it as discursive history-writing which describes the "real world" in factual ways. Revelation's prose is much more analogical and liturgical and thus resists our immediate and facile corollaries between its "other-world" visions and "this-world's" places and persons. John has been transported "in the spirit" to journey in a strange land—a land very different from his (and our) world, but nevertheless a land on which John discovers the nature of God's reign in relationship to the evils of our current existence and ultimate transformation.

Apocalypses draw upon a pool of familiar *symbols* to speak about spiritual and historical realities. Special numbers represent spiritual truth; incredible animals and non-human humans are dramatic distortions of everyday places and people. The visionary experience itself requires new frames of reference and different forms of communication. Collins's nice phrase, "literal non-literalism," is an appropriate way to speak of the symbol systems which provide apocalypses their essential content. Yet, apocalypses are not written as detached accounts of future historical events; their images do not intend to draft reality in literal or factual ways. Apocalypses view reality from an entirely different frame of reference in order to transform our understanding of human existence.[11] At the same time, the world created by symbols is not fictive; it is a non-literal but real world, with parallels to human experience and existence.

Even though symbols are not ordinary language, Revelation does not require some special cipher to unlock its "mystery." John's purpose is to reveal, not conceal; and if one follows the clues, his intended meanings become quite clear. This should come as no surprise if one recalls John's pastoral interests; pastors work for clear communication. Thus, John draws from a pool of well-known pagan myths, Jewish scriptures, and Christian traditions to cast a familiar background against which his readers come to understand and share in his visionary experience.

The ultimate purpose of Revelation's symbolism, of course, is to convey the book's message "on the end (which) serves to release the imagination from concrete reality; because they are pictures of the 'not yet,' the images are free to go their own way."[12] While Beardslee's point is surely correct, it is sometimes more appropriate to speak of visionary phenomena as "not here" rather than as "not yet"—in terms of cosmology rather than eschatology. Thus, Revelation's images are born in God's heavenly domain where ultimate truth for earth is found. The larger point must be further qualified by the frequent observation that John correlates historical fact and non-historical symbol to varying degrees (Caird, *Revelation*, pp. 60–62). For example, the messages to the seven congregations (Rev. 2–3) and the vision of Babylon's destruction (Rev. 17–18) relate to actual cities in John's "real" world. In any case, the historical plane of reference has more to do with God's salvation than with human history. Thus, the action which Revelation plots corresponds to the outworking of God's salvation in human history: the announcement of God's triumph at the exaltation of the slain Lamb (5:1—11:19) always provokes the protest of evil powers (12:1—19:10), the essential conflict which is finally resolved in God's favor and revealed by a consummating act.

In addition, symbols are evocative. Any seer wants his readers to "feel" the impact of apocalyptic language in a visceral way and realizes that their imaginative powers are excited by metaphor or myth to think about their faith in new and fresh ways.

Reading apocalypses, therefore, should be an "experience"— dramatic and emotive. Even though Revelation retells the familiar story of God's salvation, it does so in a way which evokes a renewed sense of the story's significance for life.

Apocalypses depend upon the *typologies* found in the OT and other Jewish writings.[13] Typologies speak of the "big ideas" of faith in terms of people, places, and events. While visions transcend ordinary experience, their images, however distorted and strange, come to resemble stories told by the biblical writers. In this way apocalyptic visions can be re-classified according to certain recognizable types of events or people that have theological value for the readers.

John's constant allusions to biblical stories suggest that he composes his book of visions in conversation with the OT. Not only is much of his rhetoric borrowed from the biblical prophets, but his visions can often be catalogued according to the types of people and events which the prophets themselves used to rehearse the constitutive features of salvation's history. For example, John describes his visions of divine judgment as a rehearsal of the plagues-exodus-wilderness-land events of the OT (Rev. 8–9, 16). Like the OT prophets, he re-classifies the covenant relationship between God and the community of believers as a type of marriage between God's Lamb and his Bride (Rev. 19–21). John even draws upon the most important Christian typology, the death-resurrection of Christ, in composing his vision of the two witnesses (Rev. 11).

John's conceptual continuity with prophetic faith suggests that he considered his visions in terms of God's promised salvation rather than as a spontaneous eruption of divine vindictiveness more characteristic of some Jewish apocalypses. For John, the prophetic impulses of social criticism and proclamation are more appropriate to his agenda. His message corresponds to the prophetic promise of the triumph of God's reign within history. For him, the new Israel has experienced a new exodus from sin and death and has set out on a journey for a new Jerusalem. The pilgrimage is not without hardship and heartache, because sin and death still exist within the fallen world order which surrounds them.

While Revelation is not a diachronic narrative and does not envision a sequence of events, it does view God's salvation as hav-

ing a history. John's appropriation of the promise-fulfillment motif is a tacit expression of this conviction and suggests how his
version of "Christian apocalypticism" has modified its Jewish antecedent. For John, the present has not collapsed into the future;
rather, the present moment in which the church lives is transformed by the past exaltation of Christ and is located within a
special history where God's promised salvation is worked out and
will be fully realized in the future return of the exalted Christ.

Apocalypses contain a *distinctive theology and historiography.*
Boring says that the images of Revelation are "non-logical and
non-inferential"; that is, taken literally, the images of strange
beasts or of an invisible heaven are "nonsensical" because they
cannot be verified by ordinary human experience (Boring, *Revelation*, pp. 57–58). Boring is correct; however, this does not mean
that Revelation makes no sense; its sense is rather "theo-logical."
The meaning of Revelation and other apocalypses is rendered coherent by certain convictions about God and history.

More specifically, every apocalypse, including Revelation,
is a theodicy. That is, Revelation seeks to defend the vital presence
and participation of a good and sovereign Lord God in a world
where the everyday experience is full of human misery and social injustice.[14] John composes Revelation as a cumulative case
for God by casting three integral images of God's Lamb: (1) God's
goodness has already been demonstrated in heaven by the exalted Lamb (Rev. 5); (2) God's goodness continues to be demonstrated in the history of the community that "follow(s) the Lamb
wherever he goes" (Rev. 14:1–5); and (3) God's goodness will be
demonstrated in cosmic splendor at the Lamb's triumphant parousia (Rev. 19:11—22:6a).

The real power of the secular elite and the powerlessness
of the believing community challenge its conviction that the Creator God is in control of creation. Schüssler Fiorenza is surely correct in arguing that John's concern is with the issue of power: who
really has control over history's destiny? Believers, who might
otherwise believe in the sovereignty of God over human affairs,
experience oppression and powerlessness that seem to contradict their belief in an all-powerful and caring God: God must be
either loving but weak or powerful yet uncaring. Apocalyptic
theology argues for the sovereign rule of God: God is creator and
has absolute control from the beginning of all things (Rev. 4). It

follows that God also has absolute control over the conclusion of all things (cf. Gen. 3 and Rev. 21–22). In light of this theological commitment, the problem shifts from God to human beings. At issue for John is the faulty perception of those who define power in secular terms rather than in terms of "the great reversal." The gospel teaches that God's promised salvation has been fulfilled not through a mighty Caesar but through a slain Lamb!

Apocalypses not only interpret human experience within history, but promote a particular notion of human history (J. J. Collins, *The Apocalyptic Imagination*, pp. 9–10). The apocalyptic tradition views the political, religious, and economic institutions of the social order on the brink of collapse. Apocalyptic hope is centered by "the vision of human existence as caught up in a transcendent struggle which will express itself in a real history culminating in a total victory of good."[15] This eschatological inertia toward God's inevitable triumph forces the readers to interpret the social conditions of their world in a radically different and threatening way: society is in irreversible devolution, and no institution of the social order or any of its ruling elite— not even Caesar—can save society from its own self-destruction. Ironically, society's institutions do bring a certain order to human existence; however, its orderliness ensures that chaos and death rather than shalom and life make up the fabric of society. Personal crisis has become a way of life for believers who live within the corrupt social order, precisely because their lives are "disorderly" to the extent that they refuse to worship society's myths and idols.

History's present crisis is radically redrawn, if viewed from the end of history when God's reign will finally triumph at the Lord's return from heaven, from outside of history. Those places of history and those agents of the Evil One who are responsible for history's misery and evils will be judged and removed from the new Jerusalem, where eschatological Israel lives with God and God's Lamb. Human life is utterly transformed so that death itself is destroyed. God's people will be vindicated at the end of history; they will receive their rewards of transformed life and eternal shalom for overcoming evil.[16] This synchronic interplay between the motifs of crisis-judgment-vindication represents the "deeper-logic" of apocalypticism's "vertical" view of human history: the salvation of history comes from *outside* of history, where God reigns, to transform history by abruptly ending the reign of evil and by vindicating the reign of God.

One final motif should be considered because it touches on how the seer writes his "theologized" history: apocalypses are *dualistic*. Their visions intersect two realms of human experience, two orientations toward human existence, personal and societal. They describe the radically different consequences of each domain—one leads to death, while the other leads to life; one leads to the self-destruction of the old social order, while the other leads to a new society. Within this dualistic worldview, the apocalypse seeks to give direction to the tensions all believers experience when trying to live in a fallen, secular world as members of a community of faith for whom the real world is yet to come. The various images of this conflict found in apocalyptic literature reflect the experience of a suffering people of God. The most pronounced conflict in Revelation is expressed by Christian martyrs, whose lament is "how long?" (Rev. 6:10). On the one hand, they recognize their lives on earth are dominated by the powerful enemies of God, who have even succeeded in ending their faithful witness to God (cf. Rev. 11:7-10). They are those most aware of the futility of simplistic idealism and of the real costs of Christian discipleship. Realism is the catchword of the politics of apocalypticism. On the other hand, their lamentation is rooted in a hope for their future vindication because of their commitment to God's gospel. A. Y. Collins may well be correct in arguing that Revelation's dualistic and violent rhetoric intends to heighten and intensify an awareness of the community's powerlessness in the present social order, both to evoke a sense of detachment from the evils of this world and to provide a "catharsis" of those sentiments (e.g., vengeance, discouragement) which might distract from the community's faith in God (A. Collins, *Crisis and Catharsis*, pp. 141-63).

At the center of the apocalyptic affirmations is that God's future vindication corresponds to God's past faithfulness. Likewise, for John, the future parousia of Christ corresponds to his past exaltation; thus, the past activities of God and God's Christ provide a concrete basis for present hope in the midst of present crisis. God's judgment and vindication have already taken place, already in heaven and inevitably upon earth; the future earthly realization of God's triumph over evil is only a matter of time.

Revelation as a prophetic oracle.[17] The modern distinctions that are sometimes made between an apocalyptic and a prophetic view of salvation's history, or between the literature of apocalypses (visionary) and of prophecies (oracular), would have been unintelligible to John. The current debate about the literary genre of Revelation reminds the interpreter that even now it is not easy to differentiate between the two. John himself refers to his composition in its prologue as both apocalypse (1:1) and prophecy (1:3). Evidently, the author felt that prophecy could be written with apocalyptic forms; revelation is revelation, whether through vision or oracle. John would also fail to appreciate the modern distinction between prophecy as "forthtelling" and as "foretelling"; his phrase, "words of prophecy," would have been understood both ways by his audience: prophecy is both proclamation and prediction.

But just what does John mean when he refers to his composition as "this prophecy"? Several recent studies have demonstrated that "Christian prophecy" can be understood as both a revelation tradition and a revealing phenomenon; the prophetic shape of Revelation may be understood accordingly. Especially according to Johannine Christianity, the presence and purpose of "the Spirit of prophecy" was to transmit the continuing instruction of the risen Lord to his current disciples (cf. Rev. 1:11; chs. 2–3; 4:1; 17:1; 21:10). In earliest Christianity, guidance came from the stable "Jesus tradition," consisting of memories about the historical Jesus, and from the Christian prophets whose Spirit-inspired prophecies transmitted the ongoing teaching of the Risen Jesus who continues to bear witness to the "word of God" within the believing community. Therefore, John's phrase, "word of God and testimony of Jesus Christ," suggests a more dynamic relationship between Christ and his disciples than is sometimes supposed by modern scholarship.[18] The belief in the Spirit as the carrier of instruction from the Risen Christ, rooted in the Fourth Gospel's "Upper Room Discourse" (John 14:26), was a controversial one. The important third-century Christian teacher, Gaius, who objected to the Montanistic use of John's teaching of the Spirit of prophecy, became an early opponent against the canonization of both John's Gospel and Revelation. Nevertheless, in more than one early canon list, Revelation follows the fourfold Gospel because the canonizing church recognized that certain of John's visions contained sayings from the exalted Lamb to the church (e.g., Rev. 2–3). The location of Revelation in these early canon lists suggests an elevated status, similar to the fourfold Gospel in importance for some Christians.

The recognition that Revelation belongs to the prophetic tradition has to do with its perspective toward the readers and does not oblige the interpreter to find all the distinctive forms of prophetic literature in John's composition. Beasley-Murray has identified several "prophetic-like oracles" strung together in chapter fourteen (*Revelation*, p. 22), and others have done the same in the final vision of Christ's parousia (for him, 19:1—21:8).[19] Typically, however, John introduces his various visions by apocalyptic formulae (e.g., "I looked and saw") rather than by the formulae of prophetic utterance (e.g., "Thus says the Lord our God"). And only once in Revelation does God actually speak to John (21:6–8); this simply does not square with the literary *Gattung* of the prophetic tradition. In any case, scholars tend to emphasize the theological distinctives of the prophetic tradition rather than its literary forms, which are apocalyptic. Therefore, the interpreter should understand that John's introduction of his book as "words of prophecy" indicates the overarching purpose of his composition: to transmit a word from God that is constitutive for faith and life.

Not only does John regard the overarching purpose of his composition to be prophetic, he views himself as a prophet, the mediator of the revelation for the churches. That the charismata of the Spirit shaped the religious orientation of earliest Christianity hardly needs mention. John's self-understanding no doubt was in continuity with this orientation, so that both his vision (cf. Rev. 5:4–7) and his commission to write it down (cf. Rev. 1:19) "would probably still have been understood . . . in terms of the spirit of prophecy"[20] rather than ecstatic rapture as for the apocalyptist. Sharply put, "we have in the Revelation of John a literary deposit of Spirit-inspired prophecy as is referred to . . . in early Christian writings."[21] Thus, both his prophetic vocation and the Spirit's inspiration to see the visions of divine mysteries ("in the Spirit"; Rev. 1:10) are what give him confidence that his composition has authority for the churches.[22]

There are three important theological distinctives to a "prophetic" reading of Revelation. First, unlike most apocalyptic documents of Judaism, which focus on things outside of history, Revelation shows an interest in history as the context for God's salvation. The visions contained in Revelation are not all of heaven, nor are they all about what happens after the end of history. The messages to the seven congregations remind the readers that even those visions of heaven and the new Jerusalem are commentaries about God's salvation as it is worked out within the history of God's people on earth. Second, John writes Revelation in conversation with his Bible (OT). The visions he receives are presumed to fulfill the biblical promise to Israel—which most NT writers consider a critical feature for understanding the Christ event. Third, building upon the previous two points, in calling his composition a prophecy John indicates that it contains the prediction of future historical events. Its function is to evoke a present response of devotion to God by foretelling the climax of human history at the Lamb's parousia. Of course, John believed that Christ would return to earth; this was the central tenet of early Christian eschatology. Yet, in referring to his book as a prophecy, he moves this claim of faith to a new level of certainty—from a belief in it to a prediction of it.

Therefore, we prefer to think of Revelation as a "hybrid"— one part apocalypse (forms) and another part prophecy (function), one modifying the other.[23] The prophetic shape of Revelation gives Christian hope a certain concreteness. Its message is transformed into an announcement that the messianic mission is the commencement of the age of fulfillment when the vindication of God's faithfulness will be realized. The Pastor's celebration of the exaltation of Jesus Christ, the paschal Lamb of God, yields the Prophet's prediction of his parousia. In part, the author utilizes the literary forms and themes of apocalypticism to draw attention to the church's current crisis. On this literary landscape, then, the clear and certain announcement (indeed, a divine edict!) of God's future triumph over evil within history is made more powerful and profound.

Revelation as a letter.[24] Not only did John use apocalyptic forms and themes to fashion a composition with a prophetic voice; he wrote Revelation as a pastoral letter to his audience. John's desire to fashion his visions into a letter seems a natural one, since letters are addressed a particular audience in a crisis of faith and since apocalyptic literature was intended for a suffering, oppressed people in need of exhortation. The coupling of letters with imaginative language is one way to intensify an author's exhortation by recasting the audience's crisis and their necessary response to it in fresh ways (J. J. Collins, *Apocalyptic Imagination*, p. 31).

In writing this commentary on Revelation, I will seek to develop more fully the fundamental importance of John's epistolary format to his overarching literary structure and theological program. In introducing this point, two aspects of letter-writing in the ancient world, and specifically within the earliest church, are important to note.[25]

First, a letter is not a narrative, and letter writers are not chroniclers. While some NT letters contain autobiographical sections (e.g., Gal. 1–2; 2 Cor. 10–12), the letters themselves do not function as historical autobiographies. Without doubt Revelation is informed by a historical perspective, and it predicts an ultimate historical event, the second coming of Christ. There is even the sense of time and movement, when viewed on a macro-historical scale: the composition begins with Christ's death and exaltation (Rev. 5–11), continues with a vision of the church's present difficulties (Rev. 12–13), and concludes with Christ's parousia (Rev. 19–21). Revelation consists mostly of the recapitulation of various themes, concentrated around critical "moments." The recapitulation of these themes, which link these climatic moments of salvation's history, reinforces this sense of movement from Christ's exaltation to his parousia which sandwiches and interprets the church's intervening history and its crisis. However, Revelation is not a historical narrative as such, which moves the reader chronologically from a beginning episode to a concluding one. The literalistic and reductionistic rendering of Revelation into a precise and specific narrative of future events frustrates John's epistolary intentions.

Second, a letter is "occasional" literature. A letter is not a systematic theology or academic writing, but a pastoral brief. In the case of Revelation, letters are written as a practical response to the needs of seven struggling congregations. Letters are occasioned by, and are read and understood in relationship to, a real life setting. Interpreters who suppose that Revelation was written as a blueprint of their modern historical situation are surely mistaken, as are those who fail to recover its practical message and interpret it in terms of mythopoetic abstractions. A mistake is made if the interpreter assumes this book of visions conveys esoteric meaning, hidden from its readers. John's visions were "formatted" as a letter by a prophet-pastor who seeks to form Christian disciples by addressing them clearly and directly about the crisis which threatens their devotion to God and to God's Christ.[26] By reading Revelation as a letter, the interpreter is reminded that the real battles of Christian faith are fought in local congregations. While it is proper, even necessary, to think of the seven congregations for whom John wrote down his visions from God as constituents of the timeless and invisible church catholic, they are first of all made up of real believers struggling with real problems that threatened their faith. A commentary sensitive to Revelation's epistolary form is therefore also sensitive to its pastoral intent and it will resist undue abstraction by always seeking to relate its meaning to the deeper realities of human life and Christian faith.

The History of Canonizing Revelation

The third critical period in the history of Revelation follows its course to canonization, which took several centuries to complete. In reconstructing this particular historical "moment," the interpreter is reminded that Revelation is not a literary composition in an isolated sense; it has been included in the list of twenty-six other writings as one part of the canon of Christian scriptures, the New Testament.[27] In forming an ongoing rule for Christian faith and practice, the church came to recognize the unique authority of the NT, and Revelation within it, for forming the life and faith of God's people. Simply stated, the church formed the Bible in order to form the church. According to 2 Timothy 3:16 the proper uses of the Bible for its intended role within the church are both pastoral (teaching and training) and prophetic (reproving and correcting). Thus, any interpretation of the Bible must be either pastoral or prophetic and must result in increased wisdom (2 Tim. 3:15) and good works (2 Tim. 3:17).

The purpose of this introductory section, then, is to discuss the special importance of Revelation when viewed as canonical literature. In taking up this point, I am going against the stream of modern commentaries on Revelation. These studies typically attempt to locate John's composition within the history of ancient religion or within a particular social and literary world. This more historical orientation toward biblical interpretation derives from modern epistemological assumptions that equate truth with historical fact. There is very little interest shown in interpreting Revelation from a *canonical* perspective, because the interpreter moves the primary locus of meaning from the point of origin to its position within the biblical canon and within the history of its interpretation by forefathers and foremothers of faith. The epistemological assumptions, then, are more religious since the canonical perspective assumes that the act of interpreting the Bible must be influenced, even guided, by its intended role as the biblical rule of faith for the Christian faith community. Meaning is linked to the ongoing role of the biblical canon within the church. In this regard, the particular history of Revelation during the formation of the NT canon, its position within the final form of the NT canon, and the variety of its interpretations provide a set of clues about how Revelation functions as part of the church's rule of faith, the Christian biblical canon.

Rather than clarify the various criteria the early church used to determine the canonicity of Christian writings,[28] I will simply assume that by including Revelation in the NT the early church recognized that Revelation would perform a canonical role for subsequent generations of believers. Together with the other writings which make up the Christian biblical canon, Revelation would continue to help define what it meant to be the church and to do as the church ought. Further, the early church assumed that the formation of Christian faith is possible only if all parts within the whole are taken seriously; therefore, the interpreter must resist the tendency to work only with a "canon within the canon," when one portion of the Bible is elevated in status to determine the meaning and authority of the rest; this bias will lead to serious distortions in the manner of Christian discipleship. The distinctive role Revelation plays in forming the church's faith can be discerned when the interpreter seeks to interpret Revelation in relationship to all other writings which make up the whole biblical canon; only then can the whole truth be discerned. Finally, then, the order of the different parts or units of the NT (Gospel, Acts, Pauline and non-Pauline Letters, Revelation) reflects a specific "grammar" that assigns a specific function to each successive unit of the whole NT. By following the implicit rules of this NT grammar, the interpreter is better able to make a meaning of a particular text or collection of texts that corresponds with the Bible's canonical role.

Revelation in the history of forming the NT. The interpreter can learn much about how Revelation should function as canon from the history of its canonization. H. Gamble aptly characterizes the canonization of Revelation as "fitful and uneven."[29] Until the time of Constantine, who used the book's imperial imagery for self-promotion,[30] Revelation was not recognized as canonical in some important regions of the early catholic church. Opposition to its canonicity was most keen in the East, where skeptical judgments were sustained over the recommendation of Athanasius, and continued to be exercised by some of the most influential leaders of early Christianity (e.g., Eusebius, Gaius, the Cappadocian Fathers). Later, this perspective continued among the Protestant Reformers who generally held to a low view of Revelation's suitability as canonical literature, although for different reasons (Krodel, *Revelation*, pp. 13–31). Today, there are still some non-Chalcedon (i.e., Nestorian) Christian communions who reject the canonicity of Revelation and follow the Peshitta, an ancient Syriac version of the Bible that excludes Revelation along with 2 Peter, 2–3 John, and Jude. And the Eastern Orthodox do not include readings from Revelation in their liturgy—tantamount to a rejection of its canonicity.

Actually, Revelation was not used during much of the second century; at least it was rarely cited in the writings of the early Fathers. According to Farmer, not until the emergence of the cult of martyrs during the late second and early third centuries did Revelation become prominent as part of a "martyr's canon."[31] This accords with two prominent features in the history of Revelation's canonization. First, the usefulness of Revelation was more quickly discerned by those believers on the margins of Christianity, such as the Montanists and chiliastic sects, who were largely rejected by mainstream Christians and by the surrounding society because of their sectarian tendencies. Their response toward history in general, informed in part by the ideas and images of apocalypticism, corresponded with their "outsiders" status. Their hope for history was placed at the end of history and in sources beyond history, rather than within history in the resources available from the elite of the sociopolitical order. Second, the elevation of Revelation's importance for faith among Christian sects became an issue for the leaders of mainstream Christianity, who were suspicious of Revelation's canonical status for fear that sectarian fanaticism was partially produced by their use (or abuse) of it. Also, the concerns over the apostolicity of Revelation expressed by influential Roman teachers, such as Gaius and Dionysius, were often less about the trustworthiness of Revelation per se, and more about the socioreligious legitimation of groups like the Montanists or the monastic cult of martyrs, who used Revelation as their "canon within the canon."[32] The issues at stake were often more political than canonical.

Zwingli's criticisms of Revelation are instructive in this regard. His low view of Revelation was due to its extensive use of angels, which encouraged in his mind a kind of pious mysticism among some immature believers. Also he objected to its liturgical idiom, which was not sufficiently "free" from the Roman Catholic mass to suit him. Luther as well held Revelation in low regard since its symbolism obscured Christ for the rank-and-file believer; and Calvin seemed to agree with this assessment. Luther also thought he detected authorial hubris: John thought more highly of his work than he ought! Luther did not seem to realize that his concerns were actually provoked by the traditional formulae used by apocalyptic writers to "boast" in God, who gave them visions of truth to write down.[33]

Into the modern period, these features of the early history of Revelation's canonization are repeated over and over again. Those believers who find it an important document of faith tend to be found on the margins of mainstream Christianity, in various fundamentalistic communions of faith, where their interpretation of Revelation advances their own ideas for human life and Christian faith. Because of Revelation's association with fundamentalism, mainstream Christianity is often frightened off from a serious conversation with Revelation. When Revelation is studied by liberals, too often it is to peddle an anti-fundamentalistic agenda within the church. The consequences of such interpretations are opposed to the church's essential intention for the Christian biblical canon to form a pluralistic community that is single-minded in its worship of God and love of neighbor.

The history of Revelation's canonization often illumines the history of its interpretation. The importance of Revelation was often obscured by self-serving interpretations which went unchecked by the church. If the Christian biblical canon was formed by the church to form the faith of the whole church, then any interpretation of Revelation which promotes the ideas or interests of one group at the expense of other communions should be resisted as unedifying. Throughout history, certain groups of believers have elevated the importance of Revelation as their "canon within the canon" either to promote a sectarian sociology or to justify an extreme interest in eschatology. For other believers, the presence of Revelation in the NT is a mere technicality; in practice, Revelation is never used to nurture believers or to measure their fidelity to the rule of faith. Whenever any part of the whole canon is excluded from the actual practice of Christian nurture, distortions in the church's witness to the gospel will result. A canonical perspective toward Revelation accepts its message as constitutive for and necessary to a vital faith.

Revelation as the NT conclusion. The NT canon in its final form is the product of an intentioned process. In this sense, neither the inclusion of Revelation within the NT canon nor its location within the NT canon is the result of arbitrary and abstract decisions made by a few. The shaping of the NT reflects the actual practice of the church, which came to recognize after a period of some time (two or three centuries) that certain collections of inspired writings, arranged in an inspiring way, best conveyed the rule of Christian faith to the faithful. While the interpreter should not place too much importance on the order of writings within the NT, such a perspective does allow one to construct what Albert Outler has called a "canon-logic" that provides an added dimension of meaning to the whole NT and to individual compositions within it.[34] The final placement of the different parts of the whole NT reflects a canonical grammar that gives coherence to the NT message and purposes to aid the faith community in determining how it should use this biblical message to nurture its Christian worship and witness.

In this light, I have argued elsewhere that the church has given added significance to Revelation by positioning it last in the biblical canon; in my view, Revelation is the Bible's "conclusion" and should be interpreted as such.[35] The most important theological convictions found in Revelation are highlighted when it is read as the concluding chapter in God's cosmic struggle with evil powers. The conclusion of the histories of humanity's evil and its redemption, of the creation, and of the special covenant between God and God's people are portrayed in John's visions. In this way, Revelation effects a canonical *inclusio* with the first chapter of the Bible's story, the OT book of Genesis. Genesis narrates the beginning of humanity's rebellion against God in the Garden of Eden, while Revelation narrates the concluding story of God's eventual triumph over the Evil One and all those the Evil One incites to rebellion. Genesis also indicates the good intentions of God for creation, while Revelation speaks of the realization of those intentions in another Garden—the paradise of the New Jerusalem, where the new Adam reigns with God and with his faithful followers. Further, the stature and purposes of God in Revelation are justified and understood by God's role as the creator of all things (Rev. 4); thus the Bible begins and concludes its story of God with the very conviction that begins the church's great ecumenical creeds: "We believe in God the Father Almighty, the maker of heaven and earth." Even as God is the creator of the present imperfect order, so also God is the creator of the new order, inaugurated by God's Lamb. Read as the Bible's *inclusio*, Revelation gives theological coherence to the Christian scriptures: everything from Genesis to Revelation should be interpreted by a "canon-logic" which asserts that a faithful creator God has kept the promise to restore all things for the Lord and for good.

The close relationship between different parts (i.e., writings or collections of writings) within the NT often signifies another element of the Bible's "canon-logic." For example, a consideration of the "special" relationship between the collection of NT letters and Revelation, itself a prophetic-apocalyptic letter, yields important clues for interpreting Revelation.[36] While the letters and Revelation are discrete parts of the NT canon, their common literary form calls attention to their "special" relationship within the NT. Further, their common form suggests common intentions: the intention of every NT letter is to form the distinctive witness of a Christian people. Of course, Revelation carries out its epistolary intention in a particular way; and its message not only contributes to the interpreter's comprehensive understanding of how the NT letters adapt the gospel to life, but also enhances the interpreter's ability to locate other parts of the whole truth found in the other NT letters. Let me clarify. Revelation addresses those believers whose spiritual witness is marginal. Its "prophetic" message is clear: they must repent and overcome evil or expect judgment at the revelation of God's triumph at the parousia (Rev. 2:5; 2:16; 2:21-25 et al.). Revelation also addresses those believers whose social status is marginal but whose witness has remained steadfast. Revelation encourages these believers to maintain their devotion to the Word (2:10-11; 3:10-12) with the promise that they will receive eschatological blessings upon the return of Christ (2:7; 2:17; 2:25-27 et al.). To repeat an important point already made, John's pastoral commitments are more "hortatory" than didactic: his composition, and the theological convictions it envisions, intend a *response* of faith and faithfulness. When Revelation is read canonically, its message issues a practical standard by which the ongoing community of believers measures its spiritual condition and decides then whether to repent or hope. The other NT letters can be read as contributing other elements to this essential standard.

In addition, the interpreter recognizes that Revelation forms a prophetic-apocalyptic perspective that should guide the meanings made of the letters; that is, important prophetic and apocalyptical ingredients are added to one's interpretation of any other NT letter, whether Pauline (Romans-Philemon) or General (Hebrews-Jude). From a careful reading of Revelation, the NT interpreter becomes more acutely aware that God's imminent judgment or redemption comes at the conclusion of history. As a result, the interpretation of other NT writings is focused by the ultimate consequences of responding to biblical (i.e., apostolic) advice: to reject the biblical "rule of faith" runs the risk of divine judgment and to follow it assures one of divine blessing. Further, when the interpreter relates letter and apocalypse together in mutually informing ways, the significance of Christ's exaltation and his parousia as the climax of God's certain triumph over social and spiritual evils becomes more central for faith and life. This theological conviction, which centers John's Revelation, checks and balances any interpretation we might make of the NT letters.

One final comment in regard to Revelation's role as the canon's conclusion. Revelation was first addressed to seven actual congregations; it deals with historically specific problems found in particular groups of Asian believers (cf. Rev. 2–3). When these writings are read within the context of the biblical canon, however, its time-bound and historically conditioned "address" is universalized; and the "cash value" of John's message to specific congregations must also be universalized—that is, adapted to the life and faith of its current readers. Thus, John's "true" audience is not the seven Asian congregations; it is the ongoing community of faith. Perhaps this very point, so crucial for biblical interpretation, is best made by Revelation, when the interpreter assumes that the number, seven, symbolizes wholeness or inclusiveness[37] and that the seven congregations of Revelation actually represent the church universal, analogous to the life and faith of every congregation in every age. Care must be exercised in making this point. I am not saying that this is the meaning intended by John. His intended meaning was historically conditioned, occasioned, and quite specific in application. Rather, this is a conclusion made from a canonical perspective, so that John's composition functions as a reminder that the writings found in the Christian biblical canon are normative for the "seven congregations" of the universal church that continues to bear witness to God in every age.

The History of Interpreting Revelation

The final moment is really the history of the church's interpretation of Revelation, beginning with its first readers and continuing to today whenever Revelation is picked up and read as the vehicle for "the word of God and the testimony of Jesus Christ." Writing such a complex history, covering some two millennia, would be a Heraclean task. The purpose of this introductory section is considerably more modest: five models for interpreting Revelation are summarized in order to establish the "traditional" boundaries for the church's ongoing conversation with John's Apocalypse.[38] If Revelation is a composition full of extremes and impossibilities, then the proper role of interpretation is to "moderate" its message by demonstrating how it is adaptable for life. In a sense the importance of a "history of interpretation" is similar to the importance of the Talmud within Judaism. The rabbinical writings that constitute the Talmud, a collection of mostly halakaic midrashim (or commentaries on Israel's moral code), presume that the Bible is full of impossible (although normative) moral ideals which must be constantly "re-interpreted" for daily life in order to make them intelligible and meaningful. During the history of its interpretation, believers have viewed Revelation in much the same way: the alien nature of John's images must be "translated" in order to make practical sense of Revelation for the ongoing community of faith.

Five Models of Interpretation.[39] Since the turn of this century, most commentators have included a description of exegetical methods to sketch the history of interpreting Revelation. While cataloging them under different rubrics, scholars generally introduce four different hermeneutical models and identify those who practiced each (Boring, *Revelation*, pp. 47–51). To these four, I will add a fifth model which reflects a post-critical (i.e., "canonical") perspective toward Revelation.

(1) The *end-historical*, or "futurist," model was employed by the earliest interpreters of Revelation (e.g., Irenaeus, Hippolytus, Tertullian, Justin Martyr; but see Boring, *Revelation*, p. 50), and versions of it continue to be used today by many leading conservative (esp. premillennial dispensational) interpreters of Revelation (e.g., Walvoord, Tenney). According to this view, the visions given to John predict in detail two future periods of human history, one falling seven years prior to Christ's return (Rev. 6:1—19:21) and the other one thousand years following the second coming of Christ (20:1—22:6). Except for his introduction (Rev. 1), the messages to the seven churches (Rev. 2–3), and the opening hymns of heavenly praise for God (Rev. 4) and God's Lamb (Rev. 5), John's entire description of God's wrath and eventual triumph over evil refers to world events still in the future.

The good news is that this position recognizes the prophetic nature of John's composition: the prophet John did intend to predict future events in ways similar to the OT prophet.[40] Especially dispensationalism retains John's profound sense of the imminence of Christ's parousia and God's triumph over the sources of human misery. Although Glasson regards this particular point as a problem for the *end-historical* position (Glasson, *Revelation*, p. 11), the interpreter need not deny its fundamental importance for Revelation. Further, from a canonical perspective, John's sense of "the very near future" of Christ's return must remain true for every audience that picks up Revelation to adapt its message afresh to its particular life and concerns. As was true for the first readers of Revelation, repentance and devotion are always called for in the light of God's imminent vindication. Especially in situations of hopelessness and powerlessness, when obedient responses to God become more difficult, the conviction of imminent release can be a word of motivating hope. Moreover, the realistic, even pessimistic view of the social order often linked to this model is in line with John's description of the anti-Christian kingdom.

Among the more significant problems with this hermeneutical model, however, two are important to mention. First, it fails to understand fully the apocalyptic and epistolary character of this composition. Thus, the symbolic language is misconstrued as literal prophecy, leading interpreters to propose a detailed blueprint for world history, usually referenced by current events. Typically, this blueprint is then presented as divine oracle (rather than human interpretation) in order to promote a theological or ethical agenda. The commentator's ideological and apologetic concerns tend to diminish John's pastoral concern conveyed by his composition's epistolary format.

Second, this model also demotes the significance of the "moment of origin" for controlling the interpretation of Revelation. If John's book has no significance to those for whom it was first addressed, then the interpreter is allowed to relate it on his or her own terms to his or her audience.

(2) The *church-historical*, or "historical," model of interpretation also views Revelation as predictive prophecy, although it views history in a more macroscopic way. Rather than predicting future events which correlate to specific details of John's visions, the interpreter conceives of Revelation as a symbolic description of history from Christ's death to his return. Typically, the focus of this interpretation is the interpreter's own time, which is usually posited at the end of history, near the return of Christ. Thus, the interpreter champions John's idea of history that all events, especially those considered important to the interpreter's community, are under the aegis of a ruling God; that all of human society since Christ's death stand under God's indictment; and that all humanity moves toward Christ's second advent, either for judgment or reward. Especially if viewing Revelation from a

canonical perspective, the interpreter will concede that it carries this sort of theological freight.

The chief problem with this hermeneutical model is similar to that of the end-historical model: both dismiss uncritically John's intended meaning for his readers at the close of the first century as holding any significance for his readers at the close of the twentieth. In this case, however, rather than being too ideological or sectarian, the church-historical position is faulty because it is too abstract to be of much practical use for the formation of Christian faith; in this sense, it denies the church's intent for the biblical canon. To my knowledge, however, this view has no modern proponents.

(3) The *non-historical*, or "idealist," model interprets Revelation as a work of theological or poetic power which transcends the intentions of its author. Revelation is a deposit of spiritual insight which is universally binding. Origen's allegorical treatment of Revelation,[41] or, more recently, the mythopoetic rendering of its meaning by J. Ellul and A. Farrer, are examples of this approach. P. S. Minear's work on apocalyptic may also fall under this category, although he is interested in Revelation's prophetic theology and in the historical situations for which its theology was first applied. For him, however, the charismatic nature of apocalyptic theology resists historical critical analysis because prophetic charisma formed, even required, non-historical expressions of language, actions and conceptions. Those scholars such as Bowman and Blevins, who view Revelation as a drama, or Lauchli and Shepherd, who view Revelation as liturgy, do so on form-critical and historical grounds rather than for purely aesthetic reasons.

There is some benefit to this approach. Modern interpreters tend to view Revelation "atomistically"; they are interested in making some sense of various parts or aspects of the written text. The tendency of modern methods of interpretation, characteristic of both conservative and critical scholars, is to get lost in the minutiae of this composition's manifold images, giving meaning to even the most meaningless part, and to lose the "sense" of the whole message. This model of interpretation bids the interpreter away from an overly scrupulous scrutiny of the visual text of Revelation, to hear it read aloud (1:3) or to see it performed. As a result, the student often is empowered to hear and understand John's message afresh.

However, unless the interpreter's hearing or seeing of Revelation is controlled by the theological convictions and ethical commitments of evangelical faith, meanings made will tend to be more existential and individualistic than biblical faith and devoid of eschatological meaning for the whole church. In my view, the tendency of those who practice this method is to diminish Revelation's canonical intent to "universalize" its meaning, while at the same time rejecting any interest in John's more pastoral intentions.

(4) The *contemporary-historical*, or "preterist" (i.e., past), model is preferred by most critical biblical scholars today.[42] According to this model the interpreter seeks to reconstruct the "moment of origin" as the essential locus of meaning for every subsequent moment in the history of interpretation. The assumption is that John had a message to convey to the congregations he addressed; and he wrote in a way that would have been understood by his first readers. John did not write a book for subsequent believers; neither did he write a book for a NT canon which was not yet a reality; rather, he wrote an Apocalypse for a specific audience to resolve a specific crisis.

Of course this is all true, and therefore the full utilization of critical methods is useful for any interpretation of Revelation. Especially when this perspective is coupled with a desire to understand John's theological (Caird, Beasley-Murray) and political (Schüssler Fiorenza, A. Collins) program, the results continue to be exciting. Further, if the interpreter holds to the importance of the writer as an inspired prophet of God, then there are theological reasons for taking the writer's intended meanings seriously (cf. 2 Pet. 1:20–21). There are problems associated with historical critical treatments of Revelation, however, that are addressed by the canonical critical model to which we now turn.[43]

(5) A *canonical critical* approach to biblical interpretation has more to do with a perspective toward Scripture than with a technique or method to interpret it (see above, "the history of canonizing Revelation"). In this sense, it belongs to the "post-critical" period of biblical interpretation, characterized by an approval of critical methods and an appreciation of the advances in understanding Scripture claimed by those methods. At the same time, more and more scholars now recognize that all too often a historical or literary critical understanding of Scripture is rarely translated in practical ways to help form the life and faith of the church.

Scholars tend to talk with and write for other scholars rather than for the Christian rank-and-file.

Canonical criticism is a method constructed in response to this problem. Its epistemology is more religious than positivistic; that is, the ultimate aim of biblical interpretation is to acquire knowledge that determines and shapes the identity of God's people in history. Whatever is the yield of critical methods in reconstructing the author's intentions, it must be "re-interpreted" and brought into agreement with the canon's intention: to form the faith of God's people. The distinctive contribution of canonical criticism is its efforts to recover the *idea of a canon* as a guide to biblical interpretation—to guide the interpreter to locate meaning in biblical texts that will allow Scripture to function as the church's rule of faith. Accordingly, the yield of a critical scholarship is centered and given direction by a perspective of the Bible's authorized role within the church.

Most important in this regard is the recognition that the church formed the NT as a second written testament to God's gospel, disclosed in the life of Jesus from Nazareth, and placed it together with the first testament (OT), disclosed in the life of Israel, thereby forming a distinctively *Christian* (rather than Jewish) biblical canon. The church's intention for this canon, or rule of faith, is to provide the worshiping community with a continuing guide to direct the formation of a distinctively Christian faith and life. Christians believe that God's promise of redemption from sin and death, first given to Israel and contained in the OT, looks ahead to its fulfillment, effected by Jesus from Nazareth whose story is told by NT writers. All biblical writings, whether OT or NT, are various interpretations of "the word of God and the testimony of Jesus Christ." When viewed together, the biblical canon is a composition which bears witness to God's gospel. Thus, its continuing function is to measure to what extent the people of God bear witness to that gospel, whether to encourage those who measure up or to rebuke those who do not.

This hermeneutical enterprise helps explain the relationship between the OT and the Christ event according to the NT Apocalypse. From a canonical perspective, the OT interprets John's vision as a testimony to a faithful God, who has disclosed in the slain and exalted Lamb a firm commitment to fulfill the biblical promise to restore all things. In this regard, a principal

feature of this commentary on Revelation is a concern to recover
allusions to or echoes of the OT as the primary context within
which John first understood his visions as the word of God.
In writing down his visions as midrashim (interpretations) of
various biblical texts or stories, John obligates his interpreters
to understand Revelation against this biblical background—in
continuity with and the fulfillment of OT faith. My concern for
"intertextuality"—for the relationship between OT and NT as mutually informing—is driven, then, by theological rather than literary commitments.

Our second point is that Revelation's canonical intent differs from its author's intent. The church included Revelation in
the NT as a critical part of a whole, which continues to convey
the "word of God and the testimony of Jesus Christ" to the
present community of interpreters. John's interest was focused by
the concerns of his first-century community of readers. Certainly
a canonical perspective is vitally interested in John's intended
meanings; however, its ultimate objective is to understand how
his intended meanings continue to frame the core convictions of
the Bible's "eternal gospel" for Revelation's current interpreters.

The best of many possible meanings, then, are those in continuity with John's intended meanings, in continuity with the commitments of the Bible's "eternal gospel," and adaptable to the life
and faith of current interpreters in ways that form them into God's
people. That is, the best interpretations of biblical texts are so
ranked because they conform to the Bible's story of God's covenant with Israel (theological criterion). Further, the best interpretations of biblical texts result in concrete responses of devotion
to God and love of neighbor (ethical criterion). Many historical-
literary critical interpretations of Revelation are interested in the
first rather than twentieth century; and their interest lies more
with philology than praxis. As critical as these interests are for
the hermeneutical enterprise, a canonical rendering of biblical
texts finds meanings that respond to the church's present crises.
The epistemological assumption behind this perspective is that
John's situation in the first century is analogous to the current
situation; the biblical situation is always comparable to the situation of its interpreter. Our point is that the hermeneutical program must include this as a decisive element of its stance toward
the biblical text. In fact the Bible's canonical role insists that the

the ultimate locus of meaning is the church's situation in life, and not the author's intended meaning, which is subordinate to its canonical intent.[44]

Conclusion

The purpose of this introduction to Revelation has been to establish a context within which to interpret the book. We have done so with a particular thesis in mind: *Revelation is an apocalyptic-prophetic epistle written to encourage the whole community of faith to focus its faith and life on the triumph of a sovereign God's reign which has now been disclosed through the exaltation of God's Christ.* It is God and not the Evil One who sits on heaven's throne; it is God who exercises judgment against the enemies of the Lord's reign; it is God who can make good on the Bible's promise of salvation; and it is God who will dispense the blessings of salvation to the community of those who faithfully follow the Lamb.

Our thesis suggests several ingredients of a hermeneutical model which controls our exposition of Revelation. We will not interpret John's prophetic apocalypse as a detailed prediction of the final days of salvation's history, and will we not attempt to find any period of world history lurking behind its rich imagery. Rather, we suppose that John's composition contains an interpretation of history, a "theologized" history if you will, which asserts that Christ's coronation in heaven initiates a new period of salvation's history, which is climaxed at his return to earth when God will make good on the biblical promise to transform the redeemed community into a people fit to live in the shalom and glory of God and God's Lamb forever.

We will also interpret Revelation as a letter, written by a pastor who utilizes apocalyptic forms and prophetic purposes to pastor his congregations. Letters are not historical narratives; they are written not to tell a story but to address problems that threaten faith in God. Letters interpret those circumstances facing real people that may lead them to draw new, sometimes incorrect, boundaries around their relationships with God, with one another, and with the surrounding world. Revelation is written to interpret the collision of the sacred and profane, when the faithful must own all the more their conviction that God has triumphed and that their devotion is not in vain.

Revelation interprets this conflict with a word of hope that challenges the possible objections to Christian devotion raised by the enemies of God's reign: where is this professed loving and powerful God in the midst of human poverty and suffering? Has God not heard the laments that rise up even from among God's people? There is a certain logic to these objections, because there is a certain ambiguity which attends to Christian devotion in a secular, materialistic world. On the one hand, Christians confess their devotion to a sovereign, loving God, whose fidelity and trustworthiness have been disclosed in Jesus from Nazareth. On the other hand, human experience, shaped by the powers and ideals of secularity, is often characterized by coercive power and violence that contradicts what Christians believe about a God who promises shalom and a shared life. For all practical purposes, life on planet Earth is in the hands of those who rule over the anti-Christian kingdom, visible and invisible; they seem more powerful than God.

The "theo-logic" of Revelation challenges the compelling logic of those whose assumptions about God are informed more by the realities of secular history than by the realities of salvation's history. In that the triumph of God's reign is rooted in a past event of history—the death and exaltation of Christ—there is sufficient evidence to continue to trust in God's reign and depend upon God's love. Especially on those occasions when God seems most absent, Revelation calls attention to the past and toward heaven for a realized Christology, and to the future for the full measure of its historical precipitate as the ultimate vindication of Christian hope.

The point is crucial for understanding John's reasons for writing Revelation and the church's reasons for canonizing it. For its first and current readers, Revelation is especially for those struggling believers who need to be reminded that the axis of faith in the world is *the gospel of God, which stimulates both the community's hope and its repentance, which is the triumph and demonstration of God's sovereign and righteous reign in the exalted and returning Christ.*

Outline of Revelation

I. PROLOGUE (1:1-3)

II. GREETINGS to the Seven Churches (1:4-3:22)
  A. Greetings from John of Patmos (1:4-20)
    1. To the seven churches in Asia (1:4-8)
    2. From John, commissioned to write heavenly mysteries (1:9-20)
  B. Greetings from Christ (2:1-3:22)
    1. To the church in Ephesus (2:1-7)
    2. To the church in Smyrna (2:8-11)
    3. To the church in Pergamum (2:12-17)
    4. To the church in Thyatira (2:18-29)
    5. To the church in Sardis (3:1-6)
    6. To the church in Philadelphia (3:7-13)
    7. To the church in Laodicea (3:14-22)

III. THANKSGIVING for God's Reign: The Ground of Christian Faith (4:1-11)
  A. Throne of God in Heaven: The Sovereign of the Cosmic Order (4:1-6a)
  B. The Four Living Creatures: Thanksgiving for God's Eternality (4:6b-8)
  C. The Twenty-four Elders: Thanksgiving for God as Creator (4:9-11)

IV. SERMON on the History of God's Salvation: An Exhortation to Christian Faithfulness (5:1-22:6a)
  A. The Exaltation of God's Lamb: The "Penultimate" Event of Salvation's History (5:1-11:19)
    1. The exaltation of God's Lamb (5:1-14)
      a. who is worthy to open God's scroll and its seven seals (5:1-10)
      b. who is worthy of worship with God (5:11-14)
    2. The revelation of God's wrath against the fallen creation (6:1-8:5)
      a. God's Lamb opens six seals of divine wrath (6:1-17)
      b. Interlude: Reminder of God's faithfulness to God's people
        (1) the sealing of the "remnant of God" (7:1-8)
        (2) the restoration of the "rest of Israel" (7:9-17)
      c. God's Lamb Opens the Seventh and Final Seal (8:1-11:14)
        (1) God's Lamb opens the seventh seal (8:1-5)
        (2) Angelic trumpets sound six more judgments of God (8:6-9:21)

a′ Indictment: the terrible triumph of God's rule over earth's kings and their cities (16:17–21)

b′ Evidence and Execution: The kings' whore and the seduction of secular power (17:1–18)

c′ Aftermath of Babylon's Destruction (18:1–19:10)

    1′ Angelic pronouncement of doom (18:1–3)

    2′ Babylon's response: lamentations (18:1–20)

    3′ Angelic pronouncement of doom (18:21–24)

    4′ Heaven's response: praise of God's triumph (19:1–10)

C. The Return of the Exalted Lamb: The Ultimate Event of Salvation's History (19:11–22:6a)

    1. The day of the Lamb: the final revelation of God's triumph over the evil dominion (19:11–20:15)

        a. The Lamb returns as Word of God (19:11–16)

        b. The Lamb invites his followers to a victory celebration (19:17–18)

        c. God, the Lamb, and the Lamb's people have triumphed over the beasts (19:19–21)

        d. God, the Lamb, and the Lamb's people have triumphed over Satan (20:1–10)

        e. God, the Lamb, and the Lamb's people have triumphed over Death and Hades (20:11–15)

    2. The city of God: entering God's promised shalom (21:1–22:6a)

V. The Epistolary BENEDICTION (22:6b–21)

    A. Epistolary Summary of John's Apocalypse (22:6b–7)

    B. Four Exhortations to Heed Its Message: God's Triumph Is Coming Soon (22:8–19)

        1. An exhortation from John who received the Revelation (22:8–11)

        2. An exhortation from Christ who gave the Revelation (22:12–16)

        3. An invitation to respond to the Revelation (22:17)

        4. A closing caveat: John's Revelation is "tamper-proof" (22:18–20a)

    C. The Benedictory Prayer (22:20b–21)

Notes

1. Cf. Elisabeth Schüssler Fiorenza, "Revelation," in *The New Testament and Its Modern Interpreters*, ed. E. J. Epp and G. W. McRae (Atlanta: Scholars Press, 1989), pp. 407-27, for a fine summary of the current state of historical critical research on Revelation.

2. Albert A. Bell, "The Date of John's Apocalypse: The Evidence of Some Roman Historians Reconsidered," *NTS* 25 (1978), pp. 93-102; B. M. Newman, "The Fallacy of the Domitian Hypothesis," *NTS* 10 (1963), pp. 133-39. For a survey of opinion see Pierre Prigent, "Au temps de l'Apocalypse," *RHPR* 54 (1974), pp. 455-83; 55 (1975), pp. 215-35, 341-63. For a recent defense of an early date, see K. L. Gentry, Jr., *Before Jerusalem Fell* (Tyler, Tex.: Institute for Christian Economics, 1989).

3. Dionysius and Eusebius argued against Johannine authorship, but they are notable exceptions and their interests were more polemical and ideological than historical; see Beasley-Murray, *Revelation*, pp. 32-34.

4. A similar claim can be made for the four Gospels and Acts, which are all anonymous compositions. Their authority derives from the subject matter of their narratives, recognized as vital and trustworthy for faith, rather than from their authorship per se.

5. Cf. R. A. Culpepper, *The Johannine School*, SBLDS 26 (Missoula, Mont.: Scholars Press, 1975); R. E. Brown, *The Community of the Beloved Disciple* (Paramus, N.J.: Paulist Press, 1979); E. Schüssler Fiorenza, "The Quest for the Johannine School: The Apocalypse and the Fourth Gospel," *NTS* 23 (1979), pp. 402-27; and finally D. E. Aune, who argues that John does not belong to the Johannine circle of prophets, but heads his own school of prophets within the Asian church, "The Prophetic Circle of John of Patmos," *JSNT* 37 (1989), pp. 103-16.

6. Esp. important is Colin J. Hemer, *Letters to the Seven Churches*, JSNTSup 11 (Sheffield: JSOT Press, 1986); also the series of essays which discuss the sociology of apocalypticism found in David Hellholm, ed., *Apocalypticism in the Mediterranean World and the Near East* (Tübingen: J. C. B. Mohr, 1983), pp. 641-770. Still helpful is William Ramsey's *The Letters to the Seven Churches of Asia* (Grand Rapids: Baker, 1985). For the political argot within Revelation as it relates to the audience's *Sitz im Leben*, see A. Y. Collins, "The Political Perspective of the Revelation to John," *JBL* 96 (1977), pp. 241-56.

7. One of the earliest to do so was James Kallas, "The Apocalypse—an Apocalyptic Book?" *JBL* 86 (1967), pp. 69-80.

8. To my knowledge, Schüssler Fiorenza is the first commentator who correctly understands the literary make-up of Revelation as a "prophetic-apocalyptic letter." A few others such as Krodel, who calls

Revelation a "prophetic-apocalyptic circular letter" (*Revelation*, pp. 51–61), have since followed her lead. However, our own account of how to put these three literary realities together is quite different. We prefer to arrange the book according to the letter form; Schüssler Fiorenza tends to concentrate her consideration of genre by the literary conventions of apocalypticism and so fails to exploit the rhetorical dimensions of John's composition. Krodel is better on this point, even though I finally disagree with him on how best to understand the structure of Revelation as a religious letter.

9. Cf. David Aune, "The Apocalypse of John and the Problem of Genre," *Semeia* 36 (1986), pp. 65–96; John J. Collins, "Introduction: Towards the Morphology of a Genre," *Semeia* 14 (1979), pp. 1–19; P. D. Hanson, "Apocalypse, the Genre," *IDBSup*, pp. 27–28; Lars Hartman, "Survey of the Problem of Apocalyptic Genre," in *Apocalypticism in the Mediterranean World and the Near East*, ed. D. Hellholm (Tübingen: J. C. B. Mohr, 1983), 329–43; David Hellholm, "The Problem of Apocalyptic Genre and the Apocalypse of John," *Semeia* 36 (1986), pp. 13–64.

10. The interpreter will find these common phrases deposited in Christ's exhortation to "overcome" (2:7, 11, 17, 26–29; 3:5, 12, 21) on the one hand, and in John's vision of the new Jerusalem (21:7–22:6a) on the other. Only in the final instance below do we find a parallelism which falls outside of these two sections of John's book of visions—and then still pertains to his vision of Christ's future parousia. This literary construction would seem to agree with our thesis that the *new Jerusalem is the community of overcomers* (see my commentary on Rev. 21:1—22:6a). Thus, (1) the images of the "paradise of God," focused by the "tree of life" (2:7), are parallel to 22:1–5, esp. 22:2; (2) "the second death" (2:11), is parallel to 21:8; (3) images of "name" and "stone" (2:17) are parallel to 21:27 and 21:19; (4) the subjection of the "nations" (2:26–27) is parallel to 19:15 (judgment of the nations) and 21:24 (salvation of the nations); (5) the references to the overcomer's "dress" and to "his name" in the "book of life" (3:5) echo images of the Lamb's bride and the Lamb's book of life in 21:2, 27; (6) to the faithful church in Philadelphia, Christ refers to "the new Jerusalem, which is coming down out of heaven from my God" (3:12), clearly parallel to John's vision of the new Jerusalem in 21:1–2; and (7) the image of reigning with Christ (3:21) is repeated in the millennial vision, 20:4–6.

11. Beasley-Murray compares these symbol systems to "political cartoons" which use traditional caricatures such as "Uncle Sam" or the "Russian Bear" to comment upon political life (*Revelation*, pp. 16–17).

12. William A. Beardslee, *Literary Criticism of the NT* (Philadelphia: Fortress Press, 1970), p. 57.

13. For a complete discussion of the typological methods of biblical writers, see Richard M. Davidson, *Typology in Scripture*, AUSDDS 2 (Berrien Springs, Mich.: Andrews University Press, 1981).

14. Kallas argues that Revelation's idea of suffering is non-apocalyptic in that it generally stems from divine retribution rather than from evil powers. While his conclusion is defensible if John's central vision of the dragon and the beasts (Rev. 12-13) were excluded from his composition, it is indefensible as Revelation now stands. Perhaps we could say that, like everything else in Revelation, the suffering motif of apocalypticism has been moderated by John in light of other interests and convictions.

15. Beardslee, *Literary Criticism*, p. 55.

16. For a brilliant discussion of the biblical ideal of *shalom*, or peace, see Nicholas Wolterstorff, *Until Justice and Peace Embrace* (Grand Rapids: Eerdmans, 1983). Wolterstorff rightly stresses the social aspects of this ideal; so that God's salvation promises much more than a private, spiritual experience of "peace with God." Shalom is a social reality, characterizing the political and economic structures of human existence as well. Therefore, the experience of God's shalom will end social injustice that renders some persons without power or freedom and impoverishes still others.

17. Although he exaggerates his case, see David Hill's helpful discussion, *New Testament Prophecy*, NFTL (Atlanta: John Knox Press, 1979), pp. 70-93. Also David Aune, *Prophecy in Early Christianity and the Ancient Mediterranean World* (Grand Rapids: Eerdmans, 1983); and Ulrich Müller, *Prophetie und Predigt im Neuen Testament*, SNT 10 (Gütersloh: Mohn, 1975). Schüssler Fiorenza, in her "Johannine School," understands (with Aune) that the "Johannine School" is a community of Christian prophets, with John of Patmos serving as its probable leader.

18. Cf. D. Moody Smith, *John*, PC (Philadelphia: Fortress Press, 1976), p. 84.

19. Cf. Hill, *Prophecy*, pp. 76-85, for extended discussion of prophetic forms found within Revelation.

20. Hill, *Prophecy*, p. 73.

21. Smith, *John*, p. 83; see also E. Boring, "Influence of Christian Prophecy on the Johannine Portrayal of the Paraclete and Jesus," *NTS* 25 (1978-79), pp. 113-23, who contends for a common "revelatory gestalt" shared by Revelation and the paraclete tradition in the Fourth Gospel. The prophets within the Christian community justified their role by a theology of the Paraclete, who continues to convey revelation from Christ to Christ's followers on earth through their prophecies.

22. Cf. F. F. Bruce, *The Canon of Scripture* (Downers Grove: Inter-Varsity Press, 1988), pp. 264-65.

23. Cf. George E. Ladd, "Why Not Prophetic-Apocalyptic?" *JBL* 76 (1957), pp. 192-200.

24. Cf. William G. Doty, *Letters in Primitive Christianity* (Philadelphia: Fortress Press, 1973), esp. pp. 56-57.

25. For a general discussion of the ancient genre of letter, see D. E. Aune, *The New Testament and Its Literary Environment* (Philadelphia: Westminster Press, 1987), pp. 158–225.

26. My graduate student, Ms. Tammera Adams, has identified eight categories which pertain to discipleship in Revelation and which demonstrate the author's pastoral concern. These characteristics of Christian discipleship are found in the various exhortations to the first readers, found throughout the book: (1) hear (i.e., obey and repent in the light of) the Word of the Lord (1:3; 2:17; 3:3; 22:17); (2) endure suffering (1:9; 2:2; 2:17; 3:21; 7:14ff.; 12:11; 13:10; 14:12; cf. John 16:33); (3) be faithful to the point of death (2:10; 11:3; 12:11; 14:13; 20:4ff.); (4) understand the significance of names as marks of true identity (2:17; 14:1, 9; 20:4ff.; cf. John 15:21); (5) public affirmation of apostolic definition of orthodoxy, esp. by community's teachers (2:2; 2:4,5; 2:15; 2:20); (6) evaluation leading to correction and repentance (2:5; 2:16; 2:21–22; 3:3; 3:19; 9:20–21; 16:9; 16:11); (7) public witness to gospel by "overcoming" evil and living for God (orthopraxy) (2:7; 2:11; 2:17; 2:26; 3:4–5; 3:12; 3:15–21; 5:5; 12:11; 14:4; 15:2; 17:14; 18:4; 21:7; 22:11, 14); and (8) public worship of God and God's Lamb (1:17; 4:8, 11; 5:9–10; 5:12–13; 7:10; 11:5; 11:17; 15:3; 16:5; 19:1, 5–6). For another discussion of the ethical elements of this idea, see Schüssler Fiorenza's helpful discussion of Rev. 14:1–5, "Followers of the Lamb: Visionary Rhetoric and Social-Political Situation," in *Discipleship in the New Testament*, ed. F. Segovia (Philadelphia: Fortress Press, 1985). For a discussion of the elements of public worship within Revelation, see Pierre Prigent, *Apocalypse et liturgie*, CT 53 (Neuchâtel: Delachaux & Niestle, 1964), and Samuel Lauchli, "Eine Gottesdienststruktur in der Johannesoffenbarung," *TZ* 16 (1960), pp. 359–78.

27. Among the recent, more popular introductions to the "canonical" dimension of NT interpretation, the best are H. Gamble, *The New Testament Canon: Its Making and Meaning* (Philadelphia: Fortress Press, 1985) and L. M. McDonald, *The Formation of the Christian Biblical Canon* (Nashville: Abingdon, 1988). A more technical discussion from a historical perspective is B. M. Metzger, *The Canon of the New Testament* (Oxford: Clarendon Press, 1988). Perhaps the most influential in this regard is H. von Campenhausen, *The Formation of the Christian Bible* (Philadelphia: Fortress Press, 1972). See also C. S. C. Williams, "The History of the Text and Canon of the New Testament," in *Cambridge History of the Bible*, vol. 2, ed. G. W. H. Lampe (Cambridge: University Press, 1969). For the theological and hermeneutical importance of the NT's final "canonical shape" see B. S. Childs, *The New Testament as Canon: an Introduction* (Philadelphia: Fortress Press, 1984); and for the theological and hermeneutical importance of the process of canonization see J. A. Sanders, *Canon and Community* (Philadelphia: Fortress Press, 1985). In this same regard, see R. W.

Wall, "The Problem of the Multiple Letter Canon of the New Testament," *HorBT* 8 (1986), pp. 1–31; idem, "The Promise of the Multiple Letter Canon of the New Testament," *CSR* 16 (1987), pp. 336–54.

28. Scholars often speak of the perceived apostolicity or orthodoxy and inspiration or usefulness of those writings which were included in the canon; however, definitions of these criteria remain contested, and we will use these terms in their most general sense. Thus, a writing was considered for canonical status if its content did not conflict with the apostolic tradition (i.e., the criterion of apostolicity) and if the consequences of its use were effective in forming and maintaining a distinctively Christian community in the world (i.e., the criterion of inspiration).

29. Gamble, NT *Canon*, p. 56.

30. Bruce, *Canon*, pp. 204–5.

31. Denis Farkasfalvy and William Farmer, *The Formation of the New Testament Canon* (New York: Paulist Press, 1983), p. 39.

32. Cf. Metzger, *Canon*, p. 105.

33. H. Hofmann, *Luther und die Johannes Apokalypse*, BGBE 24 (Tübingen: J. C. B. Mohr, 1982).

34. Cf. A. C. Outler, "The 'Logic' of Canon-making and the Task of Canon-criticism," in *Texts and Testaments. Essays in Honor of S. D. Currie*, ed. W. E. March (San Antonio: Trinity University Press, 1980), 263–76.

35. R. W. Wall, "Introduction: New Testament Ethics," *HorBT* 5 (1983), pp. 49–94.

36. R. W. Wall, "Problem of Multiple Letter," pp. 21–23.

37. Some commentators on Revelation have been themselves persuaded by, but are not very persuasive about, the symbolic and structural significance of the number seven—(Lohmeyer, Charles, Farrer, Schüssler Fiorenza are among them). In our view, seven has symbolic value for John but no more so than other numbers critical to his symbolic world, such as twelve. To subdivide John's book of visions into a scheme of sevens, however, is forced and artificial.

38. For an excellent history of interpretation, see Bernard McGinn, "Revelation," in *The Literary Guide to the Bible*, ed. R. Alter and F. Kermode (Cambridge, Mass.: Harvard University Press, 1987), pp. 523–41.

39. Charles' concise discussion of the various models for interpreting Revelation (*Revelation*, vol. 1, pp. clxxxiii–clxxxvii) is still unsurpassed and is usually parroted by modern commentators. Cf. his *Studies in the Apocalypse* (Edinburgh: T. & T. Clark, 1913).

40. Cf. John Barton, *Oracles of God* (London: Darton, Longman, and Todd, 1986), esp. pp. 179–213.

41. Cf. H. Crouzel, *Origen* (New York: Harper & Row, 1989), pp. 61–86.

42. Cf. Andre Feuillet's bibliographical essay, *The Apocalypse* (New York: Alba House, 1965), which discusses recent history of interpreting

Revelation (1900–1960) according to various methods and theological interests. Ugo Vanni's *L'Apocalypse johannique et l'Apocalyptique dans le Nouveau Testament*, BETL 53 (Louvain: Louvain University Press, 1980), pp. 21–46, updates Feuillet's work through 1980.

43. A more popular and constructive response to the historical critical enterprise from a canonical critical perspective is provided by James A. Sanders in "The Bible as Canon," *Christian Century* (Dec. 2, 1981), pp. 1250–55.

44. For this point see Sanders, *Canon and Community*.

§1 *Prologue (Rev. 1:1–3)*

The author's prologue to Revelation intends to establish its content as a **revelation** (*apokalypsis*) **of Jesus Christ**. The book's opening phrase has a twofold function. First, it situates the composition within a particular literary and theological tradition: apocalypticism. Within this tradition, the idea of revelation refers to a process whereby God makes known through visions the final days of salvation's history. Such visions are not like dreams; they are revelatory acts of God, mediated typically through angels and received by a seer, who, under the influence of the spirit of prophecy, is able to transmit divine revelation to the community of believers.

Second, the opening phrase validates the author's authority and as a result the importance of his composition. Much like Paul in his letter to the Galatians (1:11–16), John establishes his credentials by linking what he has written to the revelation he has received from Jesus Christ. Further, because his subject matter is derived from divine revelation, John expects his audience to recognize his composition as **the word of God and the testimony of Jesus Christ**: it is the gospel of God, given to and witnessed by Jesus Christ. Given the apocalyptic character of his composition, such an expectation is intensified because **the time is near**. What John has written down intends to unveil the mysteries of God's salvation for those who live at the end of time. Of course, the purpose of any epistolary composition, even an apocalyptic one, is pastoral; indeed, John has written down his visions with a careful eye to the theological crises of his first readers. Revelation was written to transform the way believers "see" their own worlds and as a consequence respond to God and to neighbor in truth and love.

1:1 / **John**, who writes in service of **Jesus Christ**, claims to have received divine **revelation** through visions (1) from Christ's angel, who presumably received it (2) from Christ, to whom it

was first given (3) by God for the community of Christ's disciples
on earth. This scheme, where prophetic truth has its ultimate
source in God, envisions the "vertical" theology of the Johannine tradition. Just as in John's Gospel, Jesus' mission as God's
Christ was to incarnate the truth about God which he had heard
and seen, thus ensuring its trustworthiness and effectiveness for
life and faith.

In accord with the apocalyptic tradition, Christ has conveyed the apocalypse to John through his angel (cf. 17:1–3). The
angel's immediate function is to facilitate God's wish that the revelation, which had previously been disclosed to the heavenly
Christ, now be disclosed to the church. That Jesus sends **his
angel** not only suggests the angel's subordinate role in the communication between the Lord and John, it also assumes Jesus'
exalted status as the Risen Christ of God: Jesus sent his angel
"from heaven." Further, John would no doubt have recognized
the angel from the Lord as his "celestial double"; thus, such a
vision represents the continuing and expected activity of the Risen
Christ.

John is singled out to receive the apocalypse because he
is Christ's **servant**. As with the epistolary introductions of other
biblical writers (cf. Rom. 1:1; James 1:1), John's use of the servant motif does not refer to a lowly status but ironically to his
authority to transmit divine revelation to Christ's other **servants**
on earth. To be sure, there is a degree of passivity implied by the
very terms of the phrase, **his angel to his servant John**: the revelatory process which begins with God and ends with the readership is preserved from unwanted or intrusive agents.

1:2 / This point is underscored by the subsequent description of John's vocation, which **testifies to everything he saw**;
his mission is to transmit what he sees and nothing more. This
phrase does not mean that John's composition is the product of
spontaneous inspiration; rather, the very act of seeing entails a
theological rather than a literary claim on John: his revelation is
from God and about God's reign, rather than from a human author with his own agenda to promote. Of course, we realize that
no author can be completely distanced from his or her composition. Thus, even though the raw material of this composition
was received spontaneously and involuntarily by prophetic inspiration, the very fact that it was written down in a particular

genre for deliberate reasons presumes that John's visions were
not communicated to his readers without his "intervention."

1:3 / The beatitudes of Revelation share a common perspective with the beatitudes found elsewhere in the NT: they assure the hearers of their future participation in God's promised
salvation. In this sense, the parallel beatitudes, **blessed is the one
who reads the words of this prophecy/blessed are those who hear
it and take to heart what is written in it**, do not describe a particular response to what John has written as much as they promise an eschatological reality into which those who obey its message
enter, when the **time**, now near, finally arrives.

John Barton has recently argued that in the time of the NT
the **words of prophecy** would have been perceived as containing
"mysteries" beyond apostolic instruction and even predictions of
future events. The modern critical interpretation of Revelation has
almost dismissed this element entirely, perhaps in reaction to the
literalism of fundamentalistic interpretations as characterized by
Hal Lindsey's *The Late Great Planet Earth*. Many scholars prefer
to understand the idea of prophecy as referring to a prophetic
"style"—forthtelling rather than foretelling—which prepares the
readers for criticism and conversion (Boring, *Revelation*, p. 80). If
we are true to John's intent, however, then we must read Revelation as containing the prediction of the future of God's salvation, focused especially in the promise of Christ's parousia. The
fulfillment of this promise is the very essence of the gospel, "the
word of God and the testimony of Jesus Christ."

Additional Notes §1

1:1–3 / Schüssler Fiorenza is no doubt correct in commenting
that "For the average Christian . . . Revelation has remained a book with
'seven seals' and an 'esoteric revelation'—despite its claim to be the revelation of Jesus Christ for Christian communities" (*Revelation*, p. 35). Yet,
by attending to John's introduction of his composition in 1:1–3 the reader
receives three important clues for understanding Revelation. These suggestions, adroitly introduced by the author, run against the current tide
of Revelation scholarship during the modern period. Generally, there
are two opinions asserted about the character of the composition itself.
Some argue that Revelation is the product of a pseudepigrapher's imagi-

nation, purposely cast as an apocalypse for theological or sociological intentions. More conservative commentators argue that John has written down in an objective and orderly fashion an accurate description of the visions he saw. Neither opinion takes the author's own assessment of his composition seriously enough; both are biased by assumptions about the nature of divine revelation itself.

First, John's opening words tell us that he has received visions from God; later, he is commissioned to write down the visions received (1:11, 19). Revelation is a book of visions, a description of what John actually saw and heard. What John saw and heard was then recognized and described in the terms of his traditions (biblical and of Jesus), as well as in light of his own religious and cultural experiences. A vision is never simply "seen"; any perception includes an interpretation of what is sensed. Throughout Revelation, we find echoes and images borrowed from John's Bible or from his world to present what he has seen and heard in intelligible ways. For example, when John turns to locate his commissioner, he sees "someone like a son of man"; that is, John identifies the Risen Christ in terms of a well-known biblical image from Daniel. He further edited his memories, arranging them by the ancient literary genre of letter in order to address crises of Christian faith found within particular congregations of believers.

Second, John understands his vision as "the word of God and the testimony of Jesus" (1:2); its message is completely consistent with the gospel of Christian faith he preaches and for which he is now imprisoned (1:9). Indeed, the theological convictions which center Revelation are completely consistent with the Bible's two testaments to God's glory and grace. The interpreter makes a mistake in our view by reading Revelation as a prediction of current world history or as a blueprint of a period of history yet to come. Likewise, the interpreter confuses John's purposes by assuming the importance of each element of Revelation's complex symbol systems. If Revelation is gospel, then its whole message and the meaning one makes of any part of it should always be measured by its consistency with the good news that God has triumphed over the evil powers and has fulfilled the promise to restore and bless God's covenant people, and through them all creation, through the risen and exalted Jesus Christ.

Finally, John views his composition as "words of prophecy" (1:3) and thus instructive for Christian faith and life; its raw material has a divine source, and he is inspired to write it down. Within the Johannine tradition, the act of writing inspired prophecy carries a certain measure of importance: it is the authoritative medium by which the believing community is nurtured and corrected by the word of God (cf. 1 John 1:4; 2:12–14, 21, 26; 5:13). Further, the exhortation to *hear* these "words of prophecy" suggests the first audience derived an understanding of God's triumph through Christ from those impressions recovered by listening to Revelation read aloud.

While he has seven Christian congregations in mind, there is reason to believe that the seer understood the number seven to carry universal significance. Further, the canonizing church, in recognizing the book's inspiration, included it as part of the Christian biblical canon because of its normative character for subsequent generations of believers. The point is this: the interpreter should not assume that Revelation is esoteric writing, relevant only for an ancient Christian people doing battle with the evil forces of the Roman Empire. The proper hermeneutical judgment, consistent with its author, is that Revelation is useful in forming Christian faith for today.

§2 Greetings from John of Patmos to the Seven Churches of Asia (Rev. 1:4–20)

An author's salutation is more than formal greetings; it usually contains a self-introduction and a description of the audience, which together define the relationship between the two. The author thereby deliberately creates the proper context for reading his composition as the word of God. In this light, then, John's greeting, which actually extends through chapter 3, is of considerable theological and rhetorical significance for how one interprets the rest of the book.

The epistolary relationship between the author, **John**, and his audience, **the seven churches in the province of Asia**, is immediately established by the familiar salutation, **grace and peace to you**. John then embellishes this simple address, and reasserts the authority of his communication, by conveying the regards of the triune God to his audience. At the heart of his greeting, however, is a confession about Christ (1:5–7). While bracketed by two claims about God's sovereign rule (1:4b, 8), the final triumph of God's reign and the restoration of God's people result from Jesus Christ's actions toward God (1:5a), toward God's people (1:5b–6), and toward God's enemies upon his return to earth (1:7). The function of this christological confession within the context of the apocalypse, then, is to provide a summary of core convictions about God and God's Christ which must be affirmed by the seven Asian congregations if John's Apocalypse is to be read without distortion and for spiritual benefit.

1:4 / The formal greeting, **grace and peace to you**, is typical of other NT letters. Even though this phrase is a familiar epistolary convention, it carries significant theological freight. First, the greeting embodies the promise/fulfillment typology of early Christian preaching: the age of **peace** (shalom), promised by God to a restored Israel, has been inaugurated by the transforming **grace** of God through Jesus Christ. Second, such blessings are now granted to a restored Israel, the church, which includes not only believing Jews, who are characteristically greeted by "peace," but also believing Gentiles, who are characteristically greeted by "grace."

The formation of this eschatological Israel, in whose history the grace and peace of God are made known, is by the redemptive action of the triune God. Appropriately, John bears the Holy Trinity's greetings to the seven churches, beginning with God, **who is, and who was, and who is to come**. John's formulation of God's name, based upon the name told to Moses in his theophany of the burning bush ("I AM WHO I AM"; Exod. 3:14/LXX), is important for two reasons. In continuity with the God of Moses' Israel, the God of eschatological Israel is eternal; God's sovereignty over the histories of salvation and creation is predicated by this claim (cf. Rev. 4). In addition to this tacit claim for God's sovereign rule over history, John's title suggests that God is involved within history in a purposeful way so that God, **who is to come**, awaits eschatological Israel at the consummation of the age.

John also bears greetings from the **seven spirits**. If the number seven symbolizes completeness or wholeness, then John does not have seven discrete spirits, or seven gifts (or some other manifestation) of the Holy Spirit, in mind. Rather, especially as part of a trinitarian confession, this phrase is a title for the Holy Spirit and suggests the wholeness of life which God continues to mediate through the Paraclete within the believing community (cf. John 14–16). This is further substantiated if the number seven is used to signify that which works and effects something real and concrete. According to John, the grace and peace of God are not theological abstractions. Like Paul, John suggests that divine grace always takes some form of transforming power, which is conveyed by the Spirit of the Risen Christ in the lives of those who follow after him.

1:5 / For a third time in short order, John uses the name **Jesus Christ**. His purpose is to draw his audience's attention to the common source of both their blessing and this apocalypse; their future blessing, envisioned by John's Revelation, depends upon their obedience to him. The seer's extended description of Jesus' authority that follows in verses 5–7 not only introduces the reader to the central images of John's Jesus, but it offers again an elegant justification of his composition's authority. Sharply put, to trust that Jesus is all this christological creed confirms him to be is to trust John's book of visions to be true.

The claims made for Jesus fall into three broad categories: Jesus Christ is known and confessed (1) in terms of his relationship to God (1:5a); (2) in terms of his relationship with the community of faith (1:5b–6); and (3) in terms of his relationship with those who do not belong to the believing community (1:7). His mediating role results in the restoration of the covenant between God and the community of faith, which assures them that the promise expressed by John's salutation is true: they have entered into the promised land where God's grace and peace are fully realized.

The threefold description of Jesus' relationship to God, his Father, approximates the three decisive stages of Jesus' messianic work, especially as it is interpreted by the Johannine tradition: (1) his **faithful witness** includes his entire messianic career, climaxed by his death, which embodied the liberating truth of God (John 8:12–32); (2) by his resurrection he became the **firstborn from the dead**, indicating the trustworthiness of his testimony about God; and (3) as glorified Lord, he became **the ruler of the kings of the earth** in order to inaugurate the victorious reign of God.

John frames his description of Christ's love for the believing community as a doxology: eternal glory and power belong to the exalted Christ (v. 6), not only because his messiahship revealed his devotion to God, but also because it revealed his love for God's people. The grammatical tension created by the shift from a present participle, **To him who loves us**, to two aorist participles, and **has freed us . . . and has made us**, suggests that the current benefits of Jesus' past messianic work (aorist participles) are actually rooted in his continual love for the covenant community (present participle). Therefore, "even though the present time is full of suffering and persecutions for Christians, Christ's love is now with them." (Schüssler Fiorenza, *Revelation*, p. 71).

1:6 / The concrete expressions of Jesus' messianic love are understood typologically by the OT story of the Exodus. Therefore, the community's entrance into God's grace and peace is the result of a new exodus from its captivity to sin and its subsequent restoration as a covenantal people—understood by John as **a kingdom and priests to serve his God and Father** (cf. Exod. 19:6). The meaning of the phrase, **priests to serve his God and Father,** should be considered in apposition to the more abstract idiom, **kingdom.** The essential and concrete result of Jesus' messianic love is the creation of a new people who live under God's reign as a community of servants, and who bear witness to God's rule by offering themselves to the Lord in worship. Thus, John has not diluted the communal and covenantal aspects of the Exodus typology found in the prophetic writings. No doubt he is keen to emphasize this more corporate aspect of God's love to counter early gnostic teaching, which viewed the effects of God's salvation in individualistic and interior ways.

God is referred to here, and throughout Revelation, as the God and Father **of Jesus** (2:27; 3:4, 21; 14:1), indicating the special relationship between the sovereign God and God's faithful Lamb. According to John, the entire history of God's salvation is concentrated by this relationship: Jesus' submission to God as crucified Christ ensures God's triumph over evil powers and human sinfulness. Because of this relationship, which purposes to save the entire cosmos from evil's effects, the believing community continues to confess God as the "Father" of Jesus Christ in whom it can hope to inherit the promised blessings of grace and peace.

1:7 / The community's hope will be vindicated at Christ's return when **the clouds** and **all the peoples of the earth will mourn because of him,** since then they will recognize that **those who pierced him** did so against the redemptive intentions of God for them. John has conjoined two OT texts (Dan. 7:13; Zech. 12:10) to interpret Christian hope in a manner similar to Matthew 24:30: the dramatic return of the Son of Man vindicates Christian faith before a cosmic courtroom. John does not say whether the lament, which issues forth from those who have rejected Christian faith, then results in repentance and a universal salvation; however, such a notion is not inappropriate to John (cf. Rev. 15:3–4; John 12:30–33).

1:8 / John concludes his initial salutation to the seven churches with an oracle from God that repeats his earlier confession about God's eternality: God is **who is, and who was, and**

who is to come (1:4b). Yet, in light of his confession about Jesus' messianic love, John can also add that God is **the Alpha and Omega**, the **Lord God . . . the Almighty**. Alpha is the first and Omega the last letter of the Greek alphabet. Used together they symbolize entirety or wholeness. When used as a divine title, they refer to God's sovereign rule over the history of creation. John couples this title with the OT name for a powerful God, **Lord . . . Almighty**, which signifies the rightful exercise of rulership over all people. When understood by the revelation of Christ's love for his people (cf. 22:13), the power of God over all creation clearly intends that all people enter into the grace and peace now enjoyed only by the faithful church.

1:9 / In the second half of his greetings (vv. 9–20), John expands his earlier prescript (v. 4a) by relating the remarkable christophany by which the Risen Christ commissions him to write Revelation. Such a commissioning vision is not unique to John; it is the normal vehicle by which God commissioned the OT prophets, and then Paul, who received his call through a christophany while traveling on the Damascus Road (cf. Acts 9:1–9). The function of such visions is twofold: the first and more explicit function is to clarify the nature of the prophet's task, while the second and more implicit function is to confer divine authority upon the prophet for the task at hand. The latter function would have been especially important for Paul, for example, whose apostolic authority derived not from his association with Jesus of Nazareth, but from his Damascus Road encounter with the Risen Christ. Similarly, John shares his own visionary experience with the Risen Christ, not only to state the circumstances that occasioned the writing of this book of visions, but also to evoke the recognition of his authority for doing so. Like Paul's, John's authority derives in part from his commission by divine revelation (cf. Acts 22:3–21).

God calls insiders to the prophetic task; the word of God is brought by champions who are called to represent God because they also earnestly seek after the salvation of God's people. Appropriately, then, John first establishes his ecclesial credentials for the call he will receive from Jesus by placing himself on the same level with his audience: **I, John, your brother and companion**. This identification suggests that John views himself as one who participates (i.e., as companion) with his Christian audience (i.e., as brother) in their various experiences of **suffering**, to which they respond with **patient endurance**, because they share equally in the same **kingdom** as priests (1:6).

John's use of the suffering motif has led some to find here a subtle reference to a more general persecution of Christians that occasioned the commissioning of this book. John's use of the motif, however, is best understood in terms of the sociology of an apocalyptic community to which he belongs: the suffering of God's people is understood eschatologically, in terms of their future status **in Jesus**. John's own response to suffering, then, is one of patient hope for Christ's return and God's final triumph over the very evil powers that cause human suffering (cf. Matt. 24:13–14).

The penal **island of Patmos**, off the west coast of Asia Minor, was settled by exiled political enemies of the Roman government. The exact circumstances of John's imprisonment are still contested among scholars. John understands his banishment to Patmos to be the result of his proclamation of **the word of God and the testimony of Jesus**. In a world where civil religion was considered the duty of every good citizen, the public proclamation of the Christian gospel would have been viewed as a political threat. John's own experience may help explain his interpretation of the surrounding sociopolitical order as anti-Christian and in conflict with God's sovereign reign. Perhaps it is for this reason that he describes both his composition and his imprisonment as ingredients of the same reality: **the word of God and the testimony of Jesus** (cf. 1:2). In this sense, John's imprisonment for the Christian gospel is an "acted parable" of the message of Revelation that envisions the fundamental conflict between two kingdoms, one divine and the other demonic.

1:10a / John's vision took place **on the Lord's day**, while he was celebrating the exaltation of Christ as Lord of the church. The seer was **in the Spirit**, inspired by the Spirit of prophecy to see and hear the revelation from God.

1:10b–11 / The commission itself is repeated here and again in 1:19, thus bracketing off and explaining the importance of John's vision of the Danielic "son of man," sandwiched in between (1:12–18). Scholars disagree over the identity of the one who first commissions John. While John recognizes the "son of man" who commissions him to write Revelation in 1:19 as the exalted Christ, he first hears a **loud voice like a trumpet** which, according to 4:1, belongs to an angel. In our view, the angel does not commission John; rather, its voice provides a trumpetlike fanfare for John's subsequent commission from Christ to **write on a scroll what you see and send it to the seven churches**.

1:12 / The distinctive voice prompts John to turn around in order **to see the voice that was speaking to me**. His first impression is to see **seven golden lampstands**, which Jesus later interprets for John as representing the seven churches to whom the seer has been commissioned to write a book of visions (1:20).

1:13a / This image explains the importance of John's impression that the voice belonged to **someone like a son of man,** whom he locates **among the seven lampstands**. John recognizes him as one like Daniel's **a son of man** (Dan. 7:13), choosing this identity rather than the more definitive messianic title for Jesus in the NT Gospels, "the Son of Man." John's decision seems entirely appropriate. According to the promise contained in Daniel's vision, "the one like a son of man," will come on the clouds (cf. Rev. 1:7) to receive "sovereign power" from God as the authorized representative of God's people (Dan. 7:27). John finds the fulfillment of Daniel's promise in Christ Jesus, who now stands among the lampstands, symbols for the "true" Israel of God, as exalted Lord.

1:13b–16 / John's interpretation of his vision is conveyed by his subsequent description of the commissioning Christ. It is a dramatic "light and sound show" of the Lord's power and majesty, full of echoes from the OT prophetic writings that evoke a sense of God's glory. Simply put, John describes a vision of Christ's lordship over the congregations for which he now writes.

Revelation 1:20 re-focuses the reader's attention on **the seven stars** (cf. 1:16), which are the guardian angels of the seven Asian congregations. Their presence in heaven as "celestial doubles" of these churches envisions an important theological point: the effectiveness of the church's historical witness to God's reign is guaranteed by its heavenly representation (cf. Eph. 2:6–7). Significantly, in this regard, Jesus holds the seven stars **in his right hand**, a symbol of his political authority. John's vision of the stars suggests that the church's ultimate destiny is tied to Christ rather than to Rome, whose triumph is temporary.

1:17–18 / John's response to his christophany testifies to its truth: **I fell at his feet as though dead**. Christ, who at last identifies himself, prohibits John, with some irony, from responding as he surely must: **Do not be afraid!** Yet, the reasons for comfort and assurance are found in Christ's self-introduction as **the First and the Last**. Christ addresses John as exalted Lord; he asserts divine authority, equal to "the Alpha and Omega" (cf. 1:8), thus legitimizing his representation of God's people on God's behalf. Further, he claims his authority over death; as **the Living One**, Christ has custody of the **keys of death and Hades** and is therefore able to unlock God's people from their captivity to sin and its consequences.

1:19–20 / The conjunction **therefore** makes clear that Jesus' exhortation to John in 1:17–18 prepares him for his commission found in 1:19. While the power of John's christophany is sufficient to compel him to obey the commission to **write what you have seen** (i.e., the christophany), the commission also includes **what is now and what will take place later**, thus indicating a profoundly hopeful perspective toward the visions John has not yet received. The Living One who gives the vision and then commissions John to write it down is the exalted Lord who confidently promises God's people that they too will follow in his destiny from death into life for ever and ever.

The grammar of this commissioning statement is notoriously difficult and makes any definitive interpretation of this crucial text impossible. In our opinion, the statement is most naturally divided into two parts. The first phrase is best understood as a generic formula of commission: **write what you have seen**. John is to compose a book consisting of all the visions the angel of Christ delivers to him. The next two phrases, (1) **what is now** and (2) **what will take place later**, qualify the entire composition, which in turn has immediate relevance for John's audience. Thus, everything that John writes down reflects what is already true (in heaven) and what is not yet true (on earth). This conclusion does not vitiate our contention that the main body of the composition envisions a sequence of past-present-future "moments" within salvation's history which can be observed at a macroscopic level. John's apocalypse tells the gospel *story*; however, it is instructive in each of its parts for how human life and Christian faith are currently construed. When John focuses a particular part of the whole vision, the other parts are also present. The reader, then, is asked to consider the importance of **what is now**, while retaining a sense of **what will take place later**. This dialectic between "the already but not yet" is, of course, characteristic of NT eschatology. Within John's Revelation, both the realized (christological) and not yet realized (eschatological) truths of the gospel story will constantly frame and form what constitutes a proper response to God.

According to many scholars, 1:19 organizes Revelation into discrete visions of the past, present, and future of salvation's history. Such arrangements seem artificial to us and actually disturb the dynamic interplay throughout the book between past, present and future elements of God's redemptive work. Our own interpretation of Revelation will suggest that current Christian existence, characterized by historical ambiguity and spiritual struggles, can be understood only when we look backward into the past and ahead into the future of God's promised salvation. The gospel of God, realized and promised through Jesus Christ, is never conveyed as a static set of timeless convictions; rather, it is the truth about God, disclosed once and for all in the messianic event, adapted again and again, generation after generation, to the ever-changing situations of those who share life "in Jesus," who is "the Living One."

Finally, notice that 1:20 shifts from symbolic to non-symbolic language. This feature of apocalyptic literature intends to provide the reader with a cipher for decoding more obscure images found in the immediate context of the vision. These "clues" are found frequently throughout Revelation—no doubt added by the seer—and always yield critical keys to help the reader along the way.

Additional Notes   §2

1:4 / Charles explains that the awkward grammar of the phrase, **who is, and who was, and who is to come**, reflects a Hebraic source where the phrase functioned as a formula for God's eternality (*Revelation*, vol. 1, p. 10). Morris implies that the odd grammar is itself an expression of God's transcendence (*Revelation*, pp. 48–49).

1:5 / The Greek word for **witness** is *martys* (cf. "martyr"), suggesting the costliness of Jesus' faithfulness to God.

1:6 / We disagree with Caird who understands **kingdom** in terms of "realized eschatology"; according to him, the community of believers performs the messianic tasks, embodying the reign of God on earth (*Revelation*, p. 17).

1:10a / Boring suggests that **on the Lord's Day** was an idiom for early Christianity's celebration of "Easter," which provides an even more concrete occasion for John's vision of Christ's triumph (*Revelation*, p. 82).

1:16 / Some argue that the image of **seven stars** relates directly to the emperor cult, which utilized astrology to predict future events. If this is John's intent, then the Lord's political authority, symbolized by his **right hand**, is asserted here as a repudiation of the imperial cult of Rome.

1:18 / According to Jewish mythology, Hades is the place of the dead. In this light, the phrase, **dead and Hades**, is a poetic redundancy, emphasizing the certainty of God's triumph over death in Christ.

1:19 / For a history of interpretation of this critical verse, see G. K. Beale, "The Interpretive Problem of Revelation 1:19" (unpublished paper presented at the annual meeting, Society of Biblical Literature, 1989). In Beale's view, the Lord's commissioning statement is a midrash on Dan. 2:28–29 and envisions "Daniel's eschatological understanding of human history." That is, John is asked to write down what amounts to the fulfillment of Daniel's prophecy about the ultimate triumph of God's rule. Beale intends to develop this point in his forthcoming commentary on *Revelation*, NIGTC (Grand Rapids: Eerdmans).

§3 Greetings from Christ to the Seven Churches of Asia (Rev. 2:1–3:22)

In the first chapter, John introduced himself and his composition (1:1–3; 1:9–10) and then greeted his readers who belong to seven different congregations of the Asian church (1:4; 1:11). Chapters 2 and 3 expand upon this introduction in continuation from the preceding commissioning vision (1:12–20). In this way, John's own perceptions of his audience are conveyed through the authoritative voice of "the First and the Last," who instructs the seer to write the Lord's greetings to the angelic representatives of the seven congregations.

Scholars continue to disagree over the literary suitability and thematic unity of this particular vision within the context of the entire apocalypse. These discussions, however important, tend to distract the interpreter from John's overarching purpose for these two chapters—discerned readily enough if one keeps in mind the literary form and rhetorical function of an apocalyptic letter. In short, Christ's greetings to the seven churches embellish John's own salutation to them.

This dramatic embellishment, also characteristic of Paul's letters, reflects two critical elements in understanding the author's purpose for writing to his audience. First, John's perceptions of his audience are indicated by Christ's description of their spiritual condition. John makes this clear by several common words and phrases that link together Christ's commission of him with Christ's messages to the seven churches. In particular, Christ's first words to each of the seven churches (2:1, 8, 12, 18; 3:1, 7, 14) repeat the same images used of Christ envisioned in John's commission. The net effect of this parallelism is to establish a relationship between the author and his audience that suggests the composition itself is written and read with common spiritual purpose. Second, and more importantly, Christ describes John's audience to establish the proper context within which Revelation is read and adapted to the church's faith and life. Again, John makes this point by linking chapters 2 and 3 to the book's conclusion by a set of common themes and phrases. Thus, the images found in Christ's final exhortations to overcome (2:7, 11, 17, 26–28; 3:5, 12, 21) are repeated in John's vision of Christ's parousia (19:11–22:6a). Of course, the "theo-logic" of this pattern is clear: the church's proper response to Christ's exhortations in the present crisis will result in God's redemptive response to them at Christ's return. This literary device, moreover, suggests the interrelatedness of the entire composition, and it very well may indicate that these various messages in particular function like a window through which the audience watches and interprets the rest of John's vision.

The perception of Revelation's relevancy for its reader's faith depends on the congregation to which one belongs. If the author's description of a particular congregation suits a reader, that reader will understand the importance of John's subsequent vision in ways appropriate to that congregation, whether as a pastoral word of hope (e.g., the congregation at Smyrna) or as a prophetic word of judgment (e.g., the congregation at Laodicea). Because apocalypses are interpreted in a variety of ways in part because their messages are conveyed by symbols rather than by pointed discourse, the nuances drawn from chapters 2 and 3 are more necessary to an author interested that the audience properly understand the whole work.

Each of the seven addresses to John's audience is built with a common fourfold pattern, with differing content due to the differing circumstances and characteristics of individual congregations. First, each congregation's angel, which represents it within the vision, is greeted by christological confession, indicating those characteristics of the exalted Lord which call that congregation to an appropriate kind of discipleship. The thematic interplay between these opening addresses and John's commissioning vision, noted above, impresses upon the reader the fundamental importance of the revelation that John has been commissioned to write down. Second, each congregation is then commended by Christ for its faithful attention to the demands of Christian discipleship, with the exception of the believers at Laodicea to whom no commendation is given (3:14–18). Yet, third, each congregation is also condemned for its inconsistent attention to the rigors of Christian faith, with the exception of the believers at Smyrna (2:8–10) and Philadelphia (3:8–10) who receive no censure from Christ. Finally, and of greatest rhetorical significance in our view, Christ encourages each congregation to overcome evil by obeying the message the Spirit conveys. Depending of the congregation's spiritual condition, obedience is expressed either as repentance or as hope in the light of God's sovereign and victorious reign. Its result is the promised blessings which will be revealed upon Christ's return. Thus, the closing exhortation determines how the apocalypse itself is to be understood by a particular congregation, whether as a message of indictment for spiritual laxity or as one of vindication for spiritual responsiveness. This point is made clearer by a thematic interplay, noted above, between the symbols of eternal life enshrined within Christ's closing words to the seven churches and the same or similar symbols found in the closing vision of Christ's parousia which marks God's final triumph over evil. The overarching structure of Revelation, which focuses the reader's attention on the messages to the seven churches, underscores the importance of this part of the vision. Again, the reader's orientation to the rest of the book, whether to view it as an encouraging or as a correcting word from God, is largely determined by the congregation to which one "belongs."

The canonical significance of this section is reflected by its importance during the history of interpretation. Beasley-Murray claims that "the seven letters of chapters 2–3 comprise the best known and most frequently expounded section of the book of Revelation" (*Revelation*, p. 70). Whether John understood these seven congregations as representative of the whole church is unclear from the text itself; nor does the textual history indicate that this was written as an encyclical letter to circulate beyond the seven. However, the symbolic significance of the number seven is well known, and if applied to the churches might allow for a more "catholic" rendering. From a canonical perspective this reconstruction is unnecessary, since the inclusion of Revelation in the biblical canon presumes its importance for the spiritual formation of believers in every age, who continue to seat themselves in the pews of Revelation's seven congregations to hear the word of the Lord God Almighty.

Morris finds another compositional pattern in chapters 2 and 3 that is worth noting in this regard. After calling attention to the importance of a "sevenfold arrangement" which organizes this section of John's composition for him, Morris goes on to comment that "churches 1 and 7 are in grave danger, churches 2 and 6 are in excellent shape, churches 3, 4 and 5 are middling, neither very good nor very bad" (*Revelation*, pp. 57–58). However, he offers us no theological interpretation of this literary pattern.

If we accept Morris' assessment of the spiritual condition of the Ephesian congregation, then the overarching pattern of this material is chiastic (ABCB'A'). Chiasmus calls the reader's attention to the vortex of the pattern (C), where one finds what is most important for the author: that is, John is calling our attention to those churches with a "middling" spirituality. His purpose is certainly pastoral: most congregations do not find themselves on the margins of spiritual excellence (with the congregations at Smyrna and Philadelphia) or apathy (with the congregations at Ephesus and Laodicea), but rather in the mainstream of spiritual mediocrity (with the congregations at Pergamum, Thyatira, and Sardis). This is, then, the nature of the spiritual crisis for most of John's readers, who constantly struggle against those forces and factors which might prevent the maturing of faith and keep our witness "middling."

2:1 / Appropriately, Christ first addresses Asia's most important congregation in one of the world's great cities, Ephesus. Luke's account of Ephesian Christianity warns of certain threats to its ministry of the gospel, such as religious pluralism and secular materialism (cf. Acts 19:1–41), but Acts also suggests its central importance to the advance of the Christian gospel (cf. Acts 20:13–37). If the list suggests a priority of concern, it seems fitting that John should begin with this church.

Christ repeats images envisioned earlier by John in recognition of Christ's lordship over the church: Christ **holds the seven stars in his right hand and walks among the seven golden lampstands**. Perhaps these symbols of his lordship are restated here to remind a powerful Christian congregation, accustomed to a place of privilege within the church, that even their conduct is scrutinized by the Risen Lord who keeps all congregations equally under his constant care.

2:2–3 / The catchphrase, **I know your deeds**, begins Christ's commendation of spiritual achievement. Revelation underscores the importance of good works as the substance of the church's witness to its fidelity to Christ. In Christian preaching, faith and faithfulness always belong together, even though their exact relationship is understood differently by NT writers. The deeds of **hard work and your perseverance**, especially when understood as a hard fought intolerance of **wicked men** and false **apostles**, may reflect a Jewish tradition that such diligent devotion satisfies a criterion of Israel's covenant with God. Especially in light of Christ's opening exhortation, the congregation's testing of **those who claim to be apostles but are not** expresses the submission of true disciples to their Lord.

The exact identity and teaching of these false and wicked apostles is unclear and remains contested. In 2:6 and 2:14–15, mention is made of the congregation's association with the Nicolaitans, followers of Nicolas of Antioch, according to primitive tradition. The language and its context seem to suggest that the Nicolaitans advocated too much accommodation with the surrounding social and religious order. John's use of the Balaam typology (Num. 25:1–2; cf. Jude 11) in 2:14 (cf. 2:2) would seem to suggest that Nicolaitan practices did not distinguish keenly enough between their Christian faith and pagan religion to prevent the public appearance (at the very least) of capitulation to idolatry and sexual immorality.

2:4–6 / The opening adversative, **Yet I hold this against you**, indicates a shift from commendation to condemnation. The perils of Ephesian disaffection from the rigors of Christian discipleship are made clear by Christ: **If you do not repent, I will come to you and remove your lampstand from its place**. Whatever else this warning might mean and whenever it might be realized, two things seem clear enough: first, the congregation jeopardizes its place within the eschatological community by continuing on its present course; yet, second, its restoration is still possible upon turning back to **do the things you did at first**. The peril of not returning to former spiritual disciplines is revealed in the future: the unrepentant congregation will be excluded from coming blessings. While some contend these blessings are more immediate and the potential loss is of spiritual vitality or the power to be a "real church," this interpretation seems unnatural to the immediate context. For John, the identity of true Israel is revealed at Christ's return, when even the church will be judged on how well it integrates its faith with good works.

The statement of the spiritual problem is that **you have forsaken your first love**. The catchphrase, **first love**, is best understood in theological terms and according to the Johannine tradition. In this light, love and truth form the single, integral reality of real Christianity. Specifically, the theological core, or "logos," of Johannine Christianity is that God is love and truth, and God's love and truth are incarnated in Jesus Christ (John 1:1–18). Further, the apostolic witness to the incarnated "logos," Jesus Christ, represents the normative understanding of love and truth (esp. 1 John 3:11–4:21). The deeper logic of this interpretation of the Christian gospel suggests a twofold clarification of Christ's message to Ephesus. First, any tolerance for teaching contrary to the apostolic witness to the word (cf. 2:2; 1 John 1:1–5; 2:18–27), as advanced for example by the Nicolaitans, constitutes opposition to the essential conviction of Christian preaching: God is love. To forsake one's "first love" would constitute the disavowal of this core conviction of apostolic teaching and would be considered apostasy. Second, the proper response to the belief that God is love is concrete actions of love for one another (1 John 4:20–21). The use of the Balaam typology in 2:14–15 for the Pergamum church suggests these two congregations face the same threat: forsaken love refers to an accommodation of pagan idolatry—an act of hatred against immature believers.

Idolatry confuses divine love and its obligations; idols are created to serve humanity's self-centered love and vain ambitions. Paul reminds his Corinthian readers that idolatry prevents the nurture of believers because it impedes sensitivity to their spiritual condition. Thus, to cause the immature to stumble in their Christian discipleship constitutes an act of hatred toward them and dishonors the rule of God (1 Cor. 8:9–13; 4:14–21; cf. 1 John 3:10–11).

2:7 / The concluding exhortation **to him who overcomes** (the preceding peril) is sandwiched between its condition and its consequence. The overcomer endures the present crisis because the overcomer **has an ear** to hear **what the Spirit says to the churches**. John employs an OT (LXX) idiom for faithfulness, **He who has an ear, let him hear**, echoing the demand of the Shema, "Hear, O Israel: The Lord our God, the Lord is one" (Deut. 6:4), which also means to "be careful to obey so that it may go well with you" (Deut. 6:3; cf. James 1:22–25). Indeed, this is said to be the measure of the community's "first love" (cf. Deut. 6:5). Likewise, to overcome the drift from its theological fundamental that God is love, the Ephesian congregation must renew and re-assert its faithfulness to Christ, whose exaltation confirms that God is love. And it is the Spirit of the exalted Christ who continues to speak on his behalf to the churches (cf. John 14:15–31; 1 John 4:1–6). The Paraclete's role within the community of Christ's disciples is to remind them of God's love and truth in order to convict them of their sin and to bring about their repentance in the light of God's truth (cf. John 16:12–15).

With this result, the congregation can then hope **to eat from the tree of life, which is in the paradise of God**. John foreshadows the final vision of the new Jerusalem (22:2), which symbolizes the new people of God (cf. 21:10). The eschatological consequence of the church's present faithfulness is the complete transformation of its existence. This promise is nuanced by the story of Genesis 1–3 that it echoes. In God's original paradise we find the first tree of life; there, like the Ephesian congregation, Adam and Eve forsook their first love and paid for the consequences of their sin. Not only does the triumph of God's reign through Jesus Christ anticipate God's future restoration of creation, Christ's exaltation bids the present church to bear witness to that future as God's new creation.

2:8 / Smyrna was a prosperous port city, not far north up the coastline from Ephesus. Smyrna's importance also extended to political matters because of its close and loyal association with Rome, even pre-dating Rome's rise to power. Although John issues unqualified praise for this congregation, we have no historical record of its beginning (although we do know from Acts 19:10 that Paul conducted a successful evangelistic campaign in the vicinity). And a generation after Revelation was written, Polycarp, a notable leader in the early church, was martyred in Smyrna.

The opening address repeats claims made earlier for Christ (1:17–18) that he is **the First and the Last, who died and came to life again**. A reminder of Easter is especially meaningful for this congregation which lives in poverty, has encountered intense religious opposition, and even faces imprisonment and martyrdom.

2:9–10 / The subsequent consolation, then, to **Be faithful, even to the point of death, and I will give you the crown of life** promises faithful disciples a future with the Risen Christ. Their reward, the **crown of life**, probably refers to the laurel wreath or garland given the athlete who wins at the games. As an eschatological symbol, it refers to the reward of eternal life for those who remain faithful even to death.

The prospect of death appears very real to these believers. Not only have they already experienced **afflictions**; they are about to **suffer; . . . the devil will put . . . you in prison to test you, and you will suffer persecution for ten days**. The agents of the Evil One in this case are **Jews** who lay claim to God's Israel but who belong to **a synagogue of Satan** which actively opposes the church's witness in Smyrna. Unlike the Nicolaitans, who endanger Christian faith from within, religious Jews, especially strong in Smyrna, were members of a distinct religious community which persecuted Christians as outsiders. We should assume that such persecution was part of the larger struggle between the church and synagogue in earliest Christianity resulting from Christian proclamation that the crucified rabbi, Jesus from Nazareth, is really the promised Christ of God according to Jewish tradition. Because Christians recognized what Easter confirmed, they were convinced that the church is God's "true" covenant partner. Tensions intensified in Asia with the Gentile mission and Paul's preaching of a Torah-free and tradition-free gospel (cf. Acts 21:27–28). No doubt this resistance to Christianity led John to say that unbelieving Jews **are Jews and are not**, when in fact believing Jews (and Gentiles) are (cf. Rom. 2:27–28; 9–11). Of course, his assertion should not be construed as anti-semitic, for John himself was a Jew (as were Jesus and Paul). Rather, his harsh rhetoric conveys in the strongest possible way the very same judgment made earlier of the non-Jewish Nicolaitans: those who do not follow the crucified Jesus as the Risen Christ stand outside of God's people in whose history God's promised salvation is now being fulfilled.

The Lord's opening declaration of his resurrection reassures a community that lives on the economic margins of the social order. No doubt the opposition from the Jewish community, affluent and politically influential, only intensified the church's poverty. It would make sense if some believers were tempted to return to the synagogue for economic reasons. Thus, the promise of an economic reversal is more forcefully given: **your poverty . . . you are rich**. As a motif of apocalyptic literature, the promise of a reversal in socioeconomic fortunes is an element of God's coming triumph over the Evil One. Further, the church's marginal status in this life indicates devotion to God; thus, the true people of God belong to a community of the poor whose liberation from poverty is their experience of God's shalom (cf. Luke 4:16–21).

2:11 / The faithful disciple, who **overcomes . . . the second death**, anticipates this reversal in fortune. The idea of a "second death" assumes that everyone experiences a "first death." The poverty of the church, its afflictions, and the Jewish slander against disciples (2:9), coupled with the imprisonment and possible martyrdom which awaits them (2:10), bear witness to their participation in the "first death." However, to die a second time is to be disqualified from eternal life which is yet to come. The **test** of which John speaks (2:10), then, is inevitable because it belongs to the realm of the first death. To resist temptation means to participate in the "first death" (i.e., martyrdom); but to participate in the first death is also to escape the second death and to enter into the promised reign of God's grace and peace.

2:12 / Continuing north up the coastline of the Aegean Sea, then moving inland, brings one to Pergamum, the capital of the Asian province. The city was built around a great acropolis on which the first temple of the imperial cult was built to Augustus in 29 B.C. For Christians, Pergamum symbolized secular power and civil religion; indeed, Christ identifies it as the city "where Satan has his throne . . . where Satan lives" (2:13).

The Lord possesses **the sharp, double-edged sword**, again repeating what John had seen in his earlier vision of Christ (1:16). This is yet another image of Christ's lordship, clarified later as "the sword of my mouth" (2:16) that will "fight against" the false teachings and sexual immoralities sponsored by the Nicolaitans (2:15; cf. 2:6). The **sword** symbolizes the eschatological word of God (cf. Heb. 4:12–13) by which lawlessness is exposed and judged (cf. 2 Thess. 2:8). The truth of this word has already been disclosed in the messianic mission of Jesus and confirmed at his exaltation. Thus, the apostolic proclamation of the gospel represents the ongoing standard by which non-apostolic claims to Christian faith and life, such as asserted by the Nicolaitans or those compromised by the imperial cult, are evaluated and condemned.

2:13 / With assurances of the gospel's truthfulness, Jesus thus commends the believers who **remain true to my name**, even though they evidently were pressured, perhaps by the leaders of the imperial cult, to **renounce your faith in me**. The language used by John suggests an active resistance to such adverse pressure, of the sort exemplified by **Antipas . . . who was put to death in your city**.

The contrast drawn between Antipas, who like Jesus is called **faithful witness** (1:5), and the city, **where Satan lives**, is notable. The contrast envisions the location of a conflict between God's reign, to which both Jesus and Antipas bore witness to by their deaths, and Satan's reign, to which Rome and its civil religion bear witness. Revelation exploits this contrast in terms of power. Civil religion, while bowing before idols that have no ultimate (i.e., eschatological) power, does nevertheless exercise real influence. The power of the anti-Christian kingdom, of course, is its corrupting and destructive influence upon the unfaithful. The powerful demonstration of God's rule, on the other hand, is the transformation of faithful people for the good.

The effects of God's grace within the church may well be obscured by the effects of living within a society at odds with the notions of divine truth and the character of divine love. Conflict is therefore the necessary result of fidelity to God's gospel. Even though such faithfulness results in affliction, it is nevertheless motivated by the reality of Christ's resurrection and the hope of his return. This is the point implicit in Christ's commendation: even as the faithful Antipas is a witness to Christ's death, he will ultimately participate in Christ's exaltation as well.

2:14–16 / The Lord's condemnation of some Christians in Pergamum expands the specific theological crisis which threatens the church's witness there. Both the Pergamene and Ephesian congregations are afflicted from within by Nicolaitan teaching (cf. 2:2, 6). Perhaps the Pergamene church, weakened by internal conflict, finds itself less able to contend against the outside pressures that are indicated in 2:13. Unable to muster adequate spiritual resources from vital worship to maintain a viable Christian witness, the less mature believers have become soft and susceptible to the corrupting influences inside and outside the worshiping community. The call to **repent**, then, warns against theological and ethical laxity that will result in an unfavorable judgment when Christ **will soon come to you and will fight against** his enemies in the city.

2:17 / The exaltation of Jesus Christ as Lord anticipates the outcome of his visitation: the Nicolaitans and the other agents of Satan in the city will certainly fall (cf. 2:5). The incentives to repent are clear, not only to escape execution by the **sword of my mouth** at the Lord's return (cf. 19:21), but also to receive **the hidden manna** and **a white stone with a new name written on it**. John's appeal to the manna typology recalls the story of Balaam and Balak (cf. Num. 22–25; 31:16; Jude 11; also, Ps-Philo 18), whose evils characterize the Nicolaitan heresy (cf. 2:14–15). In a sense, the city of Pergamum is for its Christian congregation like the wilderness was for the children of Israel: it is the context of spiritual struggle and testing, where the one **who overcomes** resists the request of Balak to accommodate the world's order. The gift of **hidden manna** probably draws upon rabbinic commentaries on Exodus 16:31–35 by which Jews expected to be nourished by this same manna in the age to come. For John, then, manna is yet another symbol of eschatological fulfillment, when God's people receive the promised blessings of salvation (cf. John 6:25–59).

The second reward of faithfulness, **a white stone**, is a more difficult symbol to understand. The **new name written on it**, whether Christ's (19:12; cf. 3:12) or the overcomer's, brings to mind a universe of "new things" (21:5) that will result from God's final triumph over evil—the "new" Jerusalem (3:12; 21:2), a "new" heaven and earth (21:1), "new" songs (5:9; 14:3), and so on. In addition, the adjective **white** is used elsewhere in Revelation in reference to spiritual purity, which is another eschatological credential. Thus, whatever else the **white stone** refers to, it symbolizes the future blessings poured out on the community of overcomers at Christ's return.

John recognized the significance of the stones in his visions by their function within his world. Two common uses in particular probably informed John's interpretation of the visionary stones. Stones were sometimes used as tickets for admission to public events. Perhaps John viewed the stones held by overcomers as admission tickets to Christ's victory feast (cf. 19:17–18). Especially if the interpreter decides that the **new name written on it** belongs to Christ, then the **white stone** probably has this significance for John. Stones were also used by juries, who gave an acquitted person a white stone at the trial's end. This rendering is also possible, especially if the **white stone** is linked to the "great white throne" (20:11), symbolic of God's final judgment of good and evil. If the interpreter decides that the **new name written on it** belongs to the overcomer and is therefore written in the "book of life" (20:15), then a cumulative case could be built for the **white stone** as symbolic of the overcomer's escape from "the second death" (20:14). We prefer this second view because it fits better this congregation's situation and John's use of the "sword" imagery: the disciple who resists satanic repression inside and outside the church will be acquitted by the heavenly jury and so escape God's eschatological judgment.

2:18 / The next major city to the east of Pergamum on the Roman highway through Asia was Thyatira. Known throughout the ancient world as a city of merchants and trade guilds, its local gods were dedicated to the city's economic well-being. Unlike Pergamum, which was a center of civil religion in Asia, the idolatry in Thyatira was materialism, whose power is measured by society's robust commerce. Perhaps this explains the extensive use of "tools of trade" as symbols for Christ's lordship over humanity's spiritual *and* material existence (cf. Col. 1:15–20).

The address recovers two more elements of John's commissioning vision, which depicted Christ as a "son of man" **whose eyes are like blazing fire and whose feet are like burnished bronze**. John's Christ reinterprets the earlier "a son of man" idiom from Daniel by the more definitive **the Son of God** title (cf. Ps. 2:7; but used only here in Revelation) to draw together the first and last parts (2:27) of the message to this congregation. In doing so, John focuses the reader's attention on Psalm 2 (esp. v. 8), which NT writers viewed as fulfilled by the divine Messiah Jesus (cf. Mark 1:11; 9:7; Heb. 1:2, 5; 5:5), as the biblical text that interprets the crisis recounted in this message. The Messiah's exalted status as **Son of God** confirms him as having **received authority from my Father** (2:27; cf. Ps. 2:8; Dan. 7:14; Matt. 28:18) to give the one who overcomes the crisis co-regency **over the nations** (2:26). Moreover, the previous images of **fire and . . . bronze**, along with the biblical images of **iron scepter** and **pottery** (cf. Ps. 2:9), are now understood as referring to the products of the city's industry. Thus, Christ's lordship over the faithful assures for them their final vindication over those whose values are shaped by economic rather than by biblical notions of power.

2:19 / Christ commends good works that deepen the congregation's **love and faith, your service and perseverance**. These deeds form relationships within a spiritual congregation that provide its foundation for "the long obedience in the right direction" (cf. 2:23c; Rom. 2:5–10). The first doublet envisions the church's devotion to God, the second, its devotion to each other. In contrast to the Ephesian church, this congregation's witness is growing rather than waning. The real issue, however, and the issue to which all the moral advice of Revelation is directed, is whether they will do **my will to the end** (2:26).

2:20–25 / The theological crisis threatening their steadfast growth is tied to the tolerated presence of **that woman, Jezebel**, who symbolizes the corrosive powers of false religion among the people of God. The label of self-proclaimed **prophetess** suggest that this false teacher may have been the female leader of an "emancipation movement" within the church. The Lord's warning that she **repent of her immorality** suggests that this sectarian movement within the church is in conflict with its apostolic teaching. The harsh, polemical rhetoric used by John to characterize **Jezebel**'s teaching reflects his own intolerance against such forms of religious anarchy (cf. 1 John 2:18–19). John's reference to **sexual immorality** denotes theological infidelity of the sort that **misleads my servants**. There is little evidence in the passage to aid the interpreter in reconstructing who **Jezebel** was and what she actually taught; however, the use of common catchphrases to describe this movement and those used to describe the gnosticizing Nicolaitans at Ephesus and Pergamum suggest some similarity between them.

Two additional clues are also worth considering in this regard. Christ's warning that **I will cast her on a bed of suffering** may indicate that the false teacher champions the opposite—that is, an escape from suffering. Especially if this city's materialistic values are projected onto its idols, Jezebel's heresy is the ancient equivalent of the current "gospel of prosperity" that equates the gospel with present, material blessings.

A second clue appears in John's reference to **Satan's so-called deep secrets**. It seems to suggest the promulgation of gnostic "mysteries" within earliest Christianity. Certain Christian teachers formed "study groups" to advance their own private interpretations, justifying their trustworthiness as "divine revelations" or **deep secrets** from God. Perhaps because these teachers often claimed their teaching was received through ecstatic experiences, **Jezebel** calls herself a **prophetess** (Beasley-Murray, *Revelation*, p. 92). Since the content and consequences of her teaching conflicted with apostolic witness, Jezebel was located with other false teachers under Satan's rule rather than under God's (cf. 1 John 2:18–27).

2:26–29 / Christ promises to give the overcomer **the morning star**. In John's world, Venus was called "the morning star"; and later in Revelation so is Jesus (22:16). Neither reference explains its use here; nor does Isaiah's reference to the fall of Babylon's king as the "morning star, fallen from heaven" (Isa. 14:12). However, these passages all use the star motif to symbolize sovereignty or rule. On this basis, it would seem likely that **the morning star** again symbolizes the eschatological situation of the community of overcomers by pointing to its future participation in the triumph of God's rule over all those secular and materialistic pretenders to the Lord's throne.

3:1 / John's Christ again seems mindful of the city's reputation while addressing its church. Sardis, once the leading city of the important Lydian Valley, is now a city of departed glory by the time John writes Revelation at the end of the first century. Following an earthquake that leveled much of the city in A.D. 17, Sardis struggled to regain its past stature with economic assistance from Rome. Because the city was well located at the western depot of the "King's Highway" that began at Susa on the Persian Gulf, the success of its rebuilding campaign was tied to its well-known role as a trading center for the textile industry (cf. 3:4–5). Unfortunately, like its church, Sardis had **a reputation of being alive, but** it was really **dead**.

The promise of economic vitality is tied to the city's military security, and for this Sardis depended on its seemingly impregnable acropolis. Nevertheless, it had been captured twice before (in 546 B.C. and 218 B.C.), both times because the enemy had "come like a thief" in the night when the sleeping city did "not know at what time (the enemy) would come."

In preparation for the harsh message Christ brings to this church, he claims his lordship in the strongest possible way: he **holds the seven spirits of God and the seven stars**. Both the spirits and the stars, the Holy Spirit and the angels, are agents of God's revelation and dispensers of God's transforming grace. Both are now under the jurisdiction of God's exalted Christ for ministry among Christ's disciples.

The church in Sardis, however, is a reclamation project, a community of the "living dead." These disciples, who **have a reputation of being alive, but . . . are dead**, are in such a serious state that Christ breaks his normal pattern of dispensing commendation before condemnation; his message is one of condemnation. The **seven stars** are the **angels** of God (1:20) and with God will stand in judgment over this church at the end of time (3:5)— a point which brackets and qualifies the entire message. Evidently this is a congregation content with spiritual mediocrity even though in desperate need of the revitalizing power of the Paraclete of the exalted Christ.

3:2–3 / A congregation whose life is not **complete in the sight of my God** is one that resists the Paraclete. The four imperatives, which follow the opening exhortation to **wake up!**, invite believers to a spiritual response different from the city, whose acropolis had fallen because of its lack of military readiness. In fact, the first of these imperatives, **strengthen!**, envisions an acropolis, and no doubt the one in Sardis that was built strong to protect a people from outside invasion. Apparently, the congregation does have some spiritual residue remaining, even though it **is about to die**—an ironical, perhaps hopeful demand in light of the opening assertion that "you are dead."

The next imperatives, **remember . . . obey . . . and repent,** provide the readers with three "wake-up calls" that orient them to John's Revelation. The renewal of the Spirit does not occur in a vacuum; the intended revival occurs when the book they **have received and heard** results in repentance. Like the book of Hebrews, Revelation's message calls for obedient response; and John's "realized Christology" (i.e., his conviction that the completed messianic mission begins the new age of God's salvation) provides justification for the demands as directives for readiness of the future Day. The warning that Revelation issues to the unrepentant is that **if you do not wake up . . . you will not know**. Spiritual renewal is "mind renewal" (cf. Rom. 12:1–2); to **repent** (*metanoeō*) literally refers to a person's intellectual reorientation, a "change of one's mind." The experience of conversion enables the congregation to **know . . . I will come to you**, even though **I will come like a thief**. The evidence of conversion is a change of lords, from placing one's confidence in the security of the city-state, destroyed by an enemy that came "like a thief in the night," to the returning Christ, who comes **like a thief** as the Lord over lords. Fanatical speculations about the exact time of Christ's return are replaced by a confidence in its imminence.

John uses images for Christ's parousia associated with the "Day of the Lord" in the Jesus tradition (Matt. 24:43; cf. 1 Thess. 5:2). John, however, adapts this eschatological motif to his situation as a warning rather than as a promise; the congregation at Sardis has failed to meet the condition of faithfulness that Jesus himself has set down for his return (Matt. 24:13–14; cf. Rom. 11:25–27). Most commentators agree that John's use of this motif intends to exclude the faithless from certain, unspecified blessings on the future Day. Given its more negative context, however, as well as John's consistent emphasis on the church's present fellowship (3:20) with a judging Lord (2:22–23), perhaps John intends only to warn the congregation of a more immediate and limited prospect, such as the visitation from an angry Lord, presumably mediated by his angel, and whatever that might bring.

3:4–6 / Using well-known images cast from Sardis' textile industry, Christ specifies the nature of those spiritual resources for revitalizing this dead church: **Yet you have a few people in Sardis who have not soiled their clothes**. This righteous remnant consists of the eschatological "overcomers" who are **worthy** and therefore **will walk with me, dressed in white**. The worthiness of the exalted Lamb to open the scroll and break its seals was based on his faithfulness to a redemptive God, even unto death (cf. 5:9). Likewise, the worthy remnant are characterized by their dress, made white by the blood of the Lamb, because of their vigorous faithfulness to God even with the possibility of martyrdom (cf. 7:9–17).

In contrasting the two groups of believers in Sardis, one spiritually alive and the other stagnant, John may have in mind the biblical contrast between Israel's "remnant" and the "rest of Israel." The confidence of the righteous remnant, based on

Isaiah's use of the motif, was rooted in their conviction that a faithful God would respond to their faithfulness by saving the unfaithful Jews. In fact, as Israel's spiritual exemplars, they felt their future salvation would prompt even the nations to repent and also enter into God's promised peace. A similar confidence lies behind the contrast John draws between 3:1–3 and 3:4–6: those who have **not soiled their clothes** and are spiritually alive will bring about the repentance of those who "have a reputation of being alive, but . . . are dead."

The concluding reference to **the book of life** once again draws the reader to Revelation's conclusion and to its promise of God's final triumph over death (20:12; cf. 2:17). The **book** is an important symbol because of its association with public decrees which initiate real events: the historic commencement of eternal life will be publicly (i.e., actually) decreed **before my Father and his angels** at Christ's return. The **book** is given added importance since it contains a roll of **name**s which stipulates one's eternal status, whether the Lord **will never blot** one's name **out . . . but will acknowledge** it. Christ's lordship over the church is decisive and ultimate; it is also historically specific and deals with individuals by their personal **name**. His decision about a believer's fitness to enter into God's eternal reign is not based upon a formal confession of faith; indeed, some in the Sardis church gave every outward appearance of true devotion. Rather, the criterion of the Lord Jesus' eschatological judgment is considerably more demanding, requiring the believer to be **worthy**, utterly faithful to God's eternal rule through Christ.

3:7 / Located near to Sardis, Philadelphia was a relatively new city, founded during the second century B.C. by Attalus II Philadelphus. This may be in John's mind when he writes to the Philadelphian church about the **new Jerusalem** (3:12). The "new" Philadelphia had been planned as a center for the hellenization program that was encouraged and financed by Attalus. The more conservative voices of the vibrant Jewish community in Philadelphia no doubt tried to thwart such a program and may have resisted Christianity as an element of their efforts in this regard (cf. 3:9).

For the only time in Revelation, Christ is called **holy and true**—the appellation used for God in 6:10. As an attribute of his lordship, Christ's ongoing claim upon the church is based on his oneness with God his Father—a critical emphasis of Johannine

Christology (cf. John 10:22–30). According to John, the authority of Jesus was first recognized and confessed by Peter (cf. John 6:69) and later clarified by Martha (cf. John 11:27); his teachings brought forth eternal life in those who believed (cf. John 6:63–64). The epistle 1 John brings together the realization of eternal life and sinless existence as the result of knowing "him who is **true**— even (God's) Son Jesus Christ" (1 John 5:20; cf. John 20:31).

On this basis, assurance can now be given that Christ **holds the key of David** (cf. 1:18) that **opens** what **no one can shut, and . . . shuts** what **no one can open**. This reference to **David** probably has the Jewish opponents of 3:9 in mind. No doubt they disputed the church's claim that Jesus is the promised Davidic Christ, whose **key** unlocks the door into the household of eschatological Israel (cf. Isa. 22:22). Rather than a defeated "anti-Christ," as his scandalous death might suggest to unbelieving Jews (cf. 1 Cor. 1:23), Jesus is the Messiah, **holy and true**, whose mission is to **shut . . . and . . . open** Israel's entrance into God's kingdom (cf. Luke 2:33–34).

3:8–10 / The church in Philadelphia receives unqualified commendation from the holder of the "key of David" who has **placed . . . an open door** for them into eternal life **that no one else can shut** (cf. John 6:35–40; 10:28–29). This is not a biblical justification of eternal security; rather, in the context of John's Revelation, it is an image of Christ's lordship: only the Lord has been given authority by his Father to determine for whom the door is opened and shut. Notice that Christ makes this determination on the basis of **deeds**: whether **you have kept my word and have not denied my name**. According to the biblical faith, good works are the evidence of true repentance (cf. 1 John 3:9–12; Luke 3:7–17; 10:25–28). Thus, John is keenly interested in the **deeds** which mark out a repentant and faithful witness to Christ. In this context, the assurance of eternal life is never justified by those who merely claim God's salvation but whose deeds are opposed to God's reign. In fact, they are no better than those who belong to **the synagogue of Satan** and who claim to be Jews but are liars (cf. John 8:42–47). The true Jew is the one for whom the door has been opened and not one who claims admission into the household of Israel on the basis of ethnicity or tradition (cf. John 8:31–41). Especially the preaching of primitive Jewish Christianity emphasized that God recognizes eschatological Israel by what it does and not by *sola fide* (James 2:24; cf. Rom. 2:5–10).

In Christ's parallel address to the congregation at Smyrna, that congregation's faithful witness to God is set in stark contrast to its social powerlessness. Likewise, the Philadelphian believers **have little strength,** but **I will make them** (the Jews) **come and fall down at your feet and acknowledge that I have loved you.** This is another stunning example of the apocalyptic reversal motif, not because it speaks of the transformation of a powerless people into a ruling people but rather because it turns the Jewish synagogue's polemic against the church upside down! The very Isaianic passages that promise God's salvation will come first to the nation Israel (Isa. 45:14 et al.) now justify the church's apologetic that the church is the "true" Israel of God.

The difficult situation facing the Philadelphian church is constitutive of the global **hour of trial,** described in 12:1–19:10, which will **test those who live on the earth.** The hardship and heartache that bespeak a fallen creation, cursed by God, purpose to **test** those who have already failed God in order to justify God's judgment of them at Christ's return. While believers are surely not exempt from suffering (2:10), their testing comes at the hands of evil powers rather than from God (cf. James 1:13–18) and will prove their faithfulness to Christ, resulting in a "crown" (3:11; cf. 2:10).

The messages to the other congregations indicate that the whole church is under attack inside and out. Whether John expected an empirewide persecution of Christians or an intensification of Jewish opposition and proselytism in this part of Asia cannot be decided by this particular text. In any case, John's pastoral intention is to encourage the congregation: while the world outside of the church will come under the judgment of God, the faithful church will not (cf. Rom. 1:17–18). The final, future execution of God's punishment against secular and religious powers that have marginalized this congregation of "little strength" intends to vindicate their faithfulness to **my command to endure patiently.** Revelation is read by the Philadelphian believers, then, as a word of hope that Christ **will keep** them **from the hour of trial.**

3:11–13 / Unlike the situation of disobedient congregations, where the imminent coming of Christ is perceived as a threat of punishment (2:5, 16; 3:3), the force of Christ's promise that **I am coming soon** (cf. 22:7, 20) is to encourage this congregation to **hold on** to the gospel **so that no one will take your crown** of eternal life; the expected vindication of their faithfulness and the reversal of their marginal status are at hand. Significantly, John does not resolve the tension felt between the opening address, which assures the reader that no one but the Risen Christ can open and close the door into eternal life (3:7–8), and this closing exhortation, which implies that evil powers could lead the believer away from the gospel of eternal life. God's salvation is a partnership, a covenant with God's people. The biblical idea of covenant envisions both conditional and unconditional aspects; it is a relationship entered into by God's love through the church's response of faith, but then maintained by divine love through the church's faithfulness to the Lord (cf. 1 John 2:28–3:10; 5:16–20).

The faithful congregation is comforted not by a future of orchestrated and pre-planned events but by the imminent expectation of an actual person, Jesus, who comes to make the overcomer **a pillar in the temple of my God** and to write three names to identify each one: **my God . . . the city of my God, the new Jerusalem, . . . my new name**. These are symbols of the community of overcomers, who will live in a new way toward God and each other. The heavenly **temple of my God** (11:19; 15:5–8) symbolizes a "true" Israel's worship of God, which has now commenced with Christ's exaltation and will be realized on earth when the **new Jerusalem** comes **down out of heaven from my God** at his return (cf. Heb. 12:22–29). A **name** is symbolic of essence; in this case, it indicates the identity of the community of current overcomers as the eschatological community that will experience transformed human existence at Christ's return.

3:14 / Laodicea was an affluent city. Located strategically at the intersection of three major trade routes, the city quickly became a banking and trading center, known especially for its woolen carpets and clothing. Also in Laodicea was one of the ancient world's most prominent medical schools, especially famous for its eye and ear treatments (cf. 3:18). This cultural identity is a useful metaphor for the faith of this city's Christian congregation. Their participation in the city's wealth had made them deaf and blind to their spiritual need (cf. 3:17–18). Thus, Christ reserves his severest condemnation for this congregation, failing to find anything in their witness worth commending.

The opening address posits Christ's witness to God as the exact opposite of the Laodicean church's witness to Christ. He is **the Amen . . . the faithful and true witness** to God. The Hebrew use of the liturgical **Amen** confirms as valid and binding the worshiping community's declarations of praise to God (cf. Isa. 65:16). Those theological convictions have been disclosed by Jesus, whose faithfulness to God as Messiah issues a true (*alēthinos*) historical witness to the truth about God's reign (cf. John 1:14). God's enthronement of Christ as **the ruler of God's creation** legitimizes the "amen" of the new age that God's recreating power is found only in the community which confesses that Jesus Christ is **ruler** over God's new creation, the church (cf. Col. 1:15–20).

3:15–20 / The decisiveness of Christ's witness to God's truth, indicated by the opening address, stands in marked contrast to the congregation's witness, which is **neither hot nor cold**; God demands a Christ-like witness from his disciples, a faith measured by faithfulness. The terrifying prospect of being **spit . . . out of my mouth** symbolizes God's negative verdict of a people who are unfaithful to God's **faithful and true witness**, who is the standard of eschatological judgment.

Drinking the caustic lime found in the hot springs of Hierapolis, six miles away, could make a person sick. Knowing the geography of the region helps make the point that Christ is sickened by the complacency of the Laodiceans, who say, **"I am rich; I have acquired wealth and do not need a thing,"** when in fact they are spiritually impoverished. Perhaps the congregation is afflicted by the same nascent Gnosticism found at nearby Colossae that bifurcated human life into spiritual/private (= good) and material/public (= evil) spheres. The result was to make Christ Lord only over one's personal and interior life, while tolerating the social evils that shaped one's public conduct (cf. James 4:13–5:6). This kind of religious schizophrenia is outlawed by the one who is Lord over both the private and public dimensions of human existence.

Against the dominant images of the Laodicean culture, Christ counsels the congregation to **repent** (3:19) and **realize that you are . . . poor, blind and naked**. Accordingly, they are to **buy from me gold** to **become rich** toward God (cf. Luke 12:21); they are to wear **white clothes** to **cover** their **nakedness** (cf. James 2:15); and they are to acquire **salve to put on your eyes** to **see** (cf. John 9:35–41). These symbolize repentance and also divine gifts that provide the repentant one with the spiritual goods necessary to turn around and follow Christ.

Christ warns of severe consequences that result from spiritual apathy; yet his emphasis is always on the spiritual resources that belong to the believing community and that make for a restored relationship with God. Indeed, Christ's harshest rebuke is prompted by his desire for fellowship with his people. His assurance that **I stand at the door and knock** does not anticipate the future entrance into God's kingdom; rather, it is a sign of Christ's present availability to restore fellowship with the believer who **hears my voice** (cf. John 10:1–18). Thus, the promise that Christ **will come in and eat with him, and he with me** is best understood as a symbol of his loving response to the one who is **earnest and repent**s. This supper is neither eschatological nor eucharistic; rather it celebrates the restoration of fellowship.

3:21–22 / The closing benediction recalls the opening terms for Christ's triumph and authority in the history of this congregation's life. Even as Christ has already triumphed (cf. 5:5) as God's **faithful and true witness** (3:14); even as God enthroned him, and he **sat down with my Father on his throne** as **ruler of God's creation** (3:14), so now Christ promises the community of overcomers **the right to sit with me on my throne**. The fellowship promised in 3:20 is qualified by this imagery of shared rule with the crucified and reigning Lord. Its fulfillment will conclude Revelation (20:4–6; 22:5) and thereby interprets the previous seven promises made to all the overcomers in the seven congregations as "their last and final privilege" (Beasley-Murray, *Revelation*, p. 108).

Additional Notes §3

2:2–3 / Boring finds behind John's reference to **deeds** a corrective to the kind of other-worldly, end-time speculation that dismisses civic or Christian responsibility as unimportant (*Revelation*, p. 95).

For a discussion of the different ways NT writers relate faith and works, see R. W. Wall, "Law and Gospel, Church and Canon," *Journal of the Wesleyan Theological Society* 22 (1987), pp. 38–70.

2:9 / John's reference to **Jews** is similar to Luke's use of the same term. For Luke, the phrase "the Jews" was an idiom for those obdurate, unbelieving Jews who refused to repent upon hearing the gospel. Rather than being an anti-Semitism, referring to an ethnic struggle, the term identifies certain opponents of a more "fraternal" struggle between repentant and unrepentant Israel. Cf. J. Jervell, *Luke and the People of God* (Minneapolis: Augsburg, 1972), pp. 41–74.

2:20–25 / Morris contends that the practices of the city's powerful trade guilds are implicit in this passage. In order to escape their poverty, some believers may have been tempted to condone unethical business practices (*Revelation*, p. 71).

3:4–6 / According to Hasel, the eschatological dimension of the biblical motif of a remnant is provided by Isaiah. He contends that the prophet uses this motif when the community's life is threatened with extermination: the continuing presence of a faithful people assures the nation of a faithful God. For Isaiah, however, the presence of this nucleus of dedicated believers, a remnant, at such times is a very condition for the future salvation of the whole people of God. See Gerhard F. Hasel, *The Remnant*, AUMSR 5 (Berrien Springs, Mich.: Andrews University Press, 1974), pp. 216–372.

3:10 / For the phrase, **hour of trial,** see S. Brown, " 'Hour of Trial' (Rev. 3:10)," *JBL* 86 (1966), pp. 308–14. In a recent unpublished study, "The Day of the Lord, the 'Hour' in the Book of Revelation, and Rev. 3:10," Allen Kerkeslager has argued that John's use of *hour* throughout Revelation (8:1; 9:15; 11:13; 14:7; 17:12; 18:10, 17, 19) is theologically important: it is a catchword that reminds the readers of the "day of the Lord" in prophetic tradition and of the second coming in Christian tradition. More specifically, it refers to the eschatological clash between the powers of evil and of God at the parousia and implies God's final triumph over sin and death takes place in a literal hour—so powerful is the might of God. Kerkeslager further argues that John's use of *hour* organizes and frames his vision of the trumpets, thus relating that series of judgments to the final victory of God.

§4 Thanksgiving for God's Reign: The Ground of Christian Faith (Rev. 4:1–11)

A clear break in John's book of visions is indicated by the events of 4:1. The seer sees an open door, and he hears the angel's trumpetlike voice summoning him to enter through heaven's portal. This passage into the visionary world will lead John to understand what will take place on earth. This is not to say that what follows in this chapter is unrelated to what precedes it; in fact, the various visions of this book are interrelated according to the seer's own commission (cf. 1:19). In our view, it is theology rather than chronology that provides the compositional axis to relate the visions together in a coherent fashion. And it is this chapter of wonderful doxologies that introduces the seven congregations to Revelation's essential theological conviction: God is the eternal creator in whom all things have their meaning and find their importance.

This seam in John's composition also cues the reader to a second primary section of this apocalyptic letter. According to the literary conventions of religious letters in the hellenistic world, the author's thanksgiving to the gods follows his greetings to the audience. In Paul's NT letters, thanksgivings express appreciation for his audience's faith, love, and hope in God. Since Paul usually wrote to specific audiences whose condition was well known, God is thanked (*eucharisteō*; Rom. 1:8; 1 Cor. 1:4; Phil. 1:3; 1 Thess. 1:2) for the blessings and gifts that characterize the situation of that particular audience. Thus, the hellenistic thanksgiving relates the goodness of God more directly and specifically to the author's perceptions of the audience's situation.

In recent years, scholars have come to recognize that epistolary thanksgivings are carriers of significant rhetorical freight in that they usually introduce the author's central theme or even a "table of contents" that then organizes the author's subsequent, extended response to his audience's crisis. In his pioneering work on epistolary thanksgivings, Paul Schubert (*Pauline Thanksgivings*) further suggested that the thanksgiving served a paraenetic or ethical purpose, calling the audience to live according to certain ethical ideals introduced there (see introduction). In Paul's case, for example, these ideals were often expressed in terms of his "triad of Christian virtue," faith-hope-love.

In the case of Revelation, however, John's thanksgiving follows a Jewish model and is more liturgical and theological than ethical; its tone is worshipful and hopeful and assumes that the audience's yet unspecified needs will be met by a good and powerful God. Revelation's epistolary thanksgiving is about God rather than about the spiritual needs or moral ideals of John's audience. In the NT letters of Ephesians and 1 Peter, where the author writes for several audiences, a traditional hymn of thanksgiving is substituted for the author's more personal thanksgiving (cf. Eph. 1:3–14; 1 Pet. 1:3–12). In the hymn, God is praised (*eulogētos*; Eph. 1:3; 1 Pet. 1:3; cf. Rev. 4:9) for the redemptive work accomplished on behalf of God's people in general. In both of these cases, the epistolary thanksgivings are similar in form and function to the *berakah*, the liturgical prayer of Jewish worship. Praise to God invokes confession of God as the faithful source of the community's well being and as worthy of such praise. The author's confession of God in praise, which intends to involve his readers, articulates the theological basis for the message of the whole letter, by which the readers then interpret their own situation and respond to God accordingly.

Chapter 4 of Revelation belongs to this second form of epistolary thanksgivings. Even though a *berakah* undergoes some changes in form when it moves first from the worshiping community, where it functions as a corporate prayer or hymn, to a literary composition, where it functions as an epistolary thanksgiving, its function remains the same: to express in praise the author's essential theological commitments. In the case of either model, both audience and author declare their confidence in God's saving grace and power and thereby establish a positive, more pastoral context for reading the entire letter. Because of God's goodness and kind attention to the audience, whatever threatens their faith can be overcome.

Against this literary background, the interpreter can more easily recognize and understand the importance of the thanksgiving given to God as the ruler over all creation (4:9). Formal

praise is offered by the heavenly congregation (4:8, 11) that surrounds God's throne in eternal worship. John's intent is to usher
his readers into this heavenly occasion of worship, so that they
join the twenty-four elders and four living creatures in their praise
of God. A tone of theocentric praise and worship that begins here
pervades the entire letter and evokes either hope or repentance;
the readers are caused to understand the book's foundational
theme as that idea of God which is introduced by their praise.
That is, the creator God is eternally established on the heavenly
throne (4:8), and all creation finds its moorings in God, who is
worthy to be praised (4:11).

4:1–2a / In our view, the interpreter of Revelation makes
a mistake to find meaning in every image that casts this vision
of the heavenly throne-room. The author intends a cumulative
impression of divine majesty which evokes the reader's praise of
God and realization of God's sovereignty over all things and
events. This is not to indulge the romantic notion that language
can express "truth" only in subjective and emotive discernment;
yet, it resists the positivist notion that language can carry meaning only if it describes "brute" facts. The language of John's Apocalypse is a part of both. In Revelation, metaphor is always evocative,
but it also carries within it some indication of the "real world."
In this sense, John intends to declare his essential understanding of reality that all of life is ruled over by a sovereign creator,
the God of Jesus Christ and his disciples. Yet, he also intends to
create a concrete "sense" of the fundamental importance of this
theological conviction to the worshiping community as it responds
to the Lord God Almighty in the actual circumstances of its life
with some measure of confidence that God has things under
control.

John is summoned into **heaven**, the setting of his visions.
It is a place entered only by angelic invitation and through the
door of a prophetic trance (**I was in the Spirit**). John's vision constitutes a religious experience and therefore yields spiritual power
for the seer and spiritual edification for those with an ear to "hear
what the Spirit says to the churches."

Heaven is home to God, and before Christ's heavenly enthronement (cf. Rev. 5) also to the Evil One (12:7). In that heaven
is analogous to history, the very ambiguity found in a place where

both God and the Evil One once coexisted (cf. Job 1–2) explains in part the ambiguity of Christian existence on planet Earth, where we experience the goodness of God and the treachery of social and personal evils. An element of Christian hope is that heaven will be replaced at the end of time by something "new," where God's people will experience only the shalom of God (cf. 21:1).

4:2b–6a / The invocation of heavenly praise is dominated by the image of a **throne,** the symbol of God's sovereign authority over all that God has created. God is known only as **the one who sat there** (4:3), although John colors his impression of God with **jasper and carnelian,** suggesting "luminous splendor" (Caird, *Revelation,* p. 63). Encircling God's throne is a **rainbow** that John describes as **resembling an emerald**—surely reminding the reader of a merciful God's everlasting covenant with all creatures promised to Noah (cf. Gen. 9:8–17). God's power is merciful and not coercive, indicating the Lord's desire to transform (rather than to destroy) all things. Significantly, God's promise to Noah, signaled by the rainbow, is tied to his authority as creator—the very point of the praises of the elders and creatures.

Surrounding the throne were . . . twenty-four elders, who themselves sit on **twenty-four other thrones.** The precise identification of the twenty-four elders is a well-known problem, and many solutions continue to be offered during the modern period of interpretation (cf. Morris, *Revelation,* pp. 86–87). The function of the elders within Revelation, however, seems reasonably clear: they form a heavenly chorus that continually sings God's praises on behalf of God's people. Further, the number **twenty-four,** a derivative of twelve, symbolizes the people of God, whom the elders represent in heaven by their praises to God (Boring, *Revelation,* p. 105). In that the heavenly liturgy is exemplary, these heavenly doxologies actually belong on the lips of the worshiping community on earth.

As to their particular identity, our suggestion begins with Jesus' "last will and testament" given at the Last Supper (cf. Luke 22:28–30). Jesus promises to those disciples who remain loyal to him the right to rule with him in the messianic kingdom. Jesus identifies them as rulers over an eschatological Israel, in contradistinction to the leaders of "official Judaism" who have relinquished their right to rule by their rejection of him as Messiah.

The significance of Jesus' use of "throne" in the passion narrative, then, is twofold: first, it signifies that the eschatological Israel of God consists of only those who are faithful to God's Christ (Luke 22:28; cf. Rev. 14:1–5); and, second, those who rule over eschatological Israel as their elders are those apostles to whom Jesus delivers his "testament" and in whom he has entrusted the responsibility for Israel's restoration (Luke 22:29–30; cf. Rev. 21:14).

If we suppose that John recognizes the vision of the **twenty-four elders** by the Jesus tradition, then for him the heavenly chorus of elders exemplifies the community of the "true" Israel that has remained faithful to the apostolic witness of Christ. In our view, then, the elders are not specifically the risen apostles, long since martyred; rather, they represent the community they founded and continue to nourish through their memories and teachings. This interpretation looks back to the messages delivered to the seven churches, and especially to those whose spiritual difficulties stem from forsaking apostolic teaching or from the attacks of the synagogue. The theological ground of their return or continuing fidelity to Christ is mirrored in the elders' praise of God's sovereign rule.

Coming **from the throne** John saw **flashes of lightning** and heard **rumblings and peals of thunder**. Perhaps these are indicators of God's power like on Sinai (cf. Heb. 12:22–29) or of the apocalypse of God's salvation like at Christ's death and resurrection (cf. Matt. 27:51–54; 28:2–3). In Revelation, however, these phenomena serve as fanfare for the testimonia of God's triumph (8:5; 11:19; 16:18). This interpretation seems especially apropos in the light of the immediate context that celebrates God as sovereign creator.

Before the throne were **seven lamps . . . blazing**, which are also the **seven spirits of God**, the Holy Spirit (cf. 1:4). The pentecostal use of "fire" as a metaphor for the empowerment of the Spirit may help explain John's image of "blazing lamps," here in apposition to the "sevenfold Spirit," as an element of God's reign (cf. Acts 1:6–8; 2:1–4; 1 Cor. 4:20–21). According to Johannine teaching, God sends the Paraclete to the community of Christ's disciples (John 14:16–17) both to teach (John 14:26) and to comfort (John 14:27) in light of the church's present situation. The rule of God is not removed from the experience of God's people on earth; God is always for Christ's disciples and with them in transforming power.

The **sea of glass, clear as crystal** has been interpreted in conflicting ways. In that John ties it to the **throne**, the **sea** is another symbol of God's reign. Within Revelation, the sea, like the heaven in which it is found, belongs to the old and not the new creation (21:1). It is the location of evil (13:1; cf. Ps. 74:12–14; Isa. 51:9–10), through which God's people must pass on their new Exodus to the promised land, the kingdom of God (15:1–3; cf. Exod. 14:21). In finding the **sea** in this vision of God's heavenly throne, and by *not* finding it in John's concluding vision of the new Jerusalem, the reader is made more aware that the destiny of the old order, including evil and death, is an ingredient of God's plan.

4:6b–8a / Drawing upon images found in the theophanies of Ezekiel 1 and Isaiah 6, John describes a group of four angelic beings he sees **in the center, around the throne**. As in Ezekiel's vision of the cherubim (Ezek. 1:6, 10), these **four living creatures** have the likenesses of **a lion . . . an ox . . . the face** of **a man . . . a flying eagle**, and are **covered with eyes, in front and in back**—an image of God's omniscience. Their **six wings** correspond to Isaiah's vision of the seraphs as well, which flew above God's throne (cf. Isa. 6:1–2).

While there is general agreement that these creatures are angelic, the significance of their four visages is contested among scholars. There are some who understand the four creatures by the angel myth in Jewish apocalypticism that occurs in the rabbinic midrashim on Ezekiel 1 and Isaiah 6. There are still others who understand the images by the astrology of the ancient Near East and its possible influence on the prophets Ezekiel and Isaiah, if not also upon John. In light of John's visionary world, we understand the creatures as angelic representatives, perhaps "celestial doubles," of God's animate creation, which is inherently higher than inanimate creation according to a Jewish theology of creation. Thus, within the heavenly order as John would understand it, each angel symbolizes the highest, most noble creature of its particular species in God's created order. For example, among all the birds of creation the eagle in flight "best" illustrates the glory of the creator God. Therefore, even as the twenty-four elders offer praise to God as representatives of true Israel, so also the **four**

living creatures offer praise to God as representatives of all creation; together creature and creation will participate in God's redemption of all things.

4:8b / The hymn they sing echoes the seraphs' declaration of God's holiness in Isaiah 6:3. No claim for God's rule is compelling that fails to include God's holiness. The reign of a holy God insists that all creatures on earth, represented in the throne room by the four living creatures, are accountable to God and obligated to give the Lord their worship and praise (cf. Rom. 1:19–20). John's emphasis, however, is on the creator's eternality: God is the one **who was, and is, and is to come** (cf. Rev. 1:4; Exod. 3:14). Such a confession is shorthand for the conviction that God, as creator, is Lord over all things. The title for God, **Lord God Almighty**, used repeatedly in Revelation, underscores John's conviction that God's will for creation will prevail over the evil powers. Further, in that God intended creation for good (cf. Gen. 1:31), John is confident that creation's history will proceed assuredly toward a redemptive conclusion—the theological ground of his book of visions.

4:9–10 / The doxological nature of this scene continues, even though John shifts his field of vision from the four living creatures to the twenty-four elders, whom he has already introduced in 4:4. The elders offer God their continual worship in concert with the thanksgiving declared by the creatures because God **lives for ever and ever**.

There is this difference, however: whereas the creatures praise God perpetually (4:8b), the elders' worship concludes in a particular act: **They lay their crowns before him who sits on the throne** (cf. 4:4b), a sign of their humble submission to God's rule (cf. Matt. 18:1–4). The effect is to make their subsequent and singular acclamation of God's worthiness for worship climactic and definitive for all of Revelation.

4:11 / The final and most important doxology is fashioned according to deeper logic of Jewish hymnody: the worshipful acclamation of God's **glory and honor and power** (4:11a) expresses the conviction that God **created all things** (4:11b). Notice that John changes the last item of the earlier triad of **glory, honor, and thanks** (4:9) to **power**, thereby underscoring his consistent claim for God's ultimate authority over world history and its ruling elite.

In this light, the doxology claims that the purpose of creation is in accord with God's **will** by which all things **have their being**. The humble worship of the elders in laying their golden crowns before God's throne is reflected in their exaltation of God, who has created the creation **by your will** and not for the world and its rulers (or even for the church and its elders).

The creator's purposes for creation, however, are in keeping with the character of God's reign as indicated by the cumulative force of chapter four's two concluding doxologies. The Trisagion ("Holy, Holy, Holy"; 4:8) of the living creatures attributes absolute holiness to God, suggesting that God simply will not tolerate evil and is at odds with the natural inclinations of a fallen world and the anti-Christian kingdom which rules over it. The **glory and honor and power** which the elders then attribute to God in the second doxology (4:11) suggest that it will be God, and not the powers of the evil dominion, who will ultimately determine the destiny of world history. The holy God, who abhors evil, and the **worthy** God, who is all-powerful, is **our Lord and God**. These two confessions suggest that God's final triumph over the forces of death and darkness is inevitable and our worship logical. As a shorthand way to speak of God, the heavenly doxologies are especially relevant for the readers of Revelation, who are under spiritual siege precisely because their worship of God is inhibited by confusing and painful traumas of life and faith, indicated in the two preceding chapters. For John, theodicy is finally settled in doxology, when the worshiping community on earth echoes the choruses of the heavenly community.

Additional Notes §4

For most, the confession of God as creator, which centers the thanksgiving of Revelation, seems incongruous with the epistle's evangelical message of divine judgment and redemption. This sense of incongruity is only heightened by our contention that the theological idea within the thanksgiving is foundational for the message the epistle intends to convey to its audience. How does the community's praise of God as creator, then, help explain God's work as redeemer?

The underlying assumption that God's creative actions are somehow separate and distinct from God's redemptive actions has been forged by Christian systematic theology, which makes a formal distinction between God as creator and God as redeemer. As creator, a transcendent God rules over all things, and as redeemer, an immanent God transforms all things for good. Typically, such formal distinctions are further drawn as belonging to two separate domains of human life; thus, God's rule is related to the natural order or to human history, whereas God's redemption is related to the spiritual order or to salvation's history. Further, we make epistemological distinctions on this basis so that God is known more objectively through nature and more effectively through redemption from sin.

Yet, such a systematic dichotomy is artificial. Biblical teaching weaves the redemptive and creative activities of God together as part of a whole cloth. Biblical teaching understands redemption as re-creation; thus, the redeemer is known through creation, and the creator has the right to redeem creation in a way which accords with the creator's (rather than the creature's) will. Even as God's glory and honor and power bring life into being, God's glory and honor and power liberate human life from sinful bondage, transforming life from old creaturehood into a new creation. That is, God promises in a good creation the same kind of existence that has already been realized in Christ and in the ongoing history of the redeemed community. In the consummation of that sacred history, God's exalted Christ ushers God's people back into the garden—not Eden, but the paradise of a new Jerusalem. The Bible's story, from the first garden to the last, reminds its readers that the God who gave life to all things by the power of the creative Word returns all things home by the grace of the redemptive Word, who is Christ Jesus our Lord. Praise be to the Lord God Almighty!

4:2 / Schüssler Fiorenza considers the **throne** to be Revelation's "central theological image." She argues that the symbol focuses the reader's attention on the creator of all things who is therefore *pantokrator*, ruling not only over the human soul "but to everything, to the political-societal realm and to the whole world" (*Revelation*, p. 116).

4:6b–8a / Boring agrees that the **four living creatures** represent the animate creation and contends that this meaning reflects an argument against certain gnostic teaching which considered the animate creation inherently evil (Boring, *Revelation*, p. 107).

§5   The Exaltation of God's Lamb:
The Penultimate Event of Salvation's History
(Rev. 5:1–14)

Chapter 5 marks the beginning of the third section in John's apocalyptic letter (see outline), shifting the reader's attention from epistolary thanksgiving to the main body of his composition. The study of the main body of religious letters has received little attention from scholars. They agree, however, that the importance of the body segment is substantive and rhetorical (see introduction). In this section of his letter, the writer deals with and seeks to resolve the crisis that threatens his audience's faith in God. In addition, the sermonic and paraenetic (ethical) nature of this material indicates the author's intimate awareness of those trying circumstances facing his readers. In some of Paul's letters, discrete paraenetic sections address in a specific and traditional way the audience's moral crisis (e.g., Rom. 12–14; 1 Thess. 4:1–12). In Revelation, the ethical element of John's message is less formal and more tacit, often "hidden" in the various forms of apocalyptic literature. Still, as several recent studies have demonstrated, John's pastoral orientation toward his readers shapes a work that issues a clarion call to faithfulness in the midst of real and pressing evils.

The way John draws upon the Paschal Lamb typology of the Exodus tradition (cf. Exod. 12) and structures the main body of his composition illustrates this point. The description of the present crisis, where evil powers challenge the church's faith in God (12:1–19:10), is sandwiched between two climactic moments of salvation's history—the penultimate exaltation of the slain Lamb (5:1–11:19) and the ultimate parousia of the exalted Lamb (19:11–22:5). The triumph of the slain Lamb, already realized in heaven (5:5), guarantees God's final triumph over evil on earth, finally realized at the Lamb's return (22:1–3). This interplay between salvation history's "already and not yet" interprets, even radicalizes, the "present evil age" (Gal. 1:4) when the eschatological community lives out its devotion to God in a world of existential ambiguity and spiritual struggle. The "big idea" of Revelation's sermon is centered by this interplay: the community is exhorted to respond in faithfulness to God, confident that God's victory has already taken place through the Risen Christ; and it is exhorted to resist the Evil One whose agents rule over the anti-Christian kingdom (Babylon) in trust that God will destroy it and establish an eternal reign of shalom (new Jerusalem).

5:1 / The focus of John's vision moves from the throne of God, which has centered his vision of heaven, to the slain Lamb, who now joins God beside the throne and before all those who worship them both. John views the scene and hears a crescendo of heavenly voices all of which bear witness to the worthiness of the slain Lamb. This vision depicts God's vindication of the crucified Lamb. At first, however, the mighty angel can find no one worthy enough to open God's scroll (5:1–3); the future of creation hangs in the balance, and John weeps in concern (5:4). Then a single elder identifies "the Lion of Judah (who) has triumphed" as the worthy one (5:5). At the climax of this scene, the elder's dramatic observation is confirmed by John, who sees not the victorious messianic Lion but rather the slaughtered Paschal Lamb (5:6). Finally, uniquely qualified by his death, the Lamb himself takes the scroll from God (5:7)—a confirmation of God's endorsement. These witnesses to the Lamb's worthiness settle the issue for the heavenly jury of the four creatures and twenty-four elders (cf. Rev. 4), whose choral response is a "new song" about the slain Lamb's worthiness to open the scroll (5:9–10). Other voices are added to this chorus, first by the thousands of angels who sing about the Lamb's worthiness to receive worship as Lord (5:11), and then by the entire cosmos that joins in a concluding liturgy of praise for both God and Lamb (5:13; cf. Phil. 2:9–11; Eph. 1:20–22).

Before John sees the Lamb, he sees **a scroll** in God's **right hand**. Caird suggests four possible explanations of the **writing on both sides** of God's scroll (Caird, *Revelation*, pp. 70–73). (1) If the scroll is equated with the Lamb's "book of life," the writing would be the names of those who belong to the eschatological community (cf. 21:27). Yet, the scroll clearly belongs to God, who holds it, and not to the Lamb, who receives it from God (5:7-8). The right to open it falls to the Lamb by virtue of his messianic credentials and not by virtue of his ownership or authorship of the scroll's decrees. Moreover, when the Lamb does break its seals to open it, the writing discloses the objects of divine wrath rather than the recipients of divine redemption.

(2) Ford suggests the writing contains the prophecies of divine judgment found in Revelation (*Revelation*, pp. 92-94). The visions subsequently delivered to the seer would have first been written on God's scroll and then written down (translated?) by John for a human readership. While John participates in this episode (5:3-5), there is no indication that his participation has anything to do with his vocation (1:19). John's participation in the vision has the rhetorical effect of pointing out to the reader the Lamb's most essential credential—not his triumph but his death. Further, John's visions contain more than prophecies of future events; they are visions of present realities. This vision of the Lamb celebrates an event already finished—the death and exaltation of Jesus Christ. Ford's suggestion, then, that the scroll contains only the predictions of future retribution, is unconvincing.

(3) Others contend that the scroll is equated with John's Bible (OT); indeed, the word for scroll, *biblios*, is the same word from which "Bible" is derived. If this interpretation is accepted, the scroll's text would no doubt contain those portions of the OT that formed John's prophetic "canon within his canon" (e.g., Ezekiel, Daniel, and Exodus) and would be the basis for his interpretation of the visions. While John alludes to the OT in writing down his visions and presumes that the OT promises are fulfilled through Christ, this interpretation of God's scroll makes no sense of the immediate scene. Why would Jesus' death be required of him before he opened a biblical scroll? How does the subsequent vision of divine judgments make sense of the OT, unless the interpreter assumes the validity of a Marcionite view of Scripture? (Marcion, a leader in the second-century church, argued that the OT should have no authority for Christians because it spoke only of God's wrath and not sufficiently of God's love.)

(4) In the ancient world, the sealed scroll carried official edicts or legal documents. Especially informed by chapter four's vision of the Lord God Almighty and the "new song" of vv. 9-10, John probably recognized God's scroll as containing the di-

vine decrees that announced God's triumph over evil (cf. Eph. 3:10) and the "official" conclusion of God's rivalry with the Evil One. Speculation about why there is **writing on both sides** should be resisted in making this point. What seems to impress John is the thoroughness of the scroll's decrees. For him, the scroll simply describes in detail the conclusion of salvation's history that has commenced with the faithful work of the Paschal Lamb.

The scroll's other characteristic is more important in this regard: it is **sealed with seven seals**. The number seven, a symbol for completion or a finished product, complements the earlier phrase, **writing on both sides**; together the scroll's two characteristics suggest the thoroughness of its scope and effect. Additionally, the number seven places the scroll into the eschatological field of images, with all the other "sevens" found throughout Revelation, thereby symbolizing the completion of God's promised salvation. The scroll's divine decrees cover the full range of eschatological effects that follow from Christ's work up to and including Christ's return. This explains why the one who is worthy to open the scroll is the Lamb who was slain. Jesus' death, or better his obedience to God unto death (cf. Phil. 2:8), vindicates him as God's Messiah; he is the one through whom God's eschatological judgment of sin and death and the transformation of all creation have their fulfillment.

5:2–4 / John **wept and wept**, when **no one in heaven or on earth or under the earth** was **found . . . worthy to open the scroll**. These are tears shed for a hopeless situation. Edicts must be decreed before they take effect; the promises of God's salvation cannot be fulfilled without the opening of the scroll. Not even **a mighty angel**, far better equipped than John to tour the cosmos, can find one **worthy** or able to open it. The history of salvation is at a standstill.

5:5–6 / The situation is not as hopeless as John first imagines: **one of the elders** points out **the Lion of the tribe of Judah, the Root of David**. This title combines two OT texts (Gen. 49:9; Isa. 11:1, 10), forming the biblical promise of a future messianic deliverer. From his heavenly vantage point, the elder identifies the one who already **has triumphed**. His Christology is formed "from above," where the results of Christ's triumph are already realized. Since his perspective accords with Jewish ex-

pectation of a messianic lion (cf. 4 Ezra 11:37-12:34), he may well
provide a foil for John's Christian (and for Jews, scandalous) faith
in a crucified Christ.

The Greek word for Christ's "triumph" is *nikaō* from which
"overcomer" comes. The elder's confirmation of Christ's triumph
responds to the earlier messages to the seven churches in which
the triumphant Christ exhorts the believers to "overcome." Now
the reader understands the full force of Christ's exhortation: the
hope of the church's eschatological triumph with Christ is rooted
in the heavenly confirmation that he has already triumphed over
the same evil powers which now threaten the church. The Lord
overcame the powers of sin and death, and so will his true disciples (cf. 14:1-5).

Yet, John, whose Christology is formed "from below" and
whose apprehension of the Lamb is formed by the traditions of
the historical Jesus, does not see at first glance what the elder
sees: he finds not a **Lion** but a **Lamb**. Neither does the Lamb appear as one who **has triumphed** but **as if he had been slain**. Here
is, then, the scandal and the foolishness of Christian proclamation: Christ is revealed as a slain Lamb, and not a triumphant
Lion (cf. 1 Cor. 1:22-24); a crucified one fulfills the OT promise
of messiah. Concerning this interpretative crux in Revelation,
Mounce concludes that "in one brilliant stroke John portrays the
central theme of NT revelation—victory through sacrifice"
(*Revelation*, p. 144).

It might be that John is at first confused by what he saw;
there is a certain tentativeness in his words, **as if it had been slain**.
His is the same ambivalence found within his audience, who on
the one hand confess with the elder a triumphant Christology
"from above," and who, on the other hand, share in the costliness
of a servant Christology "from below." Rhetorically, this moment
in John's christophany, full of tension and ambiguity, underscores
both the spiritual crisis and its solution for John's readership.

John, at first confused, does find the slain Lamb **standing**,
evidently no longer dead. He also finds him **in the center of the
throne** of God. Thus, it is where John finds the Lamb, as much
as what he finds there, that confirms him as worthy to open the
scroll: the Lamb is one with God (cf. 5:13; John 10:30-38). Further,
John's initial ambivalence calls attention to a reversal in the way
power is conventionally defined: Lordship is given to a Lamb.

Upon closer examination, John finds that he has **seven horns and seven eyes, which are the seven spirits of God**—the specific indicators which link the Lamb to God's kingdom as the mediator of its power and truth. The Lamb currently conveys the truth and power of God's reign to **all the earth** through the sevenfold Spirit of God, the Paraclete (cf. John 14:17; 16:7–11). This collection of images envisions the conflict between violent death and triumphant might and portrays the Christian idea of a slain but exalted Christ. At a more implicit level, the scene also portrays the experience of Christian martyrs who one day will be enthroned with Christ (cf. Rev. 6:9–11; 20:4).

5:7–8 / If John requires certain proof that the slain Lamb he sees is the same as the triumphant Lion the elder sees, then the Lamb himself provides it: **he came and took the scroll** from God. He is the only one who is able to act upon what the scroll documents. This event, which represents Christ's exaltation, results in his adoration when **the four living creatures and the twenty-four elders** fall **down before the Lamb** as they had before God earlier (Rev. 4:8–10). The **prayers of the saints** are now directed to the enthroned Lamb, because in his triumph they have been made confident of God's mercy (cf. Heb. 4:14–16).

5:9–10 / The new (i.e., eschatological) **song** sung by the heavenly chorus interprets the full significance of the Lamb's action in taking God's scroll. In this sense, the song responds to the angel's earlier question, "Who is worthy to break the seals and open the scroll?" (5:2): the slain and risen Lamb is **worthy to take the scroll and to open its seals**; he is the Messiah who is able to inaugurate the new age of God's triumph over the Evil One.

The credentials given for the Lamb's worthiness are three. First, **you were slain**. The word **slain**, *sphazō*, indicates the violent slaughtering of a Paschal lamb (Exod. 12:6; cf. 1 Cor. 5:7; 1 Pet. 1:18–19). This interpretation of Christ's death is consistent with the Exodus typology found throughout Revelation; that is, John's intent is to evoke hope for a new Exodus from sin and into God's promised kingdom of grace and peace.

Second, **with your blood you purchased men for God from every . . . nation**. The verb **purchase** (*agorazō*; cf. Rev. 3:18; 13:17) denotes a commercial transaction, typified by the purchase of people as slaves. Although some persons were purchased by pagan priests for sacral purposes, most were prisoners of war who were exported to the victor's nation (usually Roman) for economic profit. In fact, the obligation of the defeated nation was to purchase back its citizens when able.

This interprets the significance of Christ's death as payment for those held captive by self-destructive sin and the fear of death. Of course, this point is also central to the Exodus tradition in which God's people are held captive by Egypt. Even as the blood of the Paschal Lamb symbolized the effective power of God's love that liberated Israel from Egypt's evil oppression, so also Christ's death—his **blood**—liberates believers from their bondage to sin (cf. Rev. 12:10–12; Rom. 6:6–7; 1 John 2:2).

In the Christian rehearsal of the Exodus typology, the true Israel of God is not defined by an election theology that tends to exclude or demote "outsiders." In Christ, the eschatological community is an inclusive community, made up of believers from **every tribe . . . and nation**. While God created even unbelievers for good, they are currently held as the prisoners of a spiritual war, enslaved to the Evil One and used as agents of his anti-Christian kingdom. Because of Christ's death and the triumph of God it effects, these slaves are purchased back by the Lamb's blood **for God.**

Third, Christ's death resulted in a **kingdom . . . that will reign on earth**, and a community of **priests to serve our God** (cf. Rev. 1:5–6). The second stanza of this christological doxology (5:10) is chiastic (ABA'), and the reader is naturally drawn to its vortex (B), where the essential insight into Christ's death is highlighted: **priests to serve our God**. That is, Christ's death transforms a people into a servant community (cf. Mark 10:45).

The second result is informed by the first. While the first is spiritual, the second is more political but no less concrete: **you have made them into a kingdom** (A)/ **and they will reign on the earth** (A'). The community of faith represents God's rule **on earth** as an alternative to the world order and its evil powers and principalities. As important as this second reality is, for John the more pivotal consequence of the cross is servanthood rather than rule. Only when the church first understands itself as a community of **priests** will it be liberated from the notions of repressive power found in the anti-Christian kingdom, and thus be fit to reign with a redeeming God and slaughtered Lamb.

5:11–12 / Adding their number to the heavenly chorus, the angelic choir joins in a hymn of praise for the worthy Lamb. Rather than rehearsing the reasons for his exaltation as before, this doxology brings together all the elements of Christ's lordship, recognizing that he rules on God's behalf (cf. Rev. 7:12). Taken together with the previous doxology, Christ's lordship is cast in redemptive terms and is directed to those he purchased from every nation.

5:13–14 / Even though both God and the Lamb are worshiped by **every creature in heaven and on earth and under the earth and on the sea**—that is, by every life God created—the basis of their worship is different. The praise accorded the exalted Christ is due to his fidelity to God (cf. Rev. 7:10). Jesus of Nazareth submitted himself to God as God's Christ, as God's Son, as God's Servant, as God's Lamb in order to usher in the eternal age of God's blessing. God rules the entire cosmos as its creator, and it is God and not the Lamb **who sits on the throne**. John's vision and the gospel it enshrines are profoundly theocentric. Worship of and devotion to the Lord Jesus must always be understood in terms of his relationship to God.

The mighty hymns of praise sung by the heavenly chorus in honor of the slain Lamb resound with the convictions of all the apostles: the ascended Christ reigns as exalted Lord in heaven until all the evil pretenders to God's throne are vanquished from earth. The concluding, cosmic **Amen!** and the elders' worship of God and Christ together suggest a pointed finality to these heavenly proceedings. The interpreter must make meanings of John's composition that correspond to this portrait of God's triumph over evil through the faithful work of the Paschal Lamb. The correct and logical response from all creation is to join in the new song of heavenly praise!

Additional Notes   §5

The eschatology of earliest Christianity recognized that the age of fulfillment had begun with Christ. The age to come, promised by the biblical prophets, has already broken into human history because of the

messianic mission of Jesus. His life of faithfulness, climaxed by his obedient death, satisfied the demand of God, who now rights the covenantal relationship with the believing community. The life, death, and
resurrection of Jesus from Nazareth constitute the elements of a "realized"
Christology in that together they fulfill the promise of God's salvation
and trigger the pouring out of its covenant blessings on the disciples of
Christ in every age.

Indeed, Luke's Jesus announced from the beginning to the end
of his messianic mission that God's promised salvation had begun
"today" (Luke 4:21; 19:9; 23:43). And John's Jesus told his followers that
in his physical absence, his Spirit would continue to impart truth and
grace to them. Currently, then, it is in the spiritual realm of the community's righted relationship with God that the Spirit of the Risen Christ
works to transform and empower God's people in the historical realm.
However, the yield of the Spirit's activity is more than the spiritual transformation of individual believers. Certainly, the renewal of mind and
heart, in the believer and in the believing community, is realized by the
transforming grace of God as mediated in the Spirit of the Risen Christ.
Yet, the social structures of human existence are transformed as well,
so that believers are enabled by the Spirit to relate to each other in new
ways. The fruit of the Spirit is the ever-increasing capacity to love each
other and to form together a community which bears witness to the new
Jerusalem in the age to come (Cf. S. C. Mott, *Biblical Faith and Social Change*
(N.Y.: Oxford University Press, 1982). The power of God which raised
Jesus from the dead is at work in the community of his disciples to raise
up a people whose devotion to God directs the attention of the present
evil age to the future age of shalom and grace.

History tells us that the emergence of the spiritual and social realities of the coming age within the life and history of the believing community is slow and sometimes painful. Jesus not only announced the
beginning of the age of fulfillment; he also spoke of the future completion of that age and of God's salvation. Israel's rejection of his messianic mission did not delay God's salvation; it did, however, limit its
scope. The continuing presence of evil, which always encourages the rejection of the gospel, continues to limit the influence of God's grace during the present age. As long as the Evil One roams the planet, the
transformation of God's creation will not take place. Matthew's Gospel
suggests that the influence of evil upon the community of disciples results in the compromise of faith and life (Cf. J. D. Kingsbury, *Matthew:
Structure, Christology, Kingdom* [Philadelphia: Fortress Press, 1976]). Thus,
the actual realization of eschatological blessing by the church is impeded
by the surrounding social order, which is evil and seeks to undermine
God's reign and purposes. While the coming age has begun, and God's
promised salvation is now being fulfilled through the Spirit in the ongoing life of those devoted to Christ, its *telos* is still in the future. Salvation has not yet fully come, because evil still pervades and distorts
human existence. To the extent of our devotion, evil will have no influence, and the effects of God's transforming grace will be more keenly

felt. Yet, as long as evil persists, the universal and systemic yield of God's grace and experience of promised shalom will be a real impossibility.

John stands within the stream of earliest Christian eschatology. The climactic vision of Christ's parousia describes the vindication of God and Christ's true disciples which proceeds from the judgment of the anti-Christian kingdom, of its malevolent rulers, and finally of death itself. This excursus therefore seeks to frame Revelation's concluding vision as well as its vision of Christ's coronation. The inertia of God's salvation which begins with Christ's exaltation in heaven will be finally felt on earth upon his return. And it will be felt first by the same elite responsible for thwarting the progress of God's salvation in the life of God's people. Only with the destruction of evil and death can the blessings of God's salvation be fully experienced—not only by the community of overcomers but throughout the new heavens and earth. John has this eschatology in mind when shaping his book. Thus, the concluding visions of Christ's parousia begin with the destruction of evil and death before describing the final transformation of God's people which can now take place at long last. And the inevitability of such an outcome is already understood in this vision of the Lamb's enthronement: the forward movement of God's saving and judging grace, begun by the executed and exalted Messiah, simply has too much inertia for the Evil One to overcome.

5:1–14 / The messianic event, culminating in the exaltation of the crucified Lamb (5:5–7), inaugurates the new age of salvation's history when God fulfills the promises made about the restoration of Israel (5:9–10). The glorification of Jesus as Lord and Christ (5:12–13; cf. 11:15) achieves the penult in Israel's history as God's covenant people and begins the "last days" that will conclude human history and usher in the eternal age.

Christ's exaltation also marks the beginning of divine judgment (6:1–11:14): on the cross and in the empty tomb, a reigning God has said "no" to a fallen creation (see above). Any threat that the evil powers might mount on earth or in heaven against God's rule, perhaps even to soften the awful consequences of God's wrath, is noticeably absent from Revelation's visions of divine judgments. In this sense, the triumph of the slain Lamb spells the certain and unequivocal defeat of evil and death; they can offer no resistance to God's judgment against the anti-Christian kingdom. Thus, with the sounding of the seventh trumpet (11:15), the vision of Christ's exaltation that begins at 5:1 concludes with similar praises (11:15–18) at the opening of the heavenly temple (11:19,) when Israel's promised restoration, symbolized by the ark, takes place first in heaven and imminently on earth.

5:1 / Boring suggests that John adds that the scroll had **writing on both sides** "to evoke a plurality of images in the readers' ears" (*Revelation*, p. 104).

5:5–6 / M. G. Reddish has recently argued that John understands his vision of the slain Lamb in terms of the hellenistic "hero-martyr." John's intention is more pastoral: he wishes to vindicate the heroic witness of those believers who face the prospect of martyrdom. See "Martyr Christology in the Apocalypse," *JSNT* 33 (1988), pp. 85–95.

Revelation's word for lamb, *arnion*, appears once in the rest of the NT—also in the Johannine tradition (John 21:15). The alternative, *amnos*, is also found in the Fourth Gospel (1:29, 36), where different words for similar things or acts are often used without distinction. No special significance should be attached, then, to Revelation's use of *arnion* other than it refers to the Paschal Lamb.

In Revelation, **horns** are associated with political or ruling power; cf. Rev. 12:3; 13:1; 17:3. **Eyes** is a biblical metaphor for spiritual illumination or truth; cf. Zech 4:10.

5:9 / The NIV adds **men** to the phrase, **you purchased men for God**, thereby glossing over an important textual problem. Some ancient mss include the pronoun "us" (*hēmas*), rendering the phrase, "you purchased **us** for God." The decision can not be decided on textual grounds alone, since both readings enjoy significant external support. In the context of the composition itself, if we take the **elders**, who sing the song, to be angelic beings, then the pronoun should be omitted on christological grounds: Christ did not die for angels. If however we take the elders to be risen elders (i.e., apostles and prophets) of eschatological Israel, then the pronoun could be retained on the same grounds.

5:10 / The verb **they will reign**, *basileusousin*, is textually corrupted as well. A minority of ancient mss prefer the present tense, "they reign" (*basileuousin*). In our view, the meaning of the verbal idea in either its future or the present tense (as a "future present") is the same: God's transforming grace has created a royal priesthood through the slain Lamb.

5:11–12 / The terms used by the angelic choir must have created the same ambivalence in John's first readers as did his first sight of Jesus as a slaughtered Lamb for him: these are terms reserved for the Caesar by the worshipers of the imperial cult. To assign them now to a slain Lamb calls attention once again to the Gospel's challenge of cultural and social definitions of power. Power finally belongs to the one who was slain on God's behalf, and not to the Caesar of an anti-God kingdom. The praxis of power is to serve the interests of God rather than the empire; it means to love God and to bear witness to God's truth disclosed in Christ Jesus.

§6 *The Lamb Breaks Six Seals of God's Scroll (Rev. 6:1–17)*

The judgment of God against a fallen world is one yield of the death and exaltation of Christ. The breaking of the seals, which opens the scroll and declares God's decree of salvation, occurs as an essential part of Christ's entrance into the heavenly throneroom. The seal judgments, and the trumpet judgments that follow, do not depict a sequence of future historical events; rather, they symbolize together God's response to—and are in that sense co-terminus with—chapter five's exaltation of the risen Lamb. Our commentary of this passage will assume, then, that, in keeping with the overarching intentions of his entire composition, John is making a theological point rather than a historical prediction.

6:1 / There is a clear relationship between the visions of the exalted Lamb in chapter 5 and his opening of the scroll's seals in chapter 6: God's global judgment, which will result from the breaking of the first four seals, is predicated on Christ's heavenly triumph. Thus, the **four living creatures**, who worshiped the Lamb when he took God's scroll in the earlier vision (5:8), now respond to the Lamb's opening of the first four seals by executing the scroll's edict through four horsemen.

The identity of the four horsemen is linked to the identity of the four living creatures; thus, even as they represent all animate creation in heaven (4:7), so the four horsemen, who obey their demand to **Come!**, are their agents on earth. The four horsemen would indicate, then, that God's judgment extends to all animate existence; even in their realm the effects of sin are noticed. In collective rebellion against a good creator, all creatures, human and non-human, have perverted God's intentions for the world order, but have thereby prevented themselves from finding those things that can make it whole. In what follows, the world desires peace, but finds war; it works for prosperity, but it finds scarcity; it seeks life, but finds only death. The messianic event challenges this corrupted creation and promises a new earth on which the intentions of a good creator are realized (cf. 21:1–22:6a).

6:2–4 / The first two horsemen are sent out as champion warriors. They both bear weapons of warfare—the first rider **held a bow** and the second **a large sword**. The first, who also rides a **white horse**, wears the **crown**, the symbol of military conquest. The second, who rides a **fiery red** horse, is intent to engage the enemy in battle. God has given earth over to itself to engage in a global, civil war, preventing its inhabitants from attaining the very things that make for their peace and security (cf. Rom. 1:28–31). Together, the horsemen **take peace from the earth**; these symbols of military strife call attention not only to a fallen creation, which now exists under the curse of God, but also to earth's need for God's shalom.

6:5–8 / The third horseman, riding a **black horse**, is sent out by the **third living creature** holding **a pair of scales in his hand**. John here envisions a "siege economy." Creation's civil war results in a scarcity of the staples necessary to sustain human life and in the rapid inflation of prices, which makes it impossible for the poor to survive. **"A quart of wheat for a day's wages"** is the slogan of the marketplace, which is characterized by inequity and injustice. These conditions surely lead to violence, since the actual availability of **wheat . . . barley . . . oil and the wine** exists only for those wealthy enough to afford them. The scales of the third horseman measure the economic structures of a fallen world, where poor persons are deprived of food, and where the earth's poor have need for God's bounty.

The fourth horseman, sent out on a **pale horse** when **the Lamb** opens **the fourth seal**, is **named Death, and Hades was following close behind him**, gathering the victims of **sword, famine and plague, and . . . the wild beasts** (perhaps those used in the Roman persecution of Christians) into its domain. According to Revelation, both Death and Hades (the place of the dead) are destined for the lake of fire as participants in the Evil One's reign of terror (Rev. 20:14). According to this vision, however, Death and Hades are results of the horsemen's activities, and are viewed, therefore, as agents of God's salvation in accord with God's decree. This does not mean that God ordains Death along with the evil powers and activities that sponsor it and Hades. Death results from creation's rebellion against God (cf. Rom. 5:12–14). Rather Death and Hades occasion God's salvation and are therefore a necessary element of God's plan of redemption, contained in the scroll's writing.

This is why John sees the triumphant Lamb open the seals that release these disasters on earth. In this sense, the four horsemen symbolize God's redemptive grace that reverses humanity's civil wars and poverty, death and disease. Caird correctly concludes that "The heavenly voice which says, '**Come!**' is not calling disasters into existence. . . . Rather the voice is declaring that nothing can now happen, not even the most fearsome evidence of man's disobedience and its nemesis, which cannot be woven into the pattern of God's gracious purpose" (*Revelation*, p. 83).

6:9–11 / The breaking of the fifth seal narrows the field of John's vision to the community of martyred believers, **who had been slain because of the word of God and the testimony they had maintained** (cf. 1:2). He finds their **souls** (or bodies) **under the altar** of the heavenly temple, they having sacrificed their lives in worship of God while participating in the systemic breakdown of the world order.

John, whose imprisonment shares in the martyrs' sacrifice (cf. 1:9), may well be tempted to cry out with them **"How long . . . until you avenge our blood?"** The martyrs' plea, addressed to the **Sovereign Lord, holy and true**, in expectation of Christ's imminent return (6:11), seeks God's eschatological vindication of their faithfulness. Their petition is not for vengeance against their persecutors; they are more concerned about their status within God's righteous reign than within an anti-Christian kingdom ruled by those secular elite who had convicted and executed them as "the enemy." We will make note, however, that in the succeeding vision of the 144,000, John assumes that God will **avenge our blood** (cf. 7:4–8).

Further, the martyrs' cry of vindication frames their concern for theodicy and the date of its resolution: **when** will a **Sovereign Lord**, whose powerful mercy is disclosed in the slain and risen Lamb, vindicate God's reign publicly as **holy and true**? No doubt, some readers of Revelation are facing a situation similar to that described by 2 Peter 3:3–4 in which the delay of Christ's parousia has prompted their opponents (perhaps other believers?)

to scoff and ridicule Christian hope in Christ's return. Second Peter's response is to reassert the patience of God, who "is not wanting anyone to perish, but everyone to come to repentance" (2 Pet. 3:9). John envisions a God who is waiting for **the number** of martyrs . . . who are **to be killed** . . . to be **completed** as the condition for the day of vindication. Both locate the resolution of theodicy in the future; both explain this delay in terms of the future vindication of God's justice; both find here incentive for the community's confidence in God's intentions for salvation's history; both encourage a patience justified by a belief in God's sovereign control over history.

The immediate context of Revelation suggests, however, that the tragic death of faithful believers indicates the nearness of God's final triumph over their persecutors. In fact, the exaltation of the slain Lamb promises them that the last will indeed be first under God's reign, and those who lose their life for the Lamb's sake will be exalted with him. This point, so crucial in John's own understanding of his vision, will be expanded in chapter seven's scene of the eschatological remnant. That scene responds to the martyrs' plea for vindication.

The certainty of the future day of vindication is indicated by the **white robe** given each martyr. By this interim act, God already condemns the pagan tribunal that has ordered the death of **fellow servants and brothers**. Since the Christian martyrs are executed unjustly, God's indictment is viewed to be **holy and true** even according to pagan standards of truth and goodness.

6:12–17 / The opening of the sixth seal issues in a two-fold response from the elite of the social order. Since Christ's exaltation validates his teaching that the last (i.e., Christian martyrs) will become first, it also means that the first will be last. Thus, the natural disasters (6:12–14) announcing the beginnings of such a reversal (cf. Matt. 27:51; 28:2) cause even **the kings of the earth** to hide **from the face of him who sits on the throne and from the wrath of the Lamb**. The deliberate irony of the phrase **the wrath of the Lamb** catches the reader's attention. Mistaken are those explanations of this catchphrase that interpret Christ's death as an act of personal or historical judgment against those who rejected him. It is best to take the phrase quite literally as the response of God's enemies, whose terrifying experience of God's anger results in a distorted understanding of the cross as God's punishment rather than God's forgiving mercy (Caird, *Revelation*, pp. 92–93). The slain Lamb is not finally a symbol of wrath (although Beasley-Murray, *Revelation*, p. 124); he is rather the symbol of God's grace that purchased a people from death for eternal life.

The **kings . . . princes . . . generals . . . rich . . . mighty** who experience God's wrath ask a legitimate question: **"Who can stand?"** They are those who were "first" in the world system and who once held the keys to the powers and blessings of the secular kingdom. They now experience the same powerlessness of *every slave*; together they are "last" in God's kingdom. Therefore, their lament recognizes a different problem than that contained in the earlier lament of the Christian martyrs (6:10). While the lament of martyrs expresses the concern of beleaguered believers, the plea of these outsiders, who have lost their positions of secular power, is to know how to belong to the community that somehow escapes the terror of God's judgment. Would it be too far-fetched to suggest that the **kings . . . mighty** represent those unbelievers who seek to hear the gospel in response to their personal experience of creatureliness telling them that things are not right? Especially during times of calamity, those most comfortable and secure among us, who lose the resources of their comforts and securities, come to realize more concretely that death and evil pervade human existence. They are often the most inclined to ask, perhaps on behalf of all those they rule over, **Who can stand?** In any case, neither question, asked by the martyr or by the pagan elite, is merely rhetorical; each is rooted in human experience. Together they prepare the reader of Revelation for the interlude in John's vision of seals that follows in chapter seven.

Additional Notes §6

The wrath of God against the world order involves the entire, fallen creation: even as sin and evil are systemic, so also is God's judgment against both creature and his natural environment. Likewise, even as evil is all pervasive, so also is the effect of God's transforming grace. The power of God's salvation extends beyond the private and spiritual domain and into the public and social domain of human existence.

Indeed, Jesus' preaching of the messianic woes warns of an upheaval of the entire societal order (cf. John 16:17–33; Matt. 24; Mark 13; Luke 21). The sociopolitical structures and patterns of international and familial life are disrupted, resulting in war between nations and conflict within families. The absence of God's shalom across creation, whether disclosed by humanity's violence or by natural disaster, stems not only from creation's rebellion against its sovereign creator, but also from God's decision to throw a rebellious creation back to itself and its own self-corrupting and self-destructive vices. Thus, the global destruction portrayed in the seal judgments of Revelation is mediated by four horsemen, who are linked in the vision with the four living creatures, symbolic of the created order (Rev. 4:7). The very structures of human existence have been so corrupted by rebellion that calamity and death are inevitable on earth, and the apocalypse of God's salvation from heaven is necessary.

Therefore, when the eternal age is finally consummated at Christ's return, it is envisioned by John as a new creation, as a new city, as a new people, as a new sociopolitical order, which is formed out of the ashes of the old order (Babylon) into a new order (new Jerusalem) over which the creator rules with the Lamb in peace and glory. The powers of darkness have been destroyed and with them the agents of sin and death.

While the full realization of this social reality lies in the future, the church bears witness to the new order today. The essential conflict between the church and the surrounding society stems from this current conflict between old and new, between present and future, between heaven and earth, between God and the Evil One. The church's life and faith envision a future cosmic reality; but the church is necessarily at odds with current notions of power and status. The visions of judgment remind God's people that those same authorities who marginalize the faithful for their commitment to the reign of God stand under God's wrath because the executed Messiah has triumphed. Their correct response, then, is continued faithfulness to Christ and rejection of the surrounding social order, even if obedience results in martyrdom.

6:2 / Ladd contends that the identity of the first horseman is Christ, and his crown represents the positive results of "the proclamation of the gospel" in the world (*Revelation*, p. 99). However, Ladd has difficulty explaining how the symbolism of the other three horsemen agrees with that of the first.

§7 Interlude: Reminder of God's Faithfulness to God's People (Rev. 7:1–17)

In concluding the horrific judgment brought about by the opening of the sixth seal, John interposes an eschatological interlude that responds to the two questions evoked by the experience of human suffering. Whether they concern the suffering of Christian martyrs, lamented at the opening of the scroll's fifth seal, or of their persecutors, initiated by the sixth, the cries for vindication and of lamentation envision a common recognition that the social order and its ruling elite are opposed to the well-being of God's creation. Even the structures of a fallen world must be reversed and transformed before the good intentions of their creator are realized. Of course, it should be said at this point that human sinfulness is more than rebellion against the creator; human sin is also the irrational rejection of those things that the creator intended for our good.

The good news is that through the exalted Lamb God has announced the availability of that transforming power necessary to redeem all humanity and to restore all creation. This gospel interprets the present passage as a word of hope for suffering believers who cry out for vindication and also for suffering unbelievers whose plea seeks a path that leads them to shalom. The ultimate purpose of divine wrath is redemption; God's anger is always subordinate to and qualified by God's mercy. God's "Yes!" is the concluding word of history.

At first glance, this interlude in John's vision of divine wrath depicts the future day of God's vindication. Two groups of believers, one of 144,000 and another of a countless number, represent God's covenant community from a different period of Israel's history, and each is preserved for God's salvation at the end of the age. Upon closer analysis, however, the same interlude takes measure of those "who can stand" before the throne of God (cf. 6:17; 7:9) and who are led by God's Lamb "to the springs of living water," where God wipes away the tears of their earthly suffering (7:17). In this way, this eschatological portrait responds to the martyrs who lamented their difficult situation during this present evil age; and it also establishes the criteria by which the unbeliever can join the great multitude belonging to God and to the Lamb (cf. 14:1–5).

7:1–4 / The identity of the **144,000 from all the tribes of Israel** has been debated for centuries. Most agree that 144,000 is symbolic of a remnant of "true" believers. Both Jewish and Christian interpreters link the history of God's salvation to the history of a covenant community that numbers twelve (e.g., twelve tribes of Israel; twelve apostles of the church), or multiples of twelve, as here. The contested issue is whether to take the phrase **all the tribes of Israel** as a literal reference to historical Israel or as a symbol of eschatological Israel (cf. Rev. 21:12). If one assumes that the phrase refers to a spiritual Israel as elsewhere in the NT (e.g., James 1:1; 1 Pet. 1:1; cf. Rom. 9–11) including Revelation (14:1), then the 144,000 could refer to an "extra special" remnant within the church, perhaps to its martyrs who exemplify fearless devotion to God of the sort John encourages. While there is no indication in the text that the 144,000 enumerate the remnant of martyrs, it does make sense of the immediate context to identify this group with those who earlier cry out for vindication (6:10). This first part of the visionary interlude, then, responds directly to the martyrs' earlier question, "How long?" (6:10).

If we are to take the phrase more literally as referring to the saints of "old" Israel, then the 144,000 would form a "cloud of witnesses" (Heb. 12:1; cf. Heb. 11:4–38) whose faithfulness to God established the first stage of Israel's exodus from sin (Heb. 11:39–40) and movement toward their eventual destination (cf. Heb. 11:13–16), the new Jerusalem (Heb. 12:22–27). Their pilgrimage to promise is suggested by the exodus symbolism that lies behind the act of sealing the 144,000, which prepares for and awaits the coronation of the eschatological Israel as depicted in the second half of this interlude.

Some might object that this only confuses the symbolic with the historical. However, John often combines historical description with symbolic meaning (e.g., the messages to the seven churches). It is not difficult, then, to imagine that the symbolic meaning of the 144,000 might refer to a historical Israel. In this regard, it is striking that there is no reference to the Lamb in this first part of the vision; not until John envisions the "great multitude" does John also see the Lamb. This may well indicate a continuity between the Israel of God prior to and then after the Christ event as comprising the two essential and interconnected dispensations of salvation's history.

We are inclined toward the first of these two options, primarily because we prefer to understand the significance of this particular interlude as a response to the two seminal questions that emerge from the chaos of the first six seal judgments. The opening phrase, **After this I saw** (7:1), intends to convey the "theo-logical" (rather than "chrono-logical") connection between the seal judgments and eschatological salvation; the same phrase is used later in the interlude (7:9) to tie together the two discrete subgroups that make up eschatological Israel. In this sense, the two parts of the interlude refer back to the two questions: the first half (i.e., the vision of the 144,000) responds to the martyrs' question, "How long?" while the second half (i.e., the vision of the great multitude) responds to fallen humanity's lament, "Who can stand?" By combining both concerns into a single passage, John suggests that both questions are appropriate responses to the reign of God that has triumphed through the slain Lamb.

The sealing of the 144,000 is prefaced by an exchange between **four angels standing at the four corners of the earth** and **another angel . . . having the seal of . . . God**. The four angels are roughly equivalent to the four horsemen in that they are given charge over a destructive force of nature—in this case **the four winds of the earth** which have **power to harm the land and the sea** (cf. 6:13). John's purpose is not to present a retrospective of the previous seal judgments or to suggest that a remnant within the church will escape humanity's suffering; rather, he intends that the interlude takes note of God's terrifying wrath in order to understand its eschatological significance both for the Christian martyrs-to-be and for wretched humanity.

In this light, the other angel comes **from the east** in expectation of the creator's good portion (cf. Gen. 2:8) or in expression of God's reigning glory (Ezek. 43:2). And it carries **the seal of the living God** to place **on the foreheads of the servants of our God**, whom we have already identified as a remnant of Christian martyrs, even though their description is true of all believers (cf. 5:10). Surely the **seal** symbolizes divine approval, even as it symbolized political legitimacy in the ancient world. More to the point, however, is the act of sealing which marks them as a people for God's redemption (cf. Eph. 1:13–14). The purpose of this moratorium from wrath, then, is to assure those servants of God, who cry out for God's vindication, that they have already been sealed for the day of their vindication.

7:5–8 / The significance of the list enumerating the remnant of a true Israel has been long debated. The best suggestions begin by recognizing that biblical genealogies serve theological purposes and that John has shaped this one to reflect the messianic hope specific to his composition. The list accordingly begins with Messiah's tribe of **Judah** (Rev. 5:5) rather than **Reuben**, who heads most OT genealogies as Jacob's eldest son (cf. Gen. 35:23). Second, the list replaces the tribe of Dan with **Manasseh**, who was actually Joseph's son (Gen. 48). Contrary to Jacob's aspirations for Dan (Gen. 49:16–17), Dan became a champion of pagan idolatry and a symbol of Israel's religious corruption (cf. Judg. 18:30–31; 1 Kings 12:25–33). Rabbis taught that Dan actually belonged to Satan's tribe (cf. T. Dan 5:6; Jer. 8:16–17), and early Christian teachers such as Irenaeus tied Dan's tribe to the Anti-christ (cf. *Against Heresies* 5.30.2).

By editing the list in this way, John envisions not only the climactic conflict of salvation's history, which pits Christ against Anti-christ, but also its outcome: the tribe of Anti-christ is not sealed and is unprotected from the destruction of God's wrath. Indeed, not only will the martyrs be vindicated, but those who took their blood will be destroyed.

7:9–12 / The second group of believers, who also receive the salvation of God, should be distinguished from the first in two critical ways. In the interlude's first scene of the 144,000, John addresses a particular concern of his readers about the status of martyred believers (cf. 1 Thess. 4:13–18). In his subsequent vision of **a great multitude**, John shifts his pastoral concern to the situation of the unbelieving world, which seeks to know how to survive the eschatological wrath of God. In responding to their question, "Who can stand?" (6:17), he describes the qualifications of those **standing before the throne and in front of the Lamb**. Second, there is a distinction in timing. The sealing of the remnant of Christian martyrs takes place during a pause in "the great tribulation," presumably to preserve them for the future day of their vindication. It is this very day that John envisions, now that "the great tribulation" has concluded (7:13–14) and the martyrs join the "rest of Israel" to celebrate their entrance into the promised salvation of God.

John challenges the pessimism that wonders whether the church will survive its pagan surrounding and those sociopolitical forces that seek to corrupt and defeat the church's service to God. The immediate response to the question, "Who can stand?" is to indicate the twofold success of those **standing before the throne** in celebration. If numbers are a measurement of success (cf. Acts 2:47b), then the believing community's description as **a great multitude that no one could count** is a formula for its ultimate success. Further, if the pluralism of the community's constituency measures the broad appeal of its gospel, then its membership, drawn **from every nation, tribe, people and language** (cf. 5:9), is yet another formula of success, even during "the great tribulation." Their eventual victory is indicated by what they wear— **white robes** (symbolic of a right relationship with God)—by what they hold—**palm branches** (in recognition of Jesus' kingship; cf. John 12:12–13)—and by what they **cried out** in triumph—**Salvation belongs to . . . God . . . and to the Lamb**. Although such a doxology could acknowledge God's triumph over evil (cf. Rev. 12:10; 19:1), here it refers to the victorious community of saints, who are ultimately delivered from the day of God's wrath. This point has significance if the interpreter understands the present passage as a response to the question posed by the suffering lost: the vision identifies those left standing in victory rather than in defeat; it is eschatological Israel's participation in the future vindication of God's reign that **all the angels . . . elders and the four living creatures** confirm with their **Amen!** and again they said **Amen!**

7:13–14 / Once again, John actually participates in the vision (cf. 5:5–6). As before, his conversation is with **one of the elders** who calls attention to a decisive paradox which interprets everything else in the vision. The seer's previous conversation with the heavenly elder concerned the identity of the worthy Lamb. That conversation is continued here. But now it concerns a question, relevant for this particular vision: **where did they** (in the white robes) **come from?** John plays the interlocutor to the elder, who answers his own question: **these are they who have come out of the great tribulation**. The definite article used with the singular **great tribulation** envisions a particular period of *salvation* history rather than human history per se. In that the history of God's salvation is worked out within the history of God's people, the "great tribulation" corresponds to the entire history of the church—past, present, and future. The issue, then, is not whether believers escape the suffering every person must endure in a fallen world; the real issue is whether all believers are saved from God's eschatological wrath. Clearly they are, according to the evidence provided by this visionary interlude.

The present tense of the participle, "have come," looks back over this period of history as the continual gathering together of the great multitude for the salvation of God. All believers from every generation have met the single criterion that allows them to stand before God's throne and in front of the Lamb in their white robes: they **have washed their robes and made them white in the blood of the Lamb**. The elder knows well the redemptive paradox: robes are whitened by the Lamb's blood; wrath is exchanged for wrath, so that life may be purchased through death. This is what lost humanity must know in order to "stand" before the throne of a merciful God.

7:15–17 / The vision's concluding hymn celebrates a true Israel's return from its worldly exile and into the promised land of eternal life, when **God will wipe away every tear from their eyes** (cf. 21:4) and when the **Lamb . . . will be their shepherd**. Then he will lead them into God's shalom where **never again will they thirst**, because the Lamb **will lead them to springs of living water** (cf. 22:1–2). God will **spread his tent over them**, so that **the sun will not beat upon them, nor any scorching heat**. And in that future day of consummation, eschatological Israel will realize the slain Lamb's work that transformed them into priests to serve God (cf. 5:10)—to **serve him day and night in his temple**. On that future day, the worship of God will not take place in an actual building—a literal **temple**—but in a relationship with the "Lord God Almighty and the Lamb" (cf. 21:22).

The hymn resounds with biblical themes, especially of the "promised land" that appears especially good to returning exiles

(Mounce, *Revelation*, p. 175). It is a doxology of promise fulfilled, the concerns of theodicy are answered. Believers suffer in a fallen world, perhaps even more so now that the world has been judged by God through the slain Lamb. Suffering believers have a certain confidence in an exalted Lamb, however, that God's justice will prevail in the end, when their living conditions will be reversed for the good.

Additional Notes　§7

7:1 / Those who contend that the four horses of chapter 6 and the four winds of chapter 7 refer to the same reality would consider 7:1–3 a summary of earlier events (Morris, *Revelation*, p. 113; Beasley-Murray, *Revelation*, p. 142).

7:14 / Contra Ladd, who contends that the **great tribulation** predicts a future period of seven years during which the church's suffering will increase (*Revelation*, pp. 116–20). Boring rightly contends that the tribulation is symbolic and belongs to the portrait of the prophets and martyrs who profile the community of true believers (*Revelation*, p. 139). Especially in each interlude of the three septets of divine judgments found in Revelation (7:1–17; 10:1–11:14; 14:12–13; 16:15–16), John employs the "martyr" motif to make clear his pastoral interests: in a world where things do not always go well and where the church is constantly tempted by the "easy way out," the mark of true Christian piety is a long and hard obedience to God in the right direction.

§8 God's Lamb Opens the Seventh Seal (Rev. 8:1–5)

The immediate result of the breaking of the seventh and final seal is **silence in heaven for about half an hour**. Since John does not provide the reader with a cipher for this heavenly calm, various explanations have been offered: it is a rhetorical device for "dramatic silence," or the **seventh seal** symbolizes a sense of finality (Caird), or a pause in the vision itself (Swete), or the aftermath of total destruction (Rissi), or the quiet environs of worship when prayers are offered to God (Beasley-Murray). While leaning toward a combination of the first and last explanations, we do not favor any interpretation which presumes a chronology of events. In our view, the **silence** that John notes does not indicate the final episode in a series of eschatological events; rather, it cues the reader to the resumption of John's larger vision of the exaltation of the slain Lamb. Thus, the seer may be noting nothing more than another dramatic contrast in his vision's tone—from catastrophic calamity to loud celebration to a short period of silence—which first catches his attention, and then calms and prepares him for what follows.

8:1–5 / Apparently during this **half an hour**, the seer is introduced to **the seven angels . . .** who **were given seven trumpets** to sound the final measure of God's triumph over the evil world order (8:6–11:19). As John looks on, he is again interrupted by **another angel** (cf. 7:2; 10:1; 14:6ff.; 18:1), a formulaic expression found at the beginning of a parenthesis to aid the interpreter's understanding of what follows. This parenthesis functions like an "apocalyptic bridge," linking together the seal and trumpet judgments as parts of a single reality.

The new angel functions as liturgist during this particular season of heavenly worship. Since the heavenly temple has opened its doors because of Christ's exaltation (11:19; cf. Heb. 8:1–2), the angel comes **to offer** a **golden censer**, full of **much incense**, and takes his place **on the golden altar before the throne** of God. These actions establish the appropriate setting for God to hear **the prayers of all the saints**, which invokes the worship of God regnant.

The prayers offered to God are different from those brought to the Lord in bowls of incense by the four living creatures and the twenty-four elders (5:8). In this instance, the whole church makes petition for divine revelation, not unlike that offered by the prophet Elijah on Mount Carmel when he asked God to vindicate his ministry and to make God's reign known. Elijah's ultimate purpose was that "these people will know . . . you . . . and that you are turning their hearts back again" (1 Kings 18:36–37). The "fire of the Lord" which fell and consumed the altar of Ba'al in divine retribution was in fact a revelation of God's lordship over even God's enemies (1 Kings 18:38–39).

Likewise, when **the angel . . . filled** the censer **with fire from the altar, and hurled it on the earth**, the word picture mediates God's positive response to the church's petition for some clear evidence that would vindicate their devotion to God rather than to God's enemies. If the Elijah tradition provides the biblical backdrop for this as well as for the subsequent vision of the trumpet judgments, then John's pastoral purpose is understood accordingly: God's judgment against God's enemies reveals the triumph of God's rule so that those congregations, now spiritually lax, will turn their hearts back to their Lord.

§9 Angelic Trumpets Sound Six Judgments of God (Rev. 8:6–9:21)

8:6 / The significance of the **seven trumpets** has been variously appraised (Beasley-Murray, *Revelation*, pp. 152–56). According to John's Bible (OT), Israel's liturgical trumpets were sounded for a variety of reasons. They were used to convene the worshiping community (Num. 10:3), to begin pilgrimages (Num. 10:5), to call warriors for war (Num. 10:9), to celebrate the sacred feasts (Num. 10:10), to install new kings (1 Kings 1:34), and to summon Israel to repentance and renewal (Jer. 4:5). Seven trumpets were also used to destroy Jericho (Josh. 6:4, 6, 8) and to establish Israel in God's promised land. In fact, Caird thinks John has this story in mind when writing down this vision because the ark appears upon the blowing of the seventh trumpet (Rev. 11:19; cf. Josh. 6:4; Caird, *Revelation*, pp. 109–11). While John may well have thought of one or all these OT references to trumpets, primary significance should be given to the number of trumpets, **seven**, indicating that the trumpets are put to an eschatological use: they sound the fulfillment of God's promises of shalom for a restored Israel and of great wrath for God's enemies.

This interpretation is in keeping with the immediate context. Since John finds the **seven angels** in the vision of the seventh seal, the interpreter should view the vision of trumpet judgments as continuing the vision of seal judgments. This continuity is not chronological but theological; and the liturgical pause of the seventh seal makes the very theological point contained in the vision of trumpet plagues: the exaltation of the slain Lamb announces God's triumph over evil and vindicates God's lordship over all things. It is this conviction that the scroll's writing asserts; and now, with the breaking of its final seal, God's scroll is laid fully open and the validity of the church's conviction about God's reign becomes even clearer with every fanfare of the angels' trumpets.

8:7–12 / The natural disasters signaled by the first four trumpets are restricted to **a third** of the **earth . . . sea . . . springs of water . . .** and sky—a significant part of the earth but not even most of it. Military strategists would call this a "survivable" result; the plagues may cause global chaos but not destruction. God's exaltation of Christ does not issue in a devastating, final judgment of evil powers and human sin; that awaits Christ's return. Rather, when God says "No!" to sin on Christ's cross, God intends also to say "Yes!" to all humanity, and to bid all, especially the disobedient church, to repent (cf. Rev. 22:11). God's first and last word is "Yes," and that stands at the center of John's Gospel.

Several commentators have noted that this part of John's vision alludes to the plagues of the Exodus tradition. The imagery of **hail and fire mixed with blood**, which resulted when **the first angel sounded his trumpet**, echoes the seventh plague on Egypt (cf. Exod. 9:13–35). With the second trumpet **the sea turns to blood**, reminding the reader of the plague of blood (cf. Exod. 7:20–21). The vision moves from salt seawater to the springs of fresh water. The star **Wormwood** (cf. Jer. 9:15) **fell from the sky** to poison drinking water, perhaps echoing the grumbling Israel at Marah (cf. Exod. 15:23). This may convey a more pointed rebuke to the disobedient church (cf. Caird, *Revelation*, pp. 114–15). The fourth trumpet triggers a catastrophe which undeniably recalls the seventh Egyptian plague (cf. Exod. 10:21–23), when **the sun was struck,** and **. . . moon, and . . . stars** so that **a third of the day was without light, and also . . . the night**—the "darkness" of the creator's judgment of a fallen creation (cf. Gen. 1:3–5).

Thus, John recognizes the vision of the trumpets by the biblical story of the Egyptian plagues. In doing so, he offers his readers a biblical background by which to better understand how the vision of trumpets relates to their own situation. According to the OT story of Israel's exodus from Egypt, the purpose of the plagues was to assert the lordship of God over the world's most powerful ruler, the Egyptian Pharaoh. The plagues were a concrete demonstration of divine authority that intended to convince the Lord's people of God's desire to lead them to a promised land more plentiful than Egypt. Recall also from Revelation 2–3 that the unfaithfulness of John's audience is due in large measure to cultural pressures, which molded and shaped Israel into a people more like Egypt (i.e., Rome) than the kingdom of priests "made" by the Lamb (cf. Rev. 5:9–10). The biblical and societal contexts in which John's believing audiences lived, then, interpret the significance of these trumpets: the various "Pharaohs" who rule over the anti-Christian kingdom in John's world stand condemned, while the unresponsive believers found among the seven congregations, who lack devotion to God, are rebuked like the grumbling, unfaithful Israel of old.

This passage provides a good illustration of the dual role of many of John's key symbols. Images used here to describe destruction are employed elsewhere of the redemptive Lamb. The purpose of this literary device is twofold. First, John intends to convey an apocalyptic understanding of salvation that locates all things—good and bad—under God's sovereign plans for creation. Most noteworthy in this regard is **blood**, which is the focal point of the first two trumpet plagues (8:7–8), but which also symbolizes the death of Christ that purchased people from evil's marketplace and placed them in God's kingdom where they can serve the Lord rather than sin (cf. Rev. 5:9–10). The image of **sun** is used of the exalted Christ, whose "face was like the sun shining" (1:16), and also here as an object of divine judgment (8:12). The regnant Christ is called the "Morning star" (22:16; cf. 2:28), but another **great star**, an angel called **Wormwood**, is God's current agent of destruction (8:10–11). And the "springs of living water," to which the shepherding Lamb leads the eschatological sheep of God (7:17), are now poisoned by **Wormwood** (8:10–11).

Second, the multivalence of these symbols, which concentrate Revelation's redemption-destruction dualisms, calls attention to the reversal motif of apocalypticism. The landmarks of a fallen creation are also the marks of a new creation in which evil is turned upside down at the triumph of God's salvation through the Lamb.

8:13 / The portentous words of **an eagle**, spoken from the highest point in the heavens, prepare the seer for the blasts of the next two trumpets, which sound ominous fanfares to divine judgments against **the inhabitants of earth** far worse than the preceding four. In this regard, it is best to understand this verse as a preface to chapter 9 rather than as the conclusion to chapter 8.

Caird suggests two possible meanings of the **eagle** (Caird, *Revelation*, p. 117). First, it echoes God's words to Moses on Sinai

(Exod. 19:4) and continues the Exodus typology. If this is true, then the alarm of **Woe! Woe! Woe!** would sound the messianic woes that accompany the church's pilgrimage to its promised shalom. Second, the word translated **eagle** could be translated "vulture" (cf. Luke 17:37), symbolic of the earth in the throes of death. In this light, the triad of woes would again refer to the messianic woes; the point of reference, however, is the fallen world whose evils justify God's judgment against it.

The apocalyptic significance of this and other triads is symbolic: like John's use of sevens, the eagle's message conveys a sense of completion such that divine judgment accords with divine ordination. In this sense, the eagle's triad of woes refers not only to the tribulation characteristic of the present age but to the divine plan that ordains and interprets it. It does not appear, however, that John correlates the messianic woes to each of the next three trumpet judgments, since the third woe is not disclosed at the blast of the seventh trumpet (cf. 11:14) which initiates, in any case, the concluding celebration of Christ's coronation in heaven (11:15–18). According to the teaching of Jesus, these woes both begin and end with his triumph—in the empty tomb and at his parousia (cf. Matt. 24:4–31). In this light, then, we read the first two woes as referring to the fifth and sixth trumpet plagues and locate them at Christ's exaltation; that is, the period of tribulation in salvation's history commences with Christ's death and exaltation. The third woe refers to the present spiritual crisis, concentrated especially in chapters 12 and 13, that continues to confront the church until history's climactic moment, the return of Christ.

9:1–4 / At the sound of the fifth trumpet, a **star that had fallen from the sky to the earth . . . was given the key to the shaft of the Abyss**. The nature of the descending **star** is debated, although most modern scholars agree that it is angelic. Like that great angel of destruction, "Wormwood" (8:10–11), this angelic star also comes from heaven on a mission of destruction. Its mission is apparently approved by God since it is **given the key**, which suggests divine sanction (cf. Matt. 16:19; Rev. 3:7). There is a certain interplay between this angel's role in opening up the **Abyss** to release its terrors, and that of the angel who accompanies Christ at his return to lock the agents of terror back up (Rev. 20:1; cf. 1 Enoch 19:1; 20:2, where the angel is identified as *Uriel*). Both angels serve the redemptive interests of a sovereign God; both are sent to carry out divinely ordained tasks—one which concerns God's judgment upon evil and the other God's redemption from evil, and one which comes at the beginning of the last days and the other at its consummation.

Caird is no doubt correct to understand that this angelic star is responsible for those human institutions—social, political, economic and religious—which promote evil and destroy creation and creature alike. Thus, while the believing community dwells on the margins of the world order, "in the world yet not an institution of it," it is empowered by the sevenfold Paraclete that comes from the exalted Lamb to teach and to comfort. The church is not harmed by the evils released from the Abyss; they "pass over" those who **have the seal of God on their foreheads**, corrupting only those who do not.

The key given to the angelic star unlocks the shaft leading down to a bottomless pit, called the **Abyss**. The location of this pit is important but for theological rather than geographical reasons. According to ancient mythology (no doubt John's cipher in understanding what he envisioned) the **Abyss** was located below the earth and was the invisible dwelling place of evil powers, such as Tiamaet and Leviathan, and their agents of evil and death (cf. 1 Enoch 18:12-16; 21:7-10; 108:3-6). It is a place of disorder and chaos, from where forces of death and darkness come to wreak their special kind of havoc. Hence, **when** the angel **opened the Abyss, smoke rose from it like the smoke from a gigantic furnace**. Through this subterranean smokestack, agents of terror were released onto earth, promoting human sinfulness and natural catastrophes—that is, chaos in the physical world (cf. James 3:15-16).

In John's vision, therefore, he sees **locusts** coming out of the smokestack and **upon the earth**. Because they are evil agents from a spiritual world, they do not act like locusts of the natural world. In fact, they ignore **the grass of the earth or any plant or tree** and are ironically **given power like that of scorpions** to harm only those destined for their own domain—the unbelieving world. God's people are excluded from the evils of the trumpet plagues, because according to Johannine teaching "the evil one cannot harm anyone born of God" (1 John 5:18).

9:5-6 / Throughout his vision of the trumpet plagues, John has indicated that the devastation of God's judgment is not yet complete. Typically, one third of the earth is touched and destroyed. This sense of an incomplete judgment conveys God's admonition: there is still time for lost humanity to repent and turn to God before the end comes and total destruction with it (cf. 2 Pet. 3:9). The marauding locusts, therefore, **were not given power to kill, but only to torture** (the unbelievers) **for five months**. The end is not yet here; a warning is given to repent before it is too late.

The meaning of **five months** is variously understood. Some commentators have suggested this period of time refers to the locust's life cycle. This interpretation mixes together the symbolical locusts with biological ones. While we find John mixing the symbolic and real worlds elsewhere in Revelation, the present phrase is best read for its symbolic value, since elsewhere Scripture uses "five" to refer to the "short-term" (cf. Morris, *Revelation*, p. 126). In this sense, then, the reign of locusts does not exact fatal or ultimate consequences—which may explain John's next observation that people suffered **agony . . . like that of a sting of a scorpion when it strikes a man**. Their work is nasty but temporary.

In fact, from the locusts' perspective, their mission is **to torture** people; from humanity's perspective, their experience is sheer **agony**. In a poetic couplet, John speaks of humanity's response to **those days**, when **men will seek death, but will not find it**/when **they will long to die, but death will elude them**. Quite possibly, John interprets what he sees by Job's lament of his birth which this echoes (cf. Job 3:21). Thus, the theological questions raised by Job's response to his suffering might suggest another way of understanding this trumpet plague. Job felt persecuted by God. If suffering be persecution by God, then life itself is without meaning. Although Job is a righteous man, he misunderstood his suffering. Its purpose was to disclose a reigning God in control of humanity's existence. The outcome in Job's case, of course, is that he realized his limitations and acknowledged that a sovereign God places limits around human life and that human suffering reflects those very real limitations.

John's adaptation of Job's story to his own visionary situation clarifies the ultimate purpose of the suffering of humanity, which is to bring it to repentance (Morris, *Revelation*, pp. 125–26). The plagues are symbolic of limits that God places upon the unredeemed, who are without the transforming power of God's saving grace. That sinful humankind does *not* repent (cf. Rev. 9:20–21) only indicates the firm hold evil has on the world order.

9:7–11 / The recapitulation of episodes serves a rhetorical rather than a chronological purpose; it provides a second, often closer look at what is happening in order to clarify its significance. In this regard, John changes the action of the episode from aorist (9:3, 5) to present (9:10; incorrectly translated by NIV) in describing the locusts' scorpion-like appearance. No doubt this shift of tense indicates that "the scene becomes increasingly vivid to him" (Morris, *Revelation*, p. 127). As John looks again at the visionary scene before him, he recognizes the locusts to be warriors rather than torturers: they **looked like horses prepared for battle**. Because of this second look, he recognizes their mission to be more like the prophet Joel than Job. In Joel's two visions of the eschatological locusts (1:2–12; 2:1–11), they are also likened to war **horses** (cf. 2:4), **rushing into battle** (cf. 2:5), and as having **lion's teeth** (cf. 1:6). Joel reports that at sight of them, "the nations are in anguish" (2:6; cf. Rev. 9:10) because they have left the "garden of Eden" as a desert wasteland (cf. 2:3).

In the context of Joel's use of the plague typology, the images of natural devastation portray the spiritual condition of God's faithless people (1:13–20; 2:12–17). Repentance is required of them if they are to enter into the day of the Lord's eschatological salvation (cf. 2:18–32). John's allusion to this prophetic tradition, so critical in early Christian preaching (cf. Acts 2:14–21), is once again centered by the deeper-logic of his message: the purpose of suffering is repentance and ultimately the future fruit of God's salvation.

John no doubt is aware that Joel's prophecy was first given to a people struggling to live for God in an anti-God world. Their two situations are further similar in that, like Joel, John is vitally concerned that the faithless members of his Israel repent. In both cases, disobedience jeopardizes their future entrance into God's new "garden of Eden" on the day of the Lord.

John returns to Job to interpret the significance of his vision of the angelic ruler who presides over the **Abyss, whose name in Hebrew is Abaddon, and in Greek, Apollyon**. **Abaddon** means "Destroyer" in Hebrew and personifies the verbal root, "to destroy." The word is used as a synonym for "death" in Job 26:6 (cf. 28:22; Ps. 88:11) for obvious reasons. However, the Greek "equivalent," **Apollyon**, does not actually transliterate the Hebrew name, even though it approximates the Greek root for "destroy," *apollymi*, also translated "perish" (cf. John 3:16!).

Even so, the reasons for mentioning the angel's name remain unclear. Most modern commentators think that John wished to connect the angelic "Apollyon" (and the locust plague) to the Greek deity, Apollo, who was followed by the same Caesars guilty of persecuting the church (cf. Krodel, *Revelation*, pp. 203–4). Domitian, for example, believed himself to be the incarnation of Apollo, leading Beasley-Murray to conclude: "(John's) last word about the fifth trumpet was a master stroke of irony: the destructive host of hell had as its king the emperor of Rome!" (*Revelation*, pp. 162–63).

9:12 / Although the seer claims that **the first woe is past**, the reader is not clear which field John is now viewing when adding this footnote to his vision of the fifth trumpet plague. Is he recounting the prior visionary episode, which has now been concluded? Or is he saying that the historical reality which the first woe infers has passed? Because John's vision is not to be construed chronologically, he probably has the fifth plague in view, and the reader is now prepared for the blast of the sixth eschatological trumpet and John's vision of the second woe.

9:13–15 / At the sounding of the sixth trumpet the seer returns to the **golden altar that is before God** (cf. 6:9–10; 8:3), which is a place for worship and prayer. Rather than assuming, as most do, that the **golden altar** presumes that prayers are once again offered for vindication by divine judgment, we prefer to understand this symbol of true worship in contrast to the subsequent images of idolatry (9:20–21) as the essential conflict of the current cosmic battle between God and the Evil One. This contrast further brackets and interprets the significance of the second woe that is sandwiched between the images of worship and idolatry: idolatry is nothing more than the foolish rejection of God, who alone can restore people back to wholeness. Again and again John reminds his readers that rebellion against God is self-destructive. If God's chief desire is to restore humanity, and to rebel against God is to repel God's chief desires, then to sin is to forsake the spiritual powers of personal transformation.

John **heard a voice coming from the horns of the golden altar**, probably angelic and certainly sanctioned by God, which gave instructions to **release the four angels . . . at the great river Euphrates**. This group of four angels is not the same as that which earlier had held back "the four winds of the earth" (7:1). Rather these **four angels . . . are bound**, suggesting to some commentators that they are evil and experts in the art of destruction to which they are now called by God. Their captivity, however, is not the result of prior evils; rather, they **had been kept . . . and were released to kill a third of mankind**. The passive voice of the verbs John employs presumes that these angels are bound by God who has kept and now releases them **for this very hour** and the redemptive task at stake.

For biblical writers, geographical places hold theological meaning. For John and his first audience, the river **Euphrates** where the four angels will mount for their attack symbolizes two realities. First, it symbolizes a vulnerable Roman Empire. Beyond the river lay the Parthian Empire and the world's finest fighting cavalry. They had thrashed Roman armies twice in recent memory, once at Carrhae in 53 B.C. and again at Vologeses in A.D. 62, and they were not defeated by Rome until A.D. 116, two decades after John's Revelation was written and first read. The renowned Parthian skill of shooting arrows while on horseback and the snake-like tails on their horses might have helped John describe what he saw; however, this supernatural cavalry led by the four angels would suggest an even greater military presence than found in Parthia, which will surely bring the mighty Rome to its knees.

Second, the **Euphrates** is used in the OT as the eastern boundary of the promised land (cf. Gen. 15:18; Josh. 1:4). The great river, then, symbolizes the entirety of the promised land (Ladd, *Revelation*, p. 136), which for John is the entire created order. The eschatological battle is both on and for that land. The assurance of victory for God's ordained troops over the armies of pretenders to God's throne envisions the final stanza of the "new song," which claims that the blood of the slain Lamb ensures the reign of God's people "on the earth" (cf. 5:10b).

9:16–19 / John does not tell us anything about the recruitment of the troops that the four angels lead into battle; he mentions only their exact number, **two hundred million**. So vast (and unbelievable) is this number—impossible to count in any case—that John must add, **I heard their number** (cf. 7:4) before describing their appearance. The appearance of the soldiers reflects their weapons. The colors of their **breastplates were fiery red, dark blue, and yellow as sulfur**, the same as their horrific breath that consists of a toxic mixture of **fire, smoke and sulfur**. These are the constitutive elements of the eschatological lake where the evil powers (cf. 19:20; 21:8) and the "second death" (cf. 20:14) are finally cast at Christ's second coming. Although found in different visions, the same symbol system is used in both passages to portray the harsh realities of divine judgment. This interplay between John's visions of the sixth trumpet plague and of Christ's parousia is completed by his description of the horses, whose **tails were like snakes** and **heads with which to inflict injury**, the soldiers **kill a third of mankind** by the breath which **came out of their mouth**. As destructive and terrifying as this weapon is, it only foreshadows the "sharp sword" which comes from out of the mouth of the returning Lamb "to strike down the nations" (19:15; cf. 1:16). What comes from the mouth of the Lord consumes and promises to be even more devastating than this second woe for those who fail to turn to God and who reject the Lamb.

9:20–21 / Given the terrible consequences of unbelief, it would seem logical, even expected, that **the rest of mankind that were not killed by these plagues** would surely repent and turn to God. Yet, they **still did not repent of the work of their hands** . . . nor **stop worshiping demons, and idols . . . nor** (repent) . . . **of their murders, their magic arts, their sexual immorality or their thefts**. John's vice list, which enumerates social and spiritual evils, only reinforces his realistic assessment that universal conversion will not take place. The very intention of Christ's death and exaltation, and of God's judgment on the evil order hidden within Christ's triumph, goes unfulfilled (cf. 2 Pet. 3:9). Pagan religion, which **worships demons . . .** and **idols that cannot see or hear or walk**, has shaped a people who do not have "eyes to see and ears to hear" the word of God and the testimony of Jesus. The world's resistance to God's reign and to God's transforming grace found in Christ is constant and pervasive. For John, the nature of rebellion against the creator is that the spiritual resources found within the community of faithful disciples, which are the means of spiritual and societal transformation, are ignored or rejected.

In a slaughtered Lamb, so easy to dismiss, the sovereign God is disclosed as completely faithful to the promise that a fallen

world would be restored to wholeness; and God's terrible judgment only discloses the world's need for restoration. Yet, in its
response to God's warning and invitation to repent, lost
humanity's essential failure is vividly exposed: they misunder-
stand God, whose trustworthiness is revealed in the Christ who
is executed as Anti-christ. One is reminded of the pagan's folly
described by Paul: "They became fools . . . and exchanged the
truth of God for a lie, and worshiped and served created things
rather than the Creator—who is forever praised" (Rom. 1:22b, 25).
How ought God's people respond to such a desperate situation?
How ought they live as the continuing "testimony of Jesus" on
earth? John responds to these questions in the following interlude.

Additional Notes   §9

8:6 / For the history of interpreting the vision of trumpet plagues,
see J. Paulien, *Decoding Revelation's Trumpets* (Berrien Springs, Mich.: Andrews University Press, 1988).

8:13 / Rather than "vulture," other ancient mss read "angel" for
eagle. Metzger explains the scribal corruption is a harmonistic attempt
to bring the work done by this eagle into agreement with the work done
elsewhere by angels; in *Textual Commentary on the Greek New Testament*
(N.Y.: United Bible Societies, 1971), p. 743.
For the importance of **three**, see Michael Wilcock, *I Saw Heaven
Opened* (Downers Grove, Ill.: InterVarsity, 1975).

§10 Interlude: Two Reminders of God's Faithfulness (Rev. 10:1–11:14)

The role played by the interlude in each of the three visions of divine wrath is the same: to cause the readers to assess their present crisis in terms of the future realization of God's past triumph in Christ. In this sense, the crisis confronting unbelieving humanity is a theological one. Their vision is blinded by the "official" propaganda of the surrounding world order; thus, their life is anchored not by faith in a sovereign God but rather by a false confidence in the idols of the anti-Christian world.

The crisis that confronts the believing community is similar in kind. Whenever the church's witness to the gospel of God is challenged or even compromised, the fundamental issue at stake for John is theological: temptations are tests of faith in God, since every problem of faith stems from a diminishing confidence in God. The tendency is often to place confidence in the definitions of security and happiness promoted within the surrounding social order.

Thus, the interlude between the sounding of the sixth and seventh trumpets marks the return of John's attention to the believing community. Like the interlude between the breaking of the sixth and seventh seals, this vision is formed by two integrated parts, which together posit that the church's hope in the certain end of its tribulation and experience of salvation is in accord with the plan of God. Again, we are inclined to think of this interlude in terms of repeated and central themes found in the **little scroll** given to John in chapter 10 and written down in chapter 11.

Many have pursued the precise meaning of the **little scroll** without success. Most associate it with God's scroll of seven seals (5:1), containing the heavenly edict of God's triumph over earthly evil. This seems to us a reasonable conjecture for two reasons. First, the vision of the little scroll is an essential part of the vision that describes the writing on the scroll with seven seals. Second, the little scroll is given by **another mighty angel**, an obvious allusion to the first "mighty angel" who had earlier searched the universe for someone worthy enough to open the seals of God's scroll and inaugurate the new age of God's salvation.

If we are to understand the **little scroll** by the larger one that had "writing on both sides" (cf. 5:1), the adjective **little** might describe the brevity of its contents—its shorter length due perhaps to its more restricted focus on a single aspect of the larger scroll's edict. Thus, Caird says, "The great scroll contained the purposes of God in so far as they were to be achieved by the Lamb. The **little scroll** contains a new version of those same purposes in so far as they are to be achieved through the agency of the church" (Caird, *Revelation*, p. 126).

Schüssler Fiorenza agrees, suggesting that the scroll's more narrow focus concerns "the prophetic interpretation of the situation of the Christian community" (*Revelation*, p. 54). Given John's pastoral concern about the fragile status of the believing community within a secular society, he may well wish to clarify its destiny according to the redemptive plan of a faithful God, and does so by making the scroll's contents known to his readers. In this sense, "little" may also qualify the scroll's overall importance in the cosmic plan of God's salvation. Whereas God's scroll could be opened only by the worthy Lamb and contains God's "macroscopic" design for salvation's history, the shorter scroll lies open in the hand of the angel (10:8) and contains a more "microscopic" vision that intends in part to encourage his beleaguered audience.

The interpreter should also be sensitive to John's clear allusions to Ezekiel's situation, especially when analyzing this interlude. Both are prophets in exile, commissioned to eat scrolls consisting of divine revelation (cf. Rev. 10:9; Ezek. 3:1–3a); and both of their scrolls **tasted as sweet as honey in** their **mouths** (cf. Rev. 10:10; Ezek. 3:3b). These linguistic links suggest to us that John understands his own commission and current situation in the context of biblical Ezekiel's commission and situation: sharply put, John views himself a latter-day Ezekiel.

Recall that the exiled Ezekiel was told to go to an obstinate Israel with a twofold message: first a warning that death results when a righteous person turns to evil (Ezek. 3:20); but second a promise that life results when a righteous person heeds the prophet's warning and does not sin (Ezek. 3:21). Interpreted by

Ezekiel's story, the message contained in John's **little scroll** carries a comparable warning and promise to a similar people. Thus, the vision of woes contained in the scroll serves not only to condemn the world order, but also to encourage a church, struggling to remain faithful in its suffering, not to sin in order to enter eternal life. We will develop this central point in the following commentary.

10:1 / Some commentators have mistaken the **mighty angel** for the Risen Christ. To be sure, the phrases describing the angel's descent **from heaven** are elsewhere used of Christ. Luke, for example, describes Jesus as **robed in a cloud** at his ascension (cf. Acts 1:9–11); and in Revelation, John likens Christ's face to **a sun** (cf. 1:16) and his feet to **fiery pillars** (cf. 1:15). Yet, nowhere in the NT is Jesus referred to as an angelic being; and given his exalted status in Revelation, the oath made by this angel in verse 6 seems an inappropriate speech for Jesus to make.

In our view, these phrases of splendor identify this messenger as **another mighty angel**, sent from the throne of God with a message of great significance for John and his readers. His identifying characteristics also suggest that its role is continuous with that of the first "mighty angel" (5:2), who called our attention to God's scroll (5:1) and to the worthy Lamb in inaugurating the new age of God's salvation (see above). These phrases also echo Ezekiel's theophany of God's throne (cf. Ezek. 1:27–28); John already realizes that the angelic message contains yet another claim for the reign of God.

10:2–4 / The first part of the angel's message is not recorded by the seer. After John hears **the voices of the seven thunders**, a **voice from heaven** tells him, **"Seal up what the seven thunders have said and do not write it down."** Many have futilely speculated exactly what this sevenfold message contained. We gather from the number **seven** that its significance to John is eschatological. We might even suggest that John hears the seven thunders as the effects of God's ruling glory, as stipulated in Psalm 29:3–9, thereby invoking his submission before God's eternal rule (cf. Ps. 29:10–11). From this, we are left with the impression that this interlude has something to do with the triumph of God, which is the essential theme of John's Revelation. Nothing beyond this very basic speculation should be advanced with confidence.

In our view, however, the prohibition not to write down what John hears has the rhetorical effect of directing the reader to the importance of John's commission to take up the little scroll to eat it. Apparently, the seer is privy to "insider's information" that his audience lacks, and this establishes his authority to write down divine revelation that is normative for their faith.

10:5–7 / The mighty angel is now prepared to take an oath and so raises **his right hand to heaven**, swearing by God's name that **"There will be no more delay!"** Many have noted that behind this oath lies the OT text, Daniel 12:5–7, according to which John interprets this particular vision. In that Danielic text, written to address a similar situation (so Caird, *Revelation*, p. 127), two men first exchange a question, "How long will it be before these astonishing things are fulfilled?" (Dan. 12:6), and then its oath-like answer, "It will be for a time, times and half a time. When the power of the holy people has been finally broken, all these things will be completed" (Dan. 12:7). Recall that earlier in Revelation the Christian martyrs, who are parallel to Daniel's "holy people . . . finally broken," asked a question similar to the one asked by Daniel's two men and equally provocative question: "How long . . . until you judge . . . earth and avenge our blood?" (Rev. 6:10). Now John has been given additional revelation which at last provides the definitive response: there will be **no more delay**. In God's exaltation of the slain Lamb, the ultimate vindication of God's people is asserted, especially against those who are opposed to the witness and worship of God's people on earth.

The actual moment of victory will come **when the seventh angel . . . sounds his trumpet** (cf. Rev. 11:15–19). We would contend the moment of God's victory has already taken place in heaven through the triumph of Jesus' messianic mission on earth (see below). For this reason John draws on the language of the gospel in expanding on this climactic act: **the mystery of God will be accomplished** in fulfillment of the prophetic promise of God's salvation. While the phrase **mystery of God** means different things to different NT writers, it usually refers to the *content* of the gospel message, the core of which is the atoning death and exaltation of Christ. This would seem to be John's perspective since he uses the verb *euēngelisen*, which means "to preach the gospel." The prophets of old promised a time when a faithful God would redeem humanity from sin and restore all things to their proper, created order. In the Christ event, that promised time has now come (cf. Rev. 5:9–10)!

John, however, does suggest a delay in completing this new age of fulfillment. According to the preaching of the earliest church, the full measure of God's kingdom has "not yet" been realized on earth, even though it has "already" begun with the Messiah's mission on earth. Verse 7 begins, then, with a strong adversative, **But** (*alla*), which usually prefaces a contrary statement or sentiment. While Christ's coronation testifies to the fulfillment of God's promise of salvation, there is a delay in its earthly effects. The full (i.e., historical) experience of God's salvation awaits Christ's parousia.

The sort of ambiguity that results from living betwixt and between these "last days," when sin and death are defeated but still experienced and when life and holiness are real but hard possibilities, is characteristic of the church's current situation. This visionary interlude interprets the crisis that stems from the sometimes frustrating attempts to be faithful to God when the gospel's promise has "not yet" been fulfilled in human experience.

10:8–10 / John is finally instructed to **take the scroll that lies open in the hand of the angel who is standing on the sea and on the land**. The scroll contains not only divine revelation, but, having already been opened, also revelation about current events. The very structure of John's composition presumes that the scroll contains some account of the fulfillment of the prophecy mentioned in the preceding text and that it relates the gospel to John's audience (see above).

The more precise nature of the scroll's message is indicated by the next part of John's commission: **Take it and eat it. It will turn your stomach sour, but in your mouth it will be as sweet as honey.** The commission is accepted by John, and the angel's words are then fulfilled. While most commentators have understood this passage as symbolizing the ecstatic appropriation and assimilation of prophetic utterances, and virtually all have associated John's experience in this regard with Ezekiel's (cf. Ezek. 2:8–3:3), they have all noted this distinction: the scroll of divine revelation given to John turns his **stomach sour**. While both John and Ezekiel found divine revelation **as sweet as honey** (cf. Ps. 119:103), only John found it bitter (*pikrainō*). Why?

The question is more difficult if the interpreter limits the content of the **little scroll** to chapter 11. If its message extends through chapter 16, as some insist, then the souring of John's stomach could be understood as a reaction to the total destruction of the world system. This option, however, does not seem possible since John's scroll is contained within an interlude, ending with 11:14. Further, within the framework of this interlude, the scroll's message is for the church and about its salvation, and not for the anti-Christian kingdom and about its destruction.

Perhaps a solution can be found in the larger context of the parallel passage in Ezekiel. The prophet's response in receiving the hard message for an obdurate people was that he "went in bitterness and in the anger of my spirit" (Ezek. 3:14). Although the word for Ezekiel's "bitterness" does not appear in the Greek translation of the Hebrew Bible (LXX, which John's audience used), it is found in John's Hebrew Bible. John would have presumed that Ezekiel's bitterness was a visceral response to the hard prospect of convincing obstinate Israel that God's warning of death was real and severe. By assuming the role of a "new Ezekiel," John may use "sour stomach" to denote his bitter response to those congregations which have fallen from their earlier spiritual vitality. John recognizes that their situation is similar to Ezekiel's exilic community; and his existential response to his difficult commission takes its cue from the prophet of old.

More importantly, however, John's interpretation of Ezekiel's commission suggests that he understood the purpose of the little scroll's message as a warning to the believing but obstinate congregations. Failure to repent jeopardizes their participation in the eschatological salvation.

10:11 / John's commission is to **prophesy**. In all probability, John's audience would have understood John's task as predicting future events, or outcomes of biblical promises **about many peoples, nations, languages and kings**. While the essential content of the little scroll concerns the church's situation, John always locates the church's salvation within a cosmic context, where the heavenly reality predicts the earthly outcome. Thus, the salvation of God's people, in accord with the promise of a faithful God, is never removed from history. Moreover, while the outworking of God's salvation is concentrated within the history of a particular people—God's people—it involves a series of concrete interactions with the entire world order. This more global venue of God's salvation makes for a messy and uneven history: the interaction between God's people and **many peoples, nations, languages and kings** always threatens to undermine the church's devotion to God. Yet, this is precisely the place where the church comes to know and experience God's grace and peace.

11:1–2 / Many stylistic and thematic elements of this second part of the interlude differ from its first part. For this reason, most commentators think this difficult passage, which centers on the ministry and fate of the "two witnesses," is derived from some discredited Jewish apocalyptic midrash on Daniel and adapted here by John for his Christian audience (Beasley-Murray, *Revelation*, pp. 176–81). However, unless John thought it contained an authentic prediction of a temple siege and the ultimate vindication of two witnesses, and unless he thought it of value for Christian proclamation, it is difficult for us to explain why he would pick up and use a prophecy regarded as false by the Jewish community. In any case, we do not think questions of sources need to be settled before coherent meanings of this passage can be advanced.

In this regard, the more pressing need is to determine how to approach this text, whether literally or symbolically (cf. Morris, *Revelation*, p. 140), or perhaps as a "parable" of God's faithfulness to the believing community during the difficult course of its "last days." A brief survey of the text's four constitutive elements, when taken symbolically and collectively, suggests a coherence that some commentators find lacking. (1) For instance, the entire section is bracketed by two references to a people who worship God. The worshiping community, found in the heavenly temple's sanctuary (11:1), refers to the eschatological Israel, removed to a heavenly haven and protected from its earthly enemies (11:2). The concluding doxology (11:13), when a portion of those previous opponents joins the believing community in praise of God, indicates the final vindication not only of God but also of the church. (2) Sandwiched between this celebration and worship of a faithful God is a story of conflict and dark distress. Actually, the three "moments" of the story depict the action of the period of salvation's history between Christ's exaltation and parousia, and thus prepare the reader for chapters 12–22. The plot begins in a triumphant testimony of Christ's two witnesses (11:3–

6) and ends in martyrdom and mockery at the hands of the Abyss' beast and his people (11:7–10). But this conflict only presents a situation ultimately reversed for the good by the God-given "Breath of life" (11:11–12; cf. Gen. 2:7; Ezek. 37:6). (3) Yet, the setting for this drama of conflict and final resolution is no particular place and every place. From the sanctuary of heavenly worship (11:1; cf. Heb. 8:2), to the "Sodom" of earthly paganism and persecution (11:8), and finally to the apocalyptic, global "city" of fulfilled promises (11:13), John moves the reader along a mythical path that finds its reality in every age. Such conflict characterizes the church's ongoing pilgrimage to the promised land. (4) Finally, the very movement of this second part of the interlude is controlled by a profound sense of time. It is something like an inverted hour-glass, so that the first act is played out over a period of seven years (11:2–3), followed by a much shorter second act of three and a half days (11:9, 11), and climaxed by an "hour of power" (11:13). Of course, these time values hold theological rather than chronological significance for John. They together characterize the course of these "last days," and signify that all is in accord with the divine program of salvation. Further, the ever-shortening periods of time—from seven years (11:2–3) to a single hour (11:13)—create the impression of a quickening pace toward the consummation of history.

The preface to the vision of the two witnesses has the image of Ezekiel's eschatological temple as its background (Ezek. 40–48). In the biblical vision, an angel commissions Ezekiel to "pay attention" as a man used a **measuring rod** (Ezek. 40:3) in order to **measure the temple of God and the altar** for a restored Israel (cf. Ezek. 40:48–43:27). In addition to the instructions given Ezekiel, John is told to **count the worshipers there**, as though the sanctuary is already in place and eschatological Israel already dwells within it. In this way, then, John is able to convey that Ezekiel's prophecy of an eschatological temple for a restored Israel has already been fulfilled, and its fulfillment is the church. This is a theological conviction found at the core of early Christian proclamation (see Rev. 3:12; 1 Pet. 2:1–10; Eph. 2:11–22; 1 Cor. 3:16–17; Acts. 6:13–14; 7:44–50; but Rev. 21:22).

Because a faithful God has already fulfilled the biblical promise of an eschatological temple, John's task is somewhat different than Ezekiel's. John is called to measure critical sections of an extant temple in order to protect the inner sanctuary (and the believers found worshiping there) from defilement or destruction. The believers are gathered around the **altar**, where the prayers of the saints are heard by God (cf. Rev. 8:2) and where they are purified to serve God's interests (cf. Ezek. 43:13–27).

Since the **outer court . . . has been given to the Gentiles** (or non-believers; cf. Eph. 4:17), it is excluded from John's measurement and the non-believers from the purifying glory of God. According to the customs of the Second Temple in Jerusalem, only the outer court could be used by non-Jews or "unofficial" (i.e., ethnic but non-religious or outcast) Jews. They were excluded from the inner courts where the more important and solemn ceremonies of Jewish worship were conducted; only religious Jews could enter and celebrate God there.

Left unprotected from the powers and principalities of evil, the unbelieving world is corrupted to become in turn corrupting agents who **trample on** (*pateō*) **the holy city for 42 months**. Although reminiscent of Jesus' prediction that the city of Jerusalem would be "trampled on (*pateō*) by the Gentiles" (Luke 21:24), in this context both **the holy city** and **the temple of God** are symbols for God's people (cf. Rev. 21:9–10) and not a geographical location. Likewise, the rounded sum of **42 months** or **1,260 days** represents an indefinite period of time during which the increased distress and harassment for God's people underscores the imminence of Christ's return and God's coming triumph. The essential point, envisioned by John's commission to measure only the inner sanctuary, frames the second half of this interlude: the church, the restored Israel of God, will be protected by God from the corrupting influences of evil and so will persevere through these 'last days' and into God's promised shalom.

11:3–6 / The (actually, **my**) **two witnesses** make an abrupt appearance into the vision, and the reader is not forewarned about the apparent change in speaker from John to God. Since they are given only what God can dispense—the **power** to **prophesy for 1,260 days**—the oracles they proclaim must bear witness to God's reign rather than to any part of John's Revelation.

Their identity is more difficult to ascertain. While cases have been mounted for a variety of historical figures (e.g., Moses and Elijah) and theological categories (e.g., law and gospel), we are best advised to pursue symbolic meanings consistent with the conviction envisioned by John's precedent commission. This course of action seems especially prudent since the two witnesses are called **the two olive trees and the two lampstands**—obvious symbols of their important roles in the life of God's people. The background for the first symbol, **the two olive trees . . . that stand before the Lord of the earth**, is found in Zechariah's vision of two olive trees that stand on either side of the gold lampstand (Zech. 4:3, 11). In his vision, the "two olive trees" symbolize the reign of King Zerubbabel and the priesthood of Joshua, the anointed mediators of God's covenant with Israel, "who serve the Lord of all the earth" (Zech. 4:14). In the wider context of the prophet's oracle, Zechariah commends Zerubbabel's work in completing the temple (Zech. 4:9) and Joshua's ministry in purifying God's people (Zech. 3:9). They are both viewed as effective mediators of God's covenant with Israel. John looks to this wider context of Zechariah's prophecy to justify his conviction that in some sense the **two witnesses** represent the renewal and restoration of God's relationship with God's people. This spiritual reality is indicated earlier by John in the final stanza of the "new song": the exalted Lamb has made the entire redeemed community into a kingdom, to reign like Zerubbabel, made up of priests, to serve God like Joshua (Rev. 5:10; cf. 1:6).

Further, **the two lampstands**, which symbolize the church elsewhere in Revelation (cf. 1:20), suggest that **the two witnesses** are a synecdoche for the community of faithful disciples. The number **two** has significance as well, referring to the number of witnesses required by Judaism to admit evidence into a court of law. The essential ministry of "two" witnesses (cf. Deut. 19:15), in continuity with the "testimony of Jesus Christ" (1:2), is to provide a valid "testimony" (11:7; cf. 1:2) to God through their death (11:7) and God's resurrection of them (11:11).

Likewise, in the confidence of eternal life (cf. 11:11), the ministry of the faithful church is to give courageous and powerful testimony to God's salvation, even though it will provoke increased tribulation and even martyrdom. Even more specifically, the ministry of the **two witnesses** agrees with the twofold character of the redeemed community. First, the witnesses serve God (cf. 5:10). They are **clothed in sackcloth**, not to mourn the circumstances of their own tribulation but rather to submit themselves in humble dedication to the redemptive interests of God (cf. Dan. 9:3–19). Second, they reign on the earth with extraordinary power. Like the church they have received divine power to prophesy about God's certain triumph (cf. Eph. 3:10); and like Christ they hold the fiery power of the prophet Elijah (cf. 2 Kings 1:1–18) to **devour their enemies** who **must die** as "a compelling divine necessity" (Morris, *Revelation*, p. 144). Their powers extend to the natural order **to shut up the sky so that it will not rain . . . to turn the waters into blood and to strike the earth with every kind of plague**. In echoing the biblical traditions of Elijah (1 Kings 17:1; cf. James 5:17–18) and Moses (Exod. 7:20; 8:12; cf. Heb. 11:23–29), who demonstrated similar powers, John intends to interpret the church's ongoing witness to God by the OT prophetic witness. In doing so, John underscores the prophet's most important characteristic: a single-minded faithfulness to proclaim and embody the word of the Lord.

Surely the courage and power of the witnesses should characterize the church's current reign on the earth. Yet, the character of their witness is rooted in their faithfulness; faithfulness is the condition for power over sin and for courageous witness in the present dispensation. In this light, then, the **two witnesses** may well refer only to the portion of the whole church, already represented by the two faithful congregations at Smyrna and Philadelphia, which exemplify single-minded devotion to God and power over sin under difficult circumstances.

11:7–10 / Only **when they have finished their** God-ordained and empowered **testimony** can **the beast that comes up from the Abyss . . . kill them**. Two elements of this event are critical for the interpreter to consider. First, this is the first appearance of **the beast**, who personifies evil power and who figures so prominently in the rest of John's composition. His absence from Revelation until this point is consistent with the primary emphasis of the first section of John's composition on God's triumph over evil through the exalted Lamb. Second, his exit **from the Abyss** (cf. 9:1) and the onslaught of his evil work commence only after the testimony of the two witnesses is **finished** (*teleō*; cf. John 19:30). The limits of evil are established by God and ultimately serve God's purposes. In this sense, John's apocalypticism is not dualistic in either an ontological or a teleological sense. That is,

God and the Evil One are not two eternal beings of equal power, directing two different histories in an independent fashion. God reigns alone and God alone will finally vanquish all pretenders to the heavenly throne through Christ.

Therefore, while the beast makes his destructive power felt, the parameters for the exercise and effect of his evil power are set by the sovereign God. In this light, we may recognize the irony John conveys by using the verb **overpower** (*nikaō*) to describe the beast's "empty" defeat of the **two prophets**. This is the same catchword John uses in speaking of those faithful believers who form a community of "overcomers" who witness to God's triumph in Christ by "overcoming" (*nikaō*) evil. They will receive the reward of eternal life at Christ's return (2:7, 11, 17, 26; 3:5, 12, 21).

We are not to suppose for a moment that the "two witnesses," who represent the community of overcomers, are actually overcome by the **beast**. Their death is only a temporary defeat. Their final victory, as the reader will soon discover, is forthcoming. By employing the Christ typology, John identifies the place of their execution as **where also their Lord was crucified**. He is not moving from symbolism to literalism to speak of the city of Jerusalem. He is rather saying something about the theological significance of the death of the "two witnesses" (and those they represent): like Jesus they suffered an apparent defeat at the hands of his enemies, and like Jesus their execution will lead to their eventual resurrection and vindication. John's main point is therefore this: faithfulness unto death is always the ultimate measure of the disciple's faithfulness to God.

What happens when there is no longer a faithful testimony to God's gospel? What happens when social evil increases and intensifies, and the "trampling" of worshipers in the "holy city" turns ugly and ends in their martyrdom? Without the ongoing testimony of Jesus, provided by the community of faithful disciples, any **great city** can turn into a wicked **Sodom** (cf. Isa. 1:9–10; Ezek. 16:46–55) in a rather short period of time—in **three and a half days**. In this context, the **great city** does not refer to a specific city, but to any neighborhood in the "global village" where people live and work, and where pervasive evil has replaced or compromised the testimony of Jesus Christ. In such places, the force of the beast's corrupting power is felt at many levels. The worldwide celebration, when the **inhabitants of earth** exchange

gifts, suggests that special festival days have been instituted for this occasion. There is the complete breakdown of basic social conventions, so that **men . . . gaze on their bodies and refuse them burial**. In creating a public spectacle of their death and by not providing them a decent burial, the leaders of the anti-Christian kingdom have acted with unbridled disrespect. Without social manners there is left anarchy and chaos, which are the marks of the Evil One (cf. Rom. 1:29–31) and not of Christ.

11:11–13 / To this point of the interlude, John has defended the vital importance of the faithful congregation in any city: by such a testimony the congregation restrains evil and conveys the power of God's reign to the surrounding society. Without such a testimony, the destructive powers of evil would rapidly increase to create disorder and death. By envisioning the extinction of the faithful congregation (i.e., the "two witnesses"), John wishes to encourage his audience to resist the temptation of spiritual laxity, no doubt prompted by the current "trampling of the Gentiles," and to live faithfully for God.

But what of those faithful witnesses in John's churches who have already been martyred? What is their destiny? Since the **two witnesses** continue to bear witness to the word of God and the testimony of Jesus Christ right up to their execution, we would expect them to share in his resurrection from death to life as well. Perhaps because John wishes the reader to associate this scene with the resurrection of Jesus, he changes tense from present to aorist. Indeed, echoes of Jesus' glorification abound, especially of his ascension: **And they went up to heaven in a cloud, while their enemies looked on** (cf. Acts 1:9–11). Ironically, according to the Lukan narrative of Jesus' ascension, two witnesses act as interpreters for the disciples **while** they **. . . looked on**, telling them that his ascension makes certain his parousia! John may well intend the very same promise for his own audience. Actually, John's substitution of **enemies** for disciples is apropos not only because the former enemies convert and become disciples, but because they respond to the resurrection of the **two witnesses** in the same way that the disciples first responded to Jesus' resurrection: in holy **terror** (cf. Mark 16:8)!

The biblical idiom, **breath of life from God**, is employed by John for the resurrection. The phrase draws upon the OT images of God's breath, which gave life to humanity (cf. Gen. 2:7) and promised new life to an exiled Israel (cf. Ezek. 37:9–10). John's use of it here accords with his convictions about the lordship of God as creator (cf. Rev. 4:11) and the faithfulness of God in keeping the biblical promise of bringing a new Israel back to life. The reality of God's rule over the beast and of God's faithfulness to the two witnesses is finally recognized by the **survivors** of the **severe earthquake**, who **gave glory to the God of heaven**. The conversion of God's enemies is a new motif for John, but entirely consistent with the overarching theme of this part of his composition: the vindication of the exalted witnesses, as with the exalted Lamb before, issues in a demand to repent and turn to God, who is "faithful and just and will forgive us our sins and purify us from all unrighteousness" (1 John 1:9).

11:14 / The completion of the intervening vision about the death and exaltation of the two witnesses signals the end of the **second woe**. Concerning the **third woe**, however, John is much more cryptic: he says only that it is **coming soon**. Does this mean that the "third woe begins with the seventh trumpet" soon to sound? This seems hardly possible, since the seventh trumpet is a fanfare not to woes and lamentations but to a heavenly chorus of praise and thanksgiving! Does John wish to create the impression that the **third woe** is delayed and will not be revealed until after the seventh trumpet has sounded its note of praise? As we stated earlier, this interpretation makes the most sense: the **third woe** looks ahead to the second part of Revelation's main body, where the current crisis facing God's people is envisioned. The **two woes** that have passed are linked with the death and exaltation of Christ; the one remaining woe interprets the period of salvation's history in which the church now lives (and often suffers at the hands of evil powers), envisioned by John as three heavenly signs (12:1–19:10).

That two-thirds of the messianic woes have been completed indicates that God's final judgment of the fallen world has not yet occurred. Of course, the incomplete nature of the devastation wreaked by God's wrath has been an important element of both the seal and the trumpet visions. We have maintained that God's partial judgment functions as a warning to a fallen world. John's message, rooted in the Christ event, is that the world system is fallen and now lives under God's indictment; unbelievers must recognize, with the survivors of the city's earthquake (11:11–13), that they need God's mercy to "survive" and they receive "survivable" mercy through the Lamb. The same image also warns the unfaithful church to repent of its spiritual laxity before its final justification is imperiled. Further, the phrase **coming soon** rehearses Christ's promise of his imminent return, which is also found repeatedly in Revelation's "bookends" (2:5, 16; 3:11; 22:7, 12, 20). The first effect of the phrase in concluding this interlude is to convince the unbelieving or unfaithful reader of Revelation that repentance is made all the more urgent by the imminence of the history's end and evil's destruction. Further, the second effect is to give hope to the faithful that the sufferings of the **third woe**, which envisions the present age, will conclude at any moment in the collapse of the world order and in the transformation of God's people.

Finally, 11:14 marks a transition between the first and second sections of Revelation's body rather than between the interlude and the seventh trumpet. The seventh trumpet itself concludes the first section in triumphant declaration of the cosmic significance of Jesus' death and exaltation as God's Lamb, and it prepares the reader of the next section of Revelation to consider the current crisis in hope and confidence.

Additional Notes §10

10:2 / Schüssler Fiorenza extends the content of the **little scroll** to include 10:1–15:4, and she asserts that its "theme of the eschatological community . . . constitutes the center of its composition" (*Revelation*, p. 55).

10:7 / The NIV translates the verb *euēngelisen*, **he announced**, which does not reflect the evangelistic content and purpose of the seventh trumpet and its vision of celebration at the opening of the heavenly temple.

10:10 / Ladd likens the **sour** taste of John's "little scroll" to Jesus' bitter tears shed over Jerusalem when he knew his people had rejected his messianic mission (John 11:35). In a similar way, Ladd says, the prophecy contained in the scroll is of the nations' rejection of Messiah and the judgment they bring upon themselves (*Revelation*, p. 147).

11:3 / Boring actually finds a note of encouragement in that the tribulation is limited to **1,260 days**—a reasonably short period of time (*Revelation*, p. 140). John's intent may have been to link the time period to Daniel's prophecy of "a time, times, and half a time" which Morris computes to equal three and one half years (*Revelation*, p. 143).

A synecdoche is a figure of symbolic speech by which a part represents the whole or the whole one part. In this sense, the **two witnesses** symbolize the entire worshiping community which bears collective witness to God and to God's Christ. D. Hill has argued that the ministry of the **two witnesses** is in continuity with the OT prophets in "their readiness to proclaim the truth of God in the face of Jewish unbelief, and even to die for that truth"; "Prophecy and Prophets in the Revelation of St. John," *NTS* 18 (1971–72), p. 401.

§11 The Seventh Angel Sounds the Final Trumpet (Rev. 11:15–19)

The seventh trumpet blows a note of rejoicing in heaven. The heavenly chorus resumes its praise of God's reign and God's Christ, continuing the doxology sung at the Lamb's coronation (cf. Rev. 5:13). Together with the great hymns of chapter 5, John brackets his vision of divine wrath and global devastation (6:1–11:14) with dissonant images of praise (5:13; 11:15-18) for rhetorical effect—to make it even more clear that God's judgment of a sinful world is grounded in the triumph of the Lamb. The twenty-four elders who conclude this celebration with a second hymn of thanksgiving express the deeper-logic of John's theological conviction: because God's reign has begun with the exaltation of Christ (11:17), God's judgment of the dead—of earth's destroyers—has also begun (11:18). The profound summary of Paul's "message of reconciliation" is centered by the same point: Christ "died for all; (therefore) the old has gone, the new has come" (2 Cor. 5:15a, 17b)!

Most commentators contend that the seventh trumpet envisions God's future and final triumph at Christ's second coming. Thus, these anthems of praise introduce the visions found in the following chapters, rather than conclude those of the previous chapters (Mounce, *Revelation*, p. 230). While the themes of God's reign, wrath, and reward are strategic to what comes next in Revelation, they are hardly "introduced" at this point and are central to the whole composition. To justify their understanding of the seventh trumpet in terms of a futuristic eschatology, some even associate Paul's "last trumpet," which announces the coming of Christ and the resurrection of the dead (1 Cor. 15:52; 1 Thess. 4:16), with John's seventh trumpet (e.g., Beasley-Murray, *Revelation*, p. 187). While both Paul and John use the trumpet as an eschatological motif, they employ the motif in different ways with different meanings. In this passage, the trumpet accompanies hymns that consider the importance of Christ's death and exaltation rather than his second coming. At this point in his vision, John is more concerned with a realized Christology than with a futuristic eschatology. Thus, the tense of the stanzas looks to the past in thanksgiving for what has "already been realized," and not to the future in hope of what is "not yet real": God has already **begun to reign** (11:17) with the exalted Lamb (cf. 5:10); and the time (*kairos*) of God's wrath already **has come** (11:18) beginning with the vindication of the slain Lamb (cf. 6:16–17).

In accord with primitive Christian proclamation, then, John posits the assertion of God's claim over the **kingdom of the world** (11:15) at the death and exaltation of Christ, and not at his second coming, which discloses and consummates God's rule on earth. A consistent claim made throughout Revelation is that the Evil One does not reign on earth or in heaven (although many are deceived into thinking he does). The most problematic aspect of positing the seventh trumpet in the future rather than in the past is that it forces the interpreter to locate the "renewal" of God's eternal reign in the future as well. If one supposes this is the case, then one must assume that the Evil One now has charge over earth and its ruling elite; and only heaven belongs to God. The theology of Revelation would challenge this assumption: if what is true in heaven is also true on earth, and if through Christ God has triumphed in heaven, then the Evil One has already been defeated and rules nowhere.

In maintaining this point, we must add the following qualification. John's Revelation (with the entire NT) envisions a dialectic between a realized Christology and a futuristic eschatology. While death's defeat has already been realized on Christ's cross and verified in his empty tomb, death's destruction, along with the evil kingdom, is still in the future. Therefore, until the future breaks into the present at Christ's return, the effects of evil continue to distort the truth and to corrupt lives on earth.

11:15 / The first hymn, sung by presumably angelic (cf. 4:8; 12:10; 19:1) **loud voices**, looks back to the penultimate moment of salvation's history and acclaims the essential truth of Christ's death and exaltation: **the kingdom of the world has become the kingdom of our Lord and of his Christ**. Even though human existence has been corrupted by the world's rebellious rulers, the sovereignty of God the creator can be reasserted because of Christ. Through the devotion of his faithful disciples, the **kingdom of the world** is challenged by a counter-kingdom of priests, made by Christ (5:10), to end the rule of those pretenders to God's throne. It is John's expectation that a life and faith that is an alternative to the world order will yield trials and tribulation. Evil is a defeated foe even though it continues to kick and struggle in the grasp of a victorious God. The first (i.e., present) stage of this new age of God's salvation is dynamic and full of conflict simply because the realities of God's salvation are breaking into the life of faithful disciples, while at the same time a defeated evil order is passing away against its wishes.

The radical theocentrism of John's Revelation is not heard more clearly than here. The antecedent of **he will reign for ever and ever** is God rather than either Christ or both God and Christ. The effective result of the messianic mission of the faithful Jesus is to bring to an end the world's rebellion against God and to provide God with the agent worthy enough to open the sealed scroll that declares and institutes God's sovereignty over the evil powers forever. Apocalypticism is keenly interested in the formation of theological perceptions about God, about the social order, and about human suffering. By focusing the eschatological restoration of God's people on the two essential moments of the Christ event—by what has been already realized (death and exaltation) and by what has not yet been realized (parousia)—John can express the relationship between present reality and what the future will bring in order to provide his readership with a way of seeing their own suffering and their surrounding community. This, then, is the essence of his pastoral program: to provide his audience with a "hermeneutic" that interprets the very real difficulties of living as Christian disciples within a non-Christian society. Recognition of Christ's exaltation and of God's triumph over the Evil One will evoke a response of either encouragement (if faithful) or repentance (if unfaithful). Human suffering, whether the yield of interpersonal or social conflict, is always the work of an "already defeated but not yet destroyed" foe.

11:16–18 / The second hymn, sung by the **twenty-four elders**, is more specifically addressed in thanksgiving to the **Lord God Almighty**. The naming of God, **Lord God Almighty**, recalls the Trisagion (4:8; cf. 1:8). But in this use of the traditional formula, John omits its third item, "is to come," and reverses the remaining two: **the One who is and who was**. In doing so, John

emphasizes the past rather than the future, further evidence that
the seventh trumpet issues a commentary on the realized effects
of the Lamb's death and exaltation. God's **great power** does not
refer to the "final conflict in which God overpowers all his enemies" (Mounce, *Revelation*, p. 231); rather, it refers to the power
exerted when God raised Christ from the dead and exalted him
in heaven (cf. Eph. 1:19–20)—the moment when God "began his
reign." On the basis of a realized Christology, God (**who was**),
has **taken** his **great power . . . to reign** into our present (**who is**).

The second stanza is a more sweeping celebration of the
new age, from its beginning to its consummation. John begins
by rehearsing Christ's death, when the **nations were angry** and
conspired against the Lamb of God (cf. Ps. 2:1–2). God responded
in kind: the seals were broken and the trumpets were sounded
to announce that God's **wrath has come**. The elders express three
certain results of the triumph of God's reign: **your wrath has come
. . . for judging the dead, and for rewarding . . . saints . . . and
for destroying those who destroy the earth**. In one sense, this
triad of verbal infinitives (in Gk.) picks up the regressive results
of God's wrath, when a fallen creation becomes more and more
intolerable for human life and culminates in God's destruction
of the old order. In another sense, the same triad picks up the
progressive results of God's blessing, when a community of God's
servants . . . and saints . . . both great and small are rewarded,
culminating in their new life as the new Jerusalem.

This future and final judgment of the nations' rebellion and
the complete vindication of the church's faithfulness reflect a sense
of fairness. As Caird points out, this is an essential aspect of John's
idea of salvation. Not only will the faithfulness of martyrs be glori-
ously vindicated, but those who ravage the earth will themselves
be ravaged by God. Yet, this is not revenge; it is rather an act of
liberation from evil so that the faithful are free to worship God
and to live in shalom through eternity according to the intentions
of a good creator (Caird, *Revelation*, p. 144).

11:19 / The opening of **God's temple in heaven** represents a problem for those who want to place the sounding of the
seventh trumpet at Christ's parousia, since John finds no such
temple in the new Jerusalem (Rev. 21:22); and even now the faithful Christian community is the "true" temple of God (cf. 11:1).

To resolve this difficulty, some scholars are inclined to follow Minear's lead and begin the next section of John's vision at 11:19 rather than at 12:1. This clever move makes John's reference to the ark of the covenant his preface to the battles of the current age, narrated from 12:1 to 14:5. However, the grammar makes this interpretation difficult: the opening **And** (*kai*) connects this verse to the preceding anthem rather than to what follows. Most translations, including the NIV, are clear on this point. Furthermore, the opening formula of chapter 12, "A great and wondrous sign appeared in heaven," indicates the beginning of a new vision, distinct from previous visions.

In our view, the temple imagery adds a final element to the meaning of the seventh trumpet that concludes John's visionary narrative of the Lamb's exaltation and marks the transition into the visions of the current age. Where else but in a heavenly temple should one expect to find the Messianic Lamb who was slain to purchase a people for God? In fact, the notion that the first and second temples were built according to a heavenly pattern was common to Judaism's Second Temple period, especially among hellenistic rabbis. John is no doubt familiar with this teaching and draws upon it in a manner similar to the author of Hebrews (cf. Heb. 8:1–10:18) to interpret his vision of a "third" temple. The foundational philosophical assumption of rabbinical teaching in this regard is that the heavenly realm asserts what is ultimately true and real (i.e., perfect and permanent). In this sense, the theology of the cross is about the renewal of Israel's eternal relationship with God, which Christ's exaltation proves. John's use of the heavenly temple symbolism establishes the basis for Christian hope that God's salvation will win out in history: what is true in heaven will be true on earth. Further, the symbolism of the ark, which points to the covenantal relationship between God and God's people, delimits ultimate truth as essentially spiritual and relational in nature; and this too will be perfected in human experience.

If we are correct that the temple motif symbolizes a perfect and permanent realization of God's covenant with Israel within history, then we can explain John's interpretation of his vision of the heavenly temple in terms of the church's eternal relationship with the **Lord God Almighty** (cf. Rev. 11:17 and 21:22) and the Lamb (cf. Rev. 21:22). The **ark of his covenant**, on which John's sight falls, signifies the promised presence of God in the midst of a forgiven people. Since the ark stands in the inner sanctuary, where no one enters except the high priest on the Day of Atonement (cf. Lev. 16:17; Heb. 10:1–19), John's reference to it here underscores the status of the faithful: their sins are forgiven and their relationship with God will stand firm to the end because of Christ's atoning death. In this regard, we should note the opening line of the preceding hymn that calls eschatological Israel to worship. The invocation, **we give thanks** (*eucharistoumen*) **to you**, encompasses the very attitude required of the worshiping community's celebration of Christ's death in the Eucharist: "this is the blood of the new covenant."

The concluding phenomena, **flashes of lightning . . . and a great hailstorm**, symbolize God's reign (cf. 4:5). They remind the readers that the heavenly temple, its ark, its altar (cf. 8:5), its slain Lamb, and all those who are purchased by his blood are ultimately **for God** (cf. 5:9), and must therefore bear witness to God's triumph over all who oppose the testimony of Jesus Christ and his people. Significantly, the only other place in Revelation where a "hailstorm" is found is at the onset of the seventh bowl (16:21), which marks the final destruction of the anti-God kingdom. The heavenly temple is linked in this way to Babylon's fall on earth, since both events are results of God's triumph in Christ.

Additional Notes §11

11:19 / For the argument that 11:19 is the preface to the next vision, see Paul Minear, *New Testament Apocalyptic*, IBT (Nashville: Abingdon, 1981), pp. 91–101. Especially the image of the ark of the covenant alerts readers to its OT meaning as symbolic of holy war and to God's certain triumph over Israel's foes. Minear finds this an appropriate symbol for what immediately follows in Revelation: a heavenly holy war between God and Satan in which God emerges victorious.

For a discussion of the idea of a heavenly temple in hellenistic Judaism, see Harold W. Attridge, *Hebrews*, Hermeneia (Philadelphia: Fortress, 1989), pp. 222–24.

§12 Flashback: The Genesis of the Current Crisis (Rev. 12:1–12)

With the exaltation of the slain Lamb, the heavenly temple has been opened and the promise of salvation has been fulfilled (11:19); a new age of salvation's history has begun. According to the eschatology of the earliest church, Christ's death and exaltation constitute the penultimate moment of salvation's history and look ahead to the ultimate moment, the parousia of the Lord Jesus Christ, when the salvation of God's people and the restoration of God's creation will be completed in full. The church's history is worked out between those two climactic moments of salvation's history and constitutes the current moment of God's salvation.

This period of time should *not* be understood in a linear, chronological sense (Boring, *Revelation*, p. 150). Rather, the word of exhortation or judgment which the Spirit conveys to the readers of John's Revelation interprets their Christian existence within an anti-Christian world. The "Babylon" of this section of John's vision is any and every place where a congregation of believers struggles to live for God. The evils found there are found everywhere and at any time before Christ's return.

Beginning with chapter 12, John introduces new characters who challenge the reign of God and the objective value of Christ's work for life on earth—the "red dragon" and the two "beasts." He draws upon a new vocabulary which describes hostility to and warfare against God. The practical problem of theodicy is that people do not always experience the triumph of God over evil; more often than not, they experience suffering and injustice. In moving the venue of the visionary world from heaven to earth, John moves the reader into a world of real conflict between two kingdoms with the Lamb and his disciples on one side and the dragon, his agents and followers on the other. The venue of the cosmic and age old conflict is now planet Earth; and the community of the Lamb's disciples is the current target of satanic oppression.

Krodel has pointed out the variety of literary, often chiastic, relationships that tie this central section of John's vision to the visions of the Lamb's exaltation (cf. 5:9–10 and 12:10–12) and parousia (cf. 12:7–9 and 20:1–10; Krodel, *Revelation*, pp. 235–36). The interplay of these two visions with this part of John's vision provides an overarching perspective on the church's current misery. While devotion to the risen and returning Christ does not exempt the disciple from suffering—for the dragon's battle is now against the woman and her offspring—it does ensure the disciple of participation in God's final triumph over the Evil One in the age to come.

We do not disagree with those who contend that John draws upon the oppressive Roman regime of his day to describe the anti-Christian kingdom in his visionary world; however, the evil reign against which the church struggles is not isolated to one point of human history but is cosmic in space and ongoing in time. The church's constant challenge is to live for God for "as long as it is called Today," and to resist the satanic powers "that none of you may be hardened by sin's deceitfulness" (Heb. 3:13). This section of Revelation envisions any believing community, when the fundamental and ongoing crisis is its spiritual battle with all who resist the reign of God.

12:1–2 / The immediate purpose of this rehearsal of the Christ event (12:1–5), and the resulting sojourn of the church (12:6) and banishment of the Evil One to earth (12:7–12), is to summarize the precedent circumstances which caused the current moment and crisis of salvation's history. In writing down his vision of heavenly signs and warfare, John utilizes the elements of a well-known myth, found in the folklore of many cultures (cf. Beasley-Murray, *Revelation*, pp. 191–97). Many citizens of John's world assumed that the myth was literally fulfilled by the Caesar; thus, "John rewrites the old pagan myth deliberately to contradict its current political application" (Caird, *Revelation*, p. 148). That is, God's salvation of the world is based upon Christ's authority and not Caesar's, who is but another pretender to the messianic throne.

The essential features of this mythic story are as follows: at the birth of a promised ruler, an evil pretender to his throne attempts to reverse the wishes of the gods by killing the ruler at birth. The infant ruler, however, escapes and eventually kills his persistent and life-long enemy, ending his reign of terror in accord with the interests of the gods. By re-presenting the essential features of Jesus' messianic career as mythic, John allows the myth's interpretation of life to re-interpret the Christ event of the Christian gospel: even though the promised Messiah was born into conflict, he eventually triumphed, thus securing God's salvation for God's people. In fact, by extending the traditional myth to include the triumphant child's ascension into heaven (12:5b) and the Evil One's subsequent banishment from heaven to fallen earth (12:7–9), John underscores the primary importance of Christ over the "Caesars" of any age.

John envisions the inauguration of the current period of salvation's history as two celestial signs (cf. 12:1, 3); a third (15:1) will complete this period of conflict, the "third woe" (11:14). The first is **great and wondrous**, because it testifies to the salvation of God. While some have identified the **woman clothed with the sun . . . and a crown of twelve stars on her head** with astral imagery current in Greco-Roman mythology (Ford, *Revelation*, p. 197), it is best to understand her by the biblical symbols known to and used by John. For example, the number **twelve** symbolizes the twelve tribes of Israel (cf. Rev. 7); thus, the **twelve stars** symbolize God's people. The **crown** as well as the **sun . . .** and **moon** symbolize either God (cf. Isa. 60:1; Ps. 104:2; Rev. 21:22–23) or the cosmic significance of God's people (cf. T. Naph. 5:1–8) in the outworking of God's promised redemption through Christ. The point is that the vision is signaling a momentous event in God's redemption of God's people.

Most would agree that the **woman** in John's vision is the antithesis of the "great prostitute" of Babylon, who is introduced later in Revelation (17:3). Most would contend that this **woman** refers to a community rather than to an individual person such as Mary. Her exact identity, whether a religious subgroup within ethnic Israel such as messianic Judaism (cf. Luke 2:36–38) or eschatological Israel (cf. Rev. 12:5b–6), remains debated. Perhaps it is best to understand the history of God's people, where God's salvation is worked out, as a continuum. The **woman** symbolizes the faithful people of God (cf. Rev. 12:17) from whom and for whom the Messiah is born. The **woman**, then, refers to a people identified by their distinctive spirituality rather than ethnicity.

Further, the woman's birth pains and cries to God anticipate the messianic era, its restoration of true Israel (cf. Isa. 26:18 LXX; Gal. 4:19), and its judgment of evil (cf. Matt. 24:4–8).

12:3–4 / The one who opposes God's desired redemption is envisioned in **another sign: an enormous red dragon with seven heads and ten horns and seven crowns on his heads**. While the dragon conjures up allusions to OT "dragons," such as Leviathan (Ps. 74:14) or the Isaianic "sea-beasts" (cf. Isa. 27:1), or more significantly to Egypt's Pharaoh (Ezek. 29:3), its real importance is again recovered within Revelation's own symbol systems. By linking the dragon to the number **seven**, elsewhere symbolic of the ordained outworking of God's salvation, and to the **crown** motif, elsewhere symbolic of God's sovereignty, John points the reader to evil's most fundamental idolatry: the promotion of secular power over what belongs to the creator God and God's exalted Lamb. Thus, through chapter 13, John describes the principalities of the evil kingdom and its reign of terror in ironic parallel to God's reign of justice and redemption.

John's apocalyptic narrative is fashioned in terms of a dualistic understanding of history; all reality for John, whether personal or societal, is subdivided up into good and evil, for God and against God. The basic conflict, whether personal or societal, that inevitably issues from humankind's quest for self-definition stems from the contested nature of historical meaning and humanity's purpose. The rhetorical effect of this dualistic view of life helps the reader to focus more clearly on the ultimate concern of any spiritual quest: who is in charge of human existence? And Revelation draws the two possible outcomes of this spiritual quest in very precise lines. On the one hand, when the Evil One gains dominion over those who bear his mark (13:17–18) the result will be their death (13:11–16). On the other hand, when God is allowed to rule over those who bear the Lamb's name (14:1) the result will be their eternal life (14:2–5).

Although the **red dragon** has real power, as indicated by his **enormous** size, its potential effect is limited: **his tail swept a third of the stars out of the sky**. As with several judgments announced by the angelic trumpets, John uses the fraction, **a third**, to signify a limited scope or effect. The **dragon** has limits placed around its powers. This is no more apparent than in the dragon's relationship with the woman's **child**, who is about to be born.

In anticipation of his triumph over God's promised Messiah, **the dragon stood in front of the woman . . . so that he might devour her child the moment it was born** (cf. Matt. 2:16). Yet, we find that his attempt is foiled by God: God will always prevail, and God's plan calls for Messiah to deliver the true Israel from evil.

12:5–6 / The summary of God's triumph over the dragon in 12:5 must remind John's readers of the gospel's central teaching: God's sovereign rule over and redemptive interests in creation have been reasserted through Christ Jesus in triumph over the Evil One. Against the deities of pagan mythology and the gnosticizing speculations of some Christians in his audience, John introduces Jesus into the flashback as a **male child** in agreement with the messianic expectations of OT prophecy. As Messiah, he is born to **rule all the nations with an iron scepter** (cf. Ps. 2:9). His authority, however, is not exercised in a tyrannical manner; here, **rule** (*poimainein*) means to shepherd the flock of God, even though firmly by an **iron** staff.

Some scholars find difficulty with John's rehearsal of the Christ event since it seems to contend that Jesus ascends into heaven immediately after his birth. John's vision, however, is not a complete narrative of Jesus' life; it has simply telescoped the Christ event, omitting the Lord's life, death, and resurrection, to focus more directly on Jesus' exaltation and the eventual outcome of the Evil One's efforts to derail the messianic mission at its birth (cf. Mark 1:13). In this sense, 12:5 interprets the significance of chapter 5: Jesus' exaltation as the Paschal Lamb spells Satan's defeat, the end of Satan's heavenly rule. Jesus' ascendency to God's **throne** contrasts sharply with the dragon's crown (12:3) and constitutes further testimony of God's certain triumph over him.

The flight of the messianic community **into the desert to a place prepared for her by God** anticipates John's subsequent vision of the dragon's repression of God's people (12:13–13:18). Actually the **desert** motif, as employed by biblical writers, envisions two contrasting experiences. On the one hand, it is the fallen and evil place where people experience the absence of God's shalom; it is the place of tribulation and temptation. Even as this was true for the Israel of old, so too the life of the "true" Israel will be full of tribulation and temptation, when the rage of the Evil One is experienced for **1,260 days** (cf. 13:5). On the other hand, it is the place where the resources of a good God are found, where a faithful people can experience a measure of God's shalom this side of God's final victory over the Evil One (cf. Mark 1:12–13). In fact, the verb, **care** (*trephosin*), is given in the subjunctive mood, indicating that the nurture (rather than the discouragement) of the messianic community is God's real intent for their **desert** home.

12:7–9 / The exaltation of Christ into heaven, which begins the church's sojourn in the wilderness (12:6), also concludes (contra Caird, *Revelation*, pp. 152–56) the ancient **war in heaven** between **Michael**, "champion and sponsor of the people of God" (Boring, *Revelation*, p. 154; cf. Dan. 10:13, 21; 12:1; Jude 9; T. Dan 6:2; T. Levi 5:7), and **the dragon and his angels**. The dragon **was not strong enough**, losing both the battle and his **place in heaven**, and so is **hurled to the earth, and his angels with him**.

This summary of the **war in heaven** occupies a strategic place in John's vision for several reasons. First, it reports Satan's defeat as one result of Christ's triumph. However strong and troublesome Satan might seem, he is nevertheless a defeated foe. Second, the Platonic cosmology of John's hellenistic audience would lead it to assume that what has transpired in heaven will have its historical duplicate on earth. Thus, if the heavenly and invisible war between God and the Evil One has ended with God's triumph through the exalted Lamb, then the Evil One will surely be defeated by God in an earthly and visible war (cf. Rev. 19:11–21). Third, the shift of venue is from a **war in heaven . . . to the earth**, where the defeated dragon continues the struggle against God and God's people. This move of Satan from heaven to earth not only anticipates John's subsequent vision of the great dragon's hostile but failed take-over bid of the church (12:13–13:18), but it also explains why the church's suffering has not ended. More negatively, it explains the disaffection of some believers, who are deceived by the secular notions of power and security advanced by Satan (cf. Rev. 2:9, 13, 24; 3:9), **who leads the whole world astray** (cf. Rev. 20:3, 8, 10). Fourth, even as Patmos is John's penal colony, so earth is Satan's penal colony—the place of his exile from heaven, which is the center of cosmic rule. On this basis, the reader also presumes the dragon's ouster from heaven represents a demotion in his current influence over the course of human history. Finally, the Evil One's dismissal from heaven foreshadows his banishment from earth when Christ returns (cf. Rev. 20:1–3).

More subtly and quite apart from anything John may wish to say about Satan's diminished powers during the present age, the seer may also wish to contrast the status of the exalted Lamb over **Michael**. This detail of his vision may be included as part of an anti-synagogue polemic, especially if some readers are encountering keen anti-Christian opposition from the influential synagogues in southwest Asia. John no doubt recognized Michael's participation in this vision in terms of rabbinical speculation that gave him elevated importance in mediating God's covenant with religious Israel. In this way, **Michael** had come to symbolize for many religious Jews a triumphant Judaism. Such a role, however, has been given to the exalted Christ (cf. 1 Tim. 2:5), who alone champions a true Israel—made up of Christ's disciples—before God's throne.

12:10–12 / The circumstances of the church's current crisis have now been established: the exaltation of Messiah, the wilderness sojourn of the messianic community, and the banishment of the enormous red dragon from heaven to earth where the messianic community now dwells. In a concluding hymn, the **loud voice in heaven** draws from two pools of themes, first to summarize the redemption that has been realized through **the blood of the Lamb** and the **testimony** of remnant Israel (12:10–11), and then to anticipate the church's conflict with a furious **devil** during the present period of salvation's history (12:12).

The first stanza begins yet another "sudden outburst of praise" which is characteristic of Revelation (Mounce, *Revelation*, p. 242). Its theme is **the kingdom of our God**, to which both **salvation** from evil and **authority** over the Evil One belong. Its tense is present, since God's reign is a present and eternal reality, as Satan's most recent defeat clearly manifests. What is of greater importance to John is that the final disposition of the heavenly war also marks the end of the satanic case for the prosecution, which had accused **our brothers . . . before . . . God day and night** (cf. Job 1:6–22; Zech. 3:1–2). The **brothers** are not angels but faithful saints of pre-messianic Israel, like Job and Zechariah, who have prepared the world for the Messiah's promised advent (cf. Heb. 11:1–12:2; contra Morris, *Revelation*, p. 157). Further, the forensic overtones of this stanza are consistent with Johannine Christianity, where the exaltation of Christ marks a fundamental shift in the weight of evidence during the heavenly trial of God's people, from Satan's accusation (cf. John 12:31; 14:30) to the Paraclete's witness (cf. John 14:16–17; 25–27; 15:26; 16:7–8; Caird, *Revelation*, pp. 153–57).

Thus, Satan's case is thrown out of court because of two kinds of evidences: because of the **blood of the Lamb** and because of the **testimony** of those Jews martyred who refused to abandon the promises of God's prophetic **word**. While John perhaps intends to encourage Christians on the verge of martyrdom to "overcome" (*nikaō*; cf. Rev. 2–3), he is not speaking here about the testimony of Christian martyrs. John does not view the history of God's people as divided into discrete dispensations; rather, the faithful remnant of Israel and now of the church form an unbroken testimony to God's reign from creation to consummation. In this sense, the saints of old bear collective witness to a pattern of life which ultimately overcomes the evils of a fallen world (cf. Heb. 11).

John sounds a realistic, perhaps even an ominous note in the final stanza. While the **heavens** (and the eschatological community!) are now rid of their satanic accuser and can **rejoice** because he has been replaced there by the exalted advocate, it is cause for **woe to the earth and the sea, because the devil has gone down to you**. This **woe** is not the "third woe," mentioned earlier in Revelation 11:14. While the "third woe" refers implicitly to the suffering of believers, its purview is the entire current age and is ultimately concentrated on the destruction of the anti-Christian kingdom at the end of the age when Christ returns. This immediate **woe** is more limited, and refers to the very beginning of the church's suffering at the hands of the Evil One, who **is filled with fury** toward God's people.

The final phrase, **he knows that his time is short**, provides two meanings to these "last days" of salvation's history. On the one hand, it suggests the *kairos* of the church's tribulation is limited, its end imminent; on the other hand, it implies that hostilities toward believers will increase because the beast has been wounded and beaten. The first meaning generates hope, while the second meaning explains the existential experience of powerlessness. Is not this the very nature of the church's crisis this side of Christ's return?

Additional Notes §12

Schüssler Fiorenza says that Revelation "speaks not only of vengeance against the dehumanizing, anti-Christian, demonic, and political powers, but also calls the inhabitants of the earth as well as the Christians to repentance. The author insists that the Christians in no way have 'made it' but that they are still in danger of losing their share in the New Jerusalem" (*Revelation*, p. 108). In our opinion, her point is keenly felt in this central section of John's Revelation.

12:1 / Because the **woman** appears as a heavenly sign, Ladd understands the woman as the "ideal church in heaven" (*Revelation*, p. 167). This, however, makes no sense of the woman's man-child, who surely belongs to earth, as Ladd himself admits. A more interesting problem is John's use of feminine images for the church. In what sense can we understand the church as both Christ's mother and his bride (19:6–8; 21:2, 9)? Kimberly Chastain provides a model to answer this question in her unpublished paper, "Bride, Mother, Beautiful Woman: Jonathan Edwards' Feminine Images of the Church," presented at the annual meeting of the American Society of Church Historians, 1990. Chastain contends that the "mother" motif envisions the present church—nurturing and supporting believers for their struggle against sin and evil. The "bride" motif envisions the eschatological church, "repristinated" to take its place within a new and purified creation.

12:5 / In resolving the problem of the "gap" between the child's **birth** and his **snatching up to God**, Caird contends that the Christ's "birth . . . means . . . the Cross" (*Revelation*, p, 149), and Boring seems to agree (*Revelation*, p. 153). Beasley-Murray, however, considers this a slick but dubious rendering (*Revelation*, pp. 199–200), and we agree.

12:10–12 / Beasley-Murray contends that v. 11 centers John's entire composition (even though its thought is already predicted by the "new song" of Rev. 5:9–10). What is new and important about this second doxology of messianic Israel's triumph is the attention it draws to Israel's defeated foe. Perhaps the chiastic structure of the song helps to make this point:

A: " . . . For the accuser . . . has been hurled down."
  B: "They overcame him . . . "
A': " . . . the devil has gone down to you."

The Christ event has altered the relationship between the people of God and God's enemy: the devil has been "overcome" in heaven and has "gone down" to the messianic community on earth. The result is a heightened sense of the spiritual and historical struggles of living for God in an anti-God world. In this sense, the doxology offers the reader a compelling preface to the visions of that world that follow in Rev. 12:13–13:18.

§13 The War in Heaven Continues on Earth (Rev. 12:13–13:18)

John's vision of the two beasts provides a fuller commentary on the meaning of the preceding hymn in terms of both the dragon's earthly activities and the situation of the messianic community. Having been foiled in his efforts to deny Jesus his messianic vocation, and having been exiled from heaven to earth where he can no longer influence the decisions of the Cosmocrater, the dragon turns his malicious attention to God's people on earth. He is naturally upset over his recent demotion, and his response is to lash out at those who are associated with the one who brought him down. The reader already knows from the flashback (12:6; and repeated in 12:13–14) that the church's desert home symbolizes its tribulation, made even more difficult by the hostilities of the dragon. Yet, the reader also realizes that God provides resources of spiritual nurture to the embattled church to transform a desert into an oasis. Revelation 12:13–13:1a echoes the Exodus tradition to make John's point: the wilderness region is the place where Israel experiences the faithfulness of God, whose promised salvation will not go unfulfilled in spite of the best efforts of God's enemies and Israel's infidelities. God is always true to God's word.

12:13–14 / These verses recapitulate 12:6. The church's situation is interpreted as an exodus event. God's people are quickly brought on the **two wings of a great eagle** out of their bondage to evil (cf. Exod. 19:4) and ushered into a place of nurture, **prepared** by God **out of the serpent's reach**. The length of stay, **time, times and half a time**, alludes to Daniel's vision of evil repression (Dan. 7:25). In Daniel and in Revelation, the theological point is the same: the Evil One will attempt to overturn the devotion of the saints, but to no avail.

12:15–17 / Like the Pharaoh of old, the serpent follows in close pursuit, intent on destruction. As before when the Reed

Sea parted for Israel, the **earth helped the woman** again by **swallowing the river that the dragon had spewed out of his mouth**. The torrent of water no doubt is a metaphor for a torrent of evil which surrounds God's people in whatever **desert** they live. Their experiences of oppression and powerlessness, coupled with the apparent triumph of secularism and materialism, could swallow up the testimony of God's people even as the earth did to an earlier generation of the insolent in the wilderness at Korah (cf. Num. 16:30).

Such temptations to apostasy, while felt by all, are ineffective within the true Israel where believers are found **who obey God's commandments and hold to the testimony of Jesus**. However, in the *rest* of Israel, where devotion to God's reign has relaxed and accommodation to the evil order has resulted, the successes of the Evil One are more notable. A caveat is therefore given to those congregations of believers, in places such as Laodicea, where a Christian witness has waned. There, it is God rather than the great dragon who will spit them out (cf. 3:16): a holy God does not drink from the dragon's watershed!

13:1a / Those translations which follow the Greek text at this point take the first part of 13:1, **And the dragon stood on the shore of the sea**, and either include it with 12:17 (e.g., RSV) or form another verse, 12:18 (e.g., JB). The textual evidence for doing so is considerable, and the natural flow of the passage commends it as well. In either case, the scene is transitional: the **dragon** has paused after a rather unsuccessful first assault against the church (12:13–17) and looks out onto the sea, the domicile of evil and powerful beasts, to summon reinforcements for a second assault against God's people (13:1b–10).

13:1b–2 / Chapter 13 portrays two powerful and evil beasts, together with the dragon, as an unholy trinity that rules over the anti-God kingdom. Beasley-Murray, who follows M. Rissi at this point, carries this analogy still further in noting that John's description of the dragon is a deliberate parody of God; the first beast, whose fatal wound is healed, is a second parody of Christ (cf. Schüssler Fiorenza, *Revelation*, p. 55); and the second beast, the false prophet who has the authority of the first beast (cf. John 14:16) and causes fire to come from heaven (cf. Acts 2:3), is a third parody of the Holy Spirit (Beasley-Murray, *Revelation*, pp. 207–8).

They form and empower another congregation of "believers" that practices evil and worships the unholy trinity. The Christian's struggle against the anti-Christian impulses of the surrounding world order is not merely an internal and intellectual one; it is also a sociopolitical struggle between two communities that have been shaped and empowered either by malevolent powers for evil or by benevolent powers for good (cf. 1 Pet. 3:13–17). Thus, each portrait concludes with John's exhortation for Christian virtue in the face of great calamity: those who remain faithful (13:10) and wise (13:18) will be numbered among the 144,000, the eschatological remnant (14:1–5).

The first **beast** that John sees **coming out of the sea** is similar to the dragon. Like the dragon, it has all the symbols of kingly authority (**ten crowns on his horns**; cf. 17:10; Dan. 7:7) and brute power (**seven heads . . . and on each head a blasphemous name**; cf. Ps. 74:13–14). Both form and place of origin indicate that it is an agent of the Evil One. The mythic **sea**, like the Abyss (cf. 11:7; 17:8), is associated with evil monsters, such as Leviathan (cf. Job 41:1–34); and in Daniel's dream, echoed in John's description of his own vision of beasts, four terrifying beasts come up out of the sea to boast of their greatness (Dan. 7:1–14).

The "real" identity of the first beast for John remains a matter of speculation (cf. Caird, *Revelation*, pp. 162–63). In my view, it is best to recognize it as a universal symbol for secular power and cultural idols, with historical counterparts in every age. Because 13:2 alludes to Daniel's vision of four beasts/world empires (Dan. 7:4–7), the specific nature of authority envisaged by John's first beast is nationalistic and political, as with Daniel's beasts. Whenever the state or its civil rulers claims for itself absolute authority or demands the right to transcend the criticisms of the believing community, it discloses its **blasphemous** agenda (Schüssler Fiorenza, *Revelation*, p. 117).

13:3–4 / Several commentators seek to find a historical counterpart to the beast whose head **seemed to have had a fatal wound, but the fatal wound had been healed** (cf. Mounce, *Revelation*, pp. 252–53). But surely John's point is rather that "the monster is a parody of Christ" (Caird, *Revelation*, p. 164). The anti-Christian movement within history counterfeits the real power of God (cf. 2 Cor. 11:1–15), while its leaders pretend to assume the messianic throne (cf. 1 John 2:18–22). In fact, the beast's power on earth is derived from the Evil One, who **had given authority to the beast**. The beast's sociopolitical program, which pervades every political regime in any age, is inherently satanic and ultimately ends in chaos and death.

Certainly, the daily record of political abuse and social maleficence testifies to humanity's powerlessness to reverse this established evil order: **Who is like the beast? Who can make war against him?** Given this hopeless situation, then, the natural response of **the whole world** that does not hope in God (cf. 13:8) is to ascribe to the beast what belongs only to God (cf. Exod. 15:11; Isa. 40:25); without the requisite spiritual resources to resist, the lost resign themselves to follow after the beast rather than the Lamb (cf. Rev. 14:4) and to worship the beast rather than God and God's exalted Lamb (cf. Rev. 5:13).

13:5–8 / The **beast** was given two roles by the dragon **to exercise** his authority for **forty-two months** (cf. 11:2), which must be in accord with the Lord God's ordination for the church (cf. 12:6). First, it **was given a mouth** (1) **to utter proud words**, (2) **to blaspheme God**, and (3) **to slander** God's **name and his dwelling place and those who live in heaven**. In order to distinguish God's **dwelling place** from **those who live in heaven**, the NIV has decided against the Greek text which places the final phrase, **those who live in heaven**, in apposition (rather than in conjunction) with the phrase, **his dwelling place**. We agree with the Greek text in this case. The best mss omit the conjunction, **and**, and identify God's **dwelling place** with **those who live in heaven**. This textual point is important because the equation of God's domicile with God's people underscores the importance of Revelation's final scene where the new Jerusalem is not a place but a people (i.e., the Bride of the Lamb, 21:9–10; cf. Phil. 3:20; Eph. 2:6; Col. 3:1; Heb. 12:22–24). In this sense, "heaven" is conceived as the transformed and eternal relationship between God and God's people.

Second, the beast's power **over every tribe, people, language and nation** (cf. Rev. 5:9) takes the form not only of words that oppose God and God's reign, but also of coercive force and military might: **he is given authority to make war**. The result that **all inhabitants of the earth will worship the beast** is inevitable, not as a matter of predestined fate, but of societal inertia. It should be pointed out that the beast's anti-Christian rhetoric, which is much more seductive and formative as a sociopolitical force, is mentioned first and more prominently than the beast's military and more brutal, coercive powers. Still, however, those **belonging to the Lamb**, whose lives are already secured by the Lamb's death, do not **worship the beast**. Their discipleship to the Lamb is clearly indicated by their suffering at the hands of the beast, who **wages war against the saints to conquer them**.

The problematical phrase, **from the creation of the world**, qualifies **the Lamb that was slain** rather than those whose names **have not been written in the book of life** (cf. RSV). The theological conviction expressed by this phrase is not that God doubly predestines the elect to follow the Lamb unto life (cf. 14:4) and the non-elect to follow the beast unto destruction (cf. 13:3), but that God is faithful to the promise of salvation now fulfilled through the slain Lamb (cf. Rev. 5:9).

13:9–10 / John's vision of the first beast concludes with an exhortation, beginning with a formula similar to that which concluded the messages to the seven congregations: **He who has an ear, let him hear** (cf. 2:7). The readers are reminded of those messages and of those practices commended or condemned; they are reinterpreted by this vision of the beast's war of words against God and the beast's brutal repression of God's people. The citation of Jeremiah 15:2 (cf. Matt. 26:52), even though corrupted during its scribal transmission (cf. Metzger, *Textual Commentary*, pp. 747–48), provides the context for understanding the spiritual significance of the vision of the first beast. While the prophet Jeremiah originally intended this oracle to warn the pagan nations against compromising Israel's life, John uses the same oracle to warn the believing community against compromising its devotion to God. Thus, while the first couplet (v. 10a) accepts the current difficulties as the reality of living out a Christian's faith in an anti-Christian world, the second couplet (v. 10b) hopes for vindication for **saints** who "overcome" the beast's rhetorical and political threats with **patient endurance and faithfulness**.

13:11 / John then **saw another beast, coming out of the earth**, completing the trinity which rules over the evil kingdom. While John perhaps recognizes this second beast as Behemoth, the evil monster who occupies the primeval desert regions according to Jewish myth (Job 40:15–24; 1 Enoch 60:7–10; 4 Ezra

6:49–53), it is not clear how or if he then intends to use particulars of that myth to interpret the evil role of this second beast. John could have utilized the Behemoth/Leviathan myth simply as an aid in recognizing the two beasts in his vision as evil and eschatological. But this does not get the interpreter very far.

In the interpretation of Daniel's dream of the four beasts, the author refers to the beasts as "four kingdoms that **will rise from the earth**" (Dan. 7:17). While appearing very different, the second beast embodies the same evils of the first beast, exploiting all its authority toward political and institutional ends in order to establish an anti-Christian kingdom on earth. The second beast is not so much the "henchman of the first" (Morris, *Revelation*, p. 166) as the "Secretary of State" who implements or institutionalizes the dragon's evil vision. Perhaps this institutional capacity explains why this beast is later identified in more official language as the "false prophet" (16:13). It might be helpful to think of its prophetic ministry on behalf of the anti-Christian kingdom as analogous to the apostolic ministry for God's kingdom: its role is to champion the Evil One (cf. Jer. 20:11–12), to perform legitimizing signs on his behalf, and to establish the instruments and artifacts of worship in his name. John's larger point is the same as before: the very historical movements which produce the institutions of the social order have their champions and their "signs and wonders" to provide them with the appropriate credentials. They have their buildings and programs, perpetuated by those who value their self-centered enterprises most of all. Yet, insofar as these disciples place their version of institutional truth over God's gospel and their institutionalized values over God's reign, they promote idolatry. When the interests of any cultural institution seek to corrupt the single-minded devotion of the church to God's incarnate Word, the work of the anti-Christian kingdom, its beasts, and its dragon will have succeeded.

Much has been made of the description of the second beast: it has **two horns like a lamb**, appearing like the Lord Jesus, but has a satanic voice **like a dragon**. John's intent is not to associate this beast as a parody of Christ; rather, this beast, the false prophet, is an exemplar of those subtle forms of evil which deceive people into embracing lies as God's truth (cf. 13:14a). In this sense, the second beast parodies the Paraclete, who promotes the truth of God by drawing people to Christ (cf. John 14:16–27). If the task of the second beast is to lead people to the first beast, which parodies Christ (13:12), then the nature of the second beast's deceptions is to convince people that the falsehoods and fictions of secularism are viable substitutes for Christ Jesus, who incarnates what is true and real.

The contrast here between the beast's appearance and its actual words seems critical in this regard. Words give expression to the intentions and commitments of the speaker in a way that mere appearances can not; appearances can deceive the one given over to facile judgments. John may well be exhorting his readers to probe more deeply, to listen more carefully to what is said. What appears to have power or to give hope and meaning for human existence, whether embodied in Rome or promoted by the false teachers within the church, is exposed by the gospel as false and powerless for salvation. John's point is this: when the believer listens intently to the "word of God and the testimony of Jesus Christ," now conveyed through the Paraclete in Christ's absence, the false claims of Rome or of Jezebel are distinctly heard as belonging to the Evil One.

13:12-15 / The second beast's role in the anti-Christian kingdom of the Evil One, then, is analogous to the role of the Holy Spirit under God's rule. The dualism of John's view of reality is made all the more clear by his parody of the Holy Trinity: not only are there two kingdoms but two trinities—one for good and the other for evil.

But there is another sense in which the authority of the second beast is similar in significance to the authoritative teaching of Christ's first apostles. Especially according to Luke's Acts, apostolic authority is justified by three basic credentials, each alluded to in Revelation 13:12-13: (1) the apostles were successors of the Risen Christ in both ministry and authority (cf. Acts 1:1-11; Rev. 13:12a); (2) their preaching had authority in that it was centered on the resurrection of Jesus to which they were witnesses (cf. Acts 2:22-36; Rev. 13:12b); and (3) they did miraculous "signs and wonders" (cf. Acts 2:14-21; 5:12; 15:4, 12; Rev. 13:13) as concrete manifestations of God's reign. These apostolic credentials, which legitimize their witness to and proclamation of the Risen Christ, parallel those attributed to the second beast, whose power and influence was to extend the authority of the first beast, the parody of Christ.

Our point in making this observation is this: the "false prophet" may be not an outsider to Christian faith but an insider, a "false apostle" (cf. 2 Pet. 2:1–3; Mark 13:22; 2 Thess. 2:9). The most subtle secularism is the one promoted by those charged with the spiritual care of a congregation of believers, when the proclamation of the Christian gospel takes its primary cues from the surrounding social order rather than from "the word of God and the testimony of Jesus Christ." What is actually proclaimed by the false apostle, like the false prophets in the congregations of the former Israel, is spiritually corrupting and ultimately forms a life and faith that opposes the reign of God. It is in this sense that the **great and miraculous signs** are used to establish idolatry (cf. Deut. 13:1) that finally deceives rather than converts **the inhabitants of the earth**.

13:16–17a / The meaning of the **mark on** the **right hand or on** the **forehead** is contested (cf. Morris, *Revelation*, p. 168); however, in the immediate context it is analogous to the "seal" of the Lamb, marked on the foreheads of the faithful remnant (cf. 14:1–2): that is, it is a symbol of ownership or allegiance to someone in authority. The universal scope of the anti-Christian kingdom on earth is indicated by the coupling of society's opposites—**small and great, rich and poor, free and slave**—signifying **everyone**; and the nature of their devotion to evil is pervasive, touching even upon basic economic realities, **so that no one could buy or sell unless he had the mark** of the beast.

Thus, the "seal" of the Evil One secures one's place within the anti-Christian kingdom, including temporal, material well-being. At the same time, however, the "mark of the beast" brands one as an opponent of God's kingdom and as destined for eternal judgment. Not only does this sort of dualism, a feature of apocalypticism, make starkly clear the trade-offs one is faced with in everyday existence, it underscores the implicit relationship between daily choices made and allegiances held. Actual choices reflect real commitments; and decisions made in resignation and even with regret to ensure one's immediate, material well-being may well result in consequences of a tragic kind.

13:17b–18 / The **mark** is **the number of the beast** (which is **666**), and this number **is a man's number**. The **wisdom** that ciphers a name from a number would have presumed two things:

(1) numerical equivalents for letters (using an ancient method of biblical interpretation called *Gematria*); and (2) that such equivalences have magical or prophetic importance. Such wisdom was a common feature of the mystical tradition found within both Judaism and the paganism of John's day. Most scholars contend that John includes this element of his vision of the beasts in his composition because he felt his readers would be able to figure out the identity of the evil man. Countless speculations since have tried to calculate the number as a man's name, only to fail the test of common sense. Most of the best interpretations contend that the number **666** refers to the man, Nero Caesar. This equation is problematical because while the letters of Nero's name equal **666** in Hebrew they do not add up in Greek, the language of John's audience (and of Revelation).

Other scholars argue that John intends the number to function as a cryptogram and not as a puzzle to be interpreted by the procedures of *Gematria*. According to this view, the cryptographic **666** falls short of the number 777, which symbolizes divine perfection, and 888, which symbolizes Christ (since 888 is Christ's numerical equivalent). If this view stands, then **666** would symbolize the fundamental difference between falsehood, embodied in the beast, and truth, embodied in the exalted Lamb (cf. Beasley-Murray, *Revelation*, pp. 220–21).

The problem with this interpretation is that it seems to dismiss John's own interest in a specific individual, which he himself indicates with the shift from metaphor, **the number of the beast**, to the more literal, **for it is** a **man's number**. If John has the name of a certain man in mind, as the majority of scholars insist, then the only plausible "wisdom" derives from the computation of the number into a man's name by using the Hebrew rather than the Greek alphabet. (Even though most in John's audience did not know Hebrew, some no doubt did and could have explained the mystery to others. More importantly, John knew Hebrew and no doubt understood the significance of this number in his vision by Hebrew consonants rather than by Greek letters.)

Thus, we return to the consensus and agree that the only plausible name is that of "Caesar Nero." The Hebrew consonants used in spelling Nero's name, attested in an ancient document from Murabet, are *nron qsr*. The sum of each consonant's numerical equivalent (nun = 50 + resh = 200 + waw = 6 + nun

= 50 + qoph = 100 + samekh = 60 + resh = 200) is **666**. Nero is the man in John's mind.

While John and his first readers identified the evil beast with the evil Caesar, from a canonical perspective, John's Nero is the ongoing model for all of history's "Caesars" who rule over the anti-Christian kingdom and who repress the commitments and values of God's kingdom. The **wisdom** required of current readers of Revelation is to recognize the false prophets and apostles who promote humanism as the way to eternal life; such is the politics of deception, and it is the fool who is deceived by the idols of the anti-Christian kingdom.

Additional Notes §13

13:1b–2 / In my opinion, identifying the first beast with a particular "antichrist"—whether a particular Roman ruler (Schüssler Fiorenza, *Revelation*, p. 117) or some future world ruler (Morris, *Revelation*, p. 160)—is too restricting. The beast is symbolic of those ruling elite in every age who promote the sociopolitical program of the Evil One. Therefore, while John does have a particular "man" in mind, Nero (13:18; see below), when writing of the beast, he is rather the embodiment of other "beasts" who rule over the anti-Christian kingdom and its citizens.

13:10 / The NIV agrees with textual scholars by preferring the more ancient reading of *apoktanthēnai* (aorist, pass. inf.), **to be killed**, to the Majority text's *apoktenei* (fut., act., ind.), "will kill." This decision is important in this instance. If the interpreter follows the Majority text (e.g., RSV), then the passage is taken as a warning not to resort to violence to defend the church, which will only result in more violence: "if any kills by the sword, then with the sword will he also be killed." The purpose of the warning is to encourage dependency upon God's eschatological vengeance (Rom. 12:19; cf. Caird, *Revelation*, p. 170). If the translator follows the scholarly consensus (e.g., NIV), then the passage is taken as an exhortation to remain faithful even though some are destined to die as martyrs: "those who are to be killed, be killed because of your faithfulness." This same exhortation is found elsewhere in the NT (cf. 1 Pet. 3:13–17). And, in the context of Revelation, martyrs are exalted and enjoy their own eschatological rewards. For these reasons, the critical text (and the NIV) is to be preferred.

13:18 / Two more recent solutions to the puzzle of **the number of the beast** are M. Oberweis, "Die Bedeutung der neutestamentlichen 'Ratselzahlen' 666 (Apk. 13:18) und 153 (Joh 21:11)," *ZNW* 77 (1986), pp.

226–41; and M. Topham, "Hanniqolaites," *ExpT* 98 (1986), pp. 44–45. Oberweis argues that the number alludes to the fulfillment of Amos 6:1, while Topham suggests that the number has the ringleader of the troublesome Nicolaitan sect (cf. Rev. 2:6, 15) in mind. The text itself makes both views impossible to sustain. For a fine treatment of the traditional solution that John had Nero in mind, see Krodel's fine summary, *Revelation*, pp. 257–59.

§14 The Eschatological Outcomes of the Conflict: The Vindication of the Faithful (Rev. 14:1–5)

The trinity of evil ones has now been introduced as the enemy of the saints on earth (12:13–13:18). They are given the authority to overcome them (13:7) and to seduce the rest of the world into worshiping the Evil One rather than God (13:16–17). Chapter 13 concludes with a resounding note of secularism's triumph: the worldwide kingdom of the Evil One is firmly established within human history. This remains the current status of the battle between God and the Evil One on earth. Ironically, even as Christ's exaltation begins a period of escalation in humanity's conflict with evil, so also does it disclose the outcome of this battle, which has already been decided in God's favor. The doxologies of the heavenly chorus have declared it, and the dragon's banishment from God's heavenly throne room has certified it. To repeat, John's entire composition is concentrated by the central conviction of the "eternal gospel" (14:6): God's reign has triumphed over the corrupting forces of evil.

This explains why John so quickly turns from his vision of global conversion to the anti-Christian kingdom to one that envisions God's triumph over its evil powers and principalities. In this new vision of the final outcome of the war on earth between the dragon's beasts and God's people, the promised outcomes of salvation and judgment, already fulfilled in heaven, will be finally realized on earth.

This claim would not surprise John's audience. According to their cosmology, shaped by Platonic thought, what happens in heaven determines what happens on earth. In this sense, the future period of salvation's history has already been determined by what has already transpired in the heavenly realm: the "eternal gospel" is not that God will triumph at some point in the indefinite future; but that God has *already* triumphed through the Risen Christ in the definite past. This hope for God's certain but future triumph must qualify the present situation on earth where evil is temporarily in charge. The evils of the current social order, and the oppression and suffering they produce in human life, are now understood by the empty tomb and endured by God's people as manifestations of a defeated reign, destined for destruction at the end of the age.

14:1–3 / It is in light of this foundational theological conviction that the reader comes now to one of the most important passages in John's book of visions. The importance of this vision for understanding John's message is surprising, since Mounce has correctly summarized the consensus of biblical scholarship which characterizes this passage as "the most enigmatic in the book" (*Revelation*, p. 266). Two of its elements, however, seem clearly significant. First, John uses images that contrast to the previous description of the beast's followers (13:5–18) and their eschatological destiny (14:8–11). The function of this contrast, which continues the contrast between the Lamb and the beast, is to help the reader interpret the "eternal gospel." It will soon be announced by the first of three angels (14:6–7) in contrast to the oppressive and idolatrous Babylon whose destruction is announced by a second angel (14:8). The true Israel, which is established by faith in the claims of the eternal gospel, represents an alternative to Babylon and will ultimately endure. Babylon and those who worship the beast will be destroyed by God (14:8–11). In the light of this contrast, then, the tacit (and logical) imperative is made clear: **follow the Lamb wherever he goes** (14:4). Viewed from the perspective of its contrasting images, this passage focuses John's account of Christian discipleship that is worked out within an historical situation of human suffering and abundant evil.

Second, the literary structure of this passage is carefully crafted to develop the theme of Christian discipleship: John first describes what he sees and hears (14:1–3) and then interprets his vision for his audience (14:4–5). Every single item of John's account of his vision is a deliberate contrast to what he has just described as the reign of evil in chapter 13: the oppression has been exchanged for liberation, evil for good, suffering for celebration. John's explanation of his vision, then, establishes the conditions for the eschatological reversal of history's painful circumstances. By utilizing contrasting images, John invites the rhetorical question—for whom is this experience of liberation a reality?—

and its requisite answer: the remnant of faithful disciples who resist the various seductions of Babylon and follow the Lamb wherever he goes!

The leading actors in this drama are already familiar to the reader. John has introduced the exalted **Lamb** in chapter 5. He is the worthy one whose exaltation has disclosed God's victory over evil (cf. 5:1–8); and he is the Paschal Lamb whose death has purchased a people for God in order that they might co-rule on a new earth and co-serve God's redemptive interests forever (cf. 5:9–10). John has also introduced this kingdom of priests in chapter 7 as the **144,000 who had** the Lamb's **name and his Father's name written on their foreheads** (cf. 7:3–4).

It is fitting that John sees them **standing on Mount Zion**. In the OT, **Mount Zion** refers to the location where God's promise of Israel's restoration is fulfilled; for John, then, it is a place of profound eschatological significance (cf. Ladd, *Revelation*, p. 189). John uses this geographical reference as a theological idiom, similar to the writer of Hebrews who speaks of Mount Zion first in non-historical and transcendent ways (Heb. 11:10; 12:22) and then as the place where God's eternal kingdom is located on earth (Heb. 12:25–28; cf. Isa. 24:21–23). Especially given the predictive nature of John's composition (cf. 1:3), his use of **Mount Zion** probably refers here to the historical and eschatological (rather than a spiritual and existential) fulfillment of God's promised restoration of the true Israel (Schüssler Fiorenza, *Revelation*, p. 186).

Rather than having the number/name of the beast, branded on their right hand and forehead, the **144,000 . . . had** the Lamb's **name and his Father's name written on their foreheads**. The two names identify the faithful remnant as belonging to God's reign, which the Lord shares with his Father (cf. 3:12; 5:13; 11:15; however, cf. 22:4). The beast's blasphemous and slanderous words (13:6) are in contrast to the lyrics John hears sung by the 144,000 (cf. 15:2–4). The images of **rushing waters** and **harpists playing the harps**, which accompany the heavenly voices, suggest soothing and melodious words of divine praise.

John identifies their lyrics as belonging to **a new song** that the redeemed chorus sings **before the throne** of God. If we understand that the words of this **new song** are in continuity with those of the earlier "new song" found in 5:9–10, as well as with the remnant's subsequent songs of "Moses and the Lamb" found in

15:3–4, then this particular eschatological hymn also celebrates God's deliverance of the faithful Israel from its evil enemy. Only those who have been purchased for God by the slain Lamb **could learn the song**. Their capacity stems from being **redeemed from the earth** and establishes a final and most critical contrast with 13:7a, which told of the beast's triumph over the saints on earth. The song and its **loud** volume expose the beast's victory over the saints as short-lived; those martyrs killed by the Evil One are destined for Mount Zion.

14:4–5 / In giving meaning to his description of the heavenly scene, John is concerned only to identify the 144,000. He does so with three statements, each a commentary on the conditions of Christian discipleship and the current crisis facing the people of God. The first statement casts the faithful remnant as a community of **pure** constituents: they are those **who did not defile themselves with women**. The interpreter must initially resolve two interrelated exegetical problems: what is (1) the meaning of **pure**, which normally refers to sexual virginity; and (2) the identity of the **women**, whether John's intent is misogynistic. The kind of asceticism that asserts that abstinence from sexual relations is the evidence of Christian devotion argues against NT teaching (cf. 1 Cor. 7:1–7) and is nowhere indicated in either Revelation or the larger Johannine tradition. It is better to view the community's sexual chastity as metaphorical of its "pure" (or sanctified) relationship with God. This conclusion is consistent with OT rhetoric which often compares the faithfulness or unfaithfulness of Israel to sexual fidelity or infidelity (e.g., Jer. 18:13; Hos. 5:4). To keep **pure**, then, is to resist those evils which undermine the community's covenantal relationship with God.

In line with this conclusion, the **women** symbolize opposition to God (Schüssler Fiorenza, *Revelation*, pp. 190–91). To view them literally would require us to think of the church as exclusively male and of celibacy as a condition for Christian discipleship. The interpreter can more precisely equate the **women** to the evil women of Revelation: the false prophetess, Jezebel, who misleads immature believers in the congregation at Thyatira into sexual immorality (i.e., spiritual infidelity) and idolatry (2:20); and the great prostitute of Babylon (17:1), who intoxicates the inhabitants of earth with the "wine of her adulteries" (17:2). Together, they symbolize the moral and theological evils, found inside and outside the church, that seduce unfaithful believers from the way of the Lamb.

In light of these preliminary conclusions, the first condition of faithful discipleship is to resist beliefs and behaviors that corrupt the community's devotion to God. Schüssler Fiorenza is right in saying that the expression points to "the cultic purity of the Lamb's followers" as well as to their holiness (cf. 21:9–11), which bears concrete witness to the character of God's reign (*Revelation*, p. 190).

The second condition stipulates that **they follow** (*akoloutheō*) **the Lamb wherever he goes**. This is the only appeal to "formal" discipleship terminology found outside of the Gospels and Acts in the NT. For this reason alone, John's phrase is a focus of our attention since it offers up another element for a normative (i.e., biblical) definition of Christian discipleship. According to John, Christian discipleship requires more than cultic purity; it requires a consistent and pervasively faithful walk along the way pioneered by the teaching of the exalted Christ (cf. Heb. 12:2), now conveyed through his Spirit (cf. John 14:26).

The final statement speaks less of the believers "sacrificial offering of themselves to God" (Mounce, *Revelation*, pp. 270–71) and more of God's partnership with the believers as they walk on the Lamb's way. The verbal idea is passive (**were purchased**), suggesting that it is God who extracts the faithful church from out of the marketplace of evil Babylon and sets it on the path to God's shalom as **firstfruits to God and the Lamb** (cf. Jer. 2:3; Ladd, *Revelation*, p. 192). God's salvation is the experience of a covenantal people, who live and worship in a relationship of shared responsibility. Faithful disciples of the sort who make up the 144,000 are untainted by the lies and fictions of secularism and materialism, and they are **blameless** and therefore acceptable to God. However, their eschatological fitness is not only the result of their faithful response to God and God's Lamb; their faithfulness is a real possibility because of God's empowering and enabling grace. From this pastoral perspective, then, John's Revelation is written in order to respond to the fundamental concern of Christian formation: what does it mean to follow the Lamb wherever he goes?

Additional Notes §14

Boring says that while chapters 12–13 were descriptive of the period of tribulation present when John wrote Revelation, chapters 14–16 are predictive of how things "finally will be" (Boring, *Revelation*, p. 168).

14:1–5 / We agree with Schüssler Fiorenza that this text underscores the fundamental decision facing John's audience: "either to worship the anti-divine powers embodied by Rome and to become 'followers' of the beast or to worship God and to become 'companions' of the Lamb on Mt. Zion" (*Revelation*, p. 181).

14:1 / Ford points out that biblical references to **Mount Zion** are usually tied to a "Warrior-God" (cf. Jer. 25:30; Ezek. 43:1–9). Some Jews reinterpreted this in accord with their expectation of a political messiah, whose reign and power over the nations will be established there (*Revelation*, p. 240). If this is so, perhaps John uses **Mount Zion** in an ironical way, for it is not a warrior-like Messiah who receives the scepter of power from God, but a slain Lamb.

14:4 / Ford shows in some detail that the OT and intertestamental references to celibacy are not gender specific and most often have a "religious" and not sexual idea in mind (*Revelation*, pp. 242–44). Schüssler Fiorenza joins Ford's argument, objecting to the assumption held by some that the "followers of the Lamb are a class of exclusively male ascetics" (*Revelation*, p. 190).

§15   The Eschatological Outcomes of the Conflict: The Judgment of the Faithless (Rev. 14:6–20)

14:6–7 / The function of angels throughout Revelation is to facilitate God's redemptive program; this is the role, then, of **another angel** that John saw **flying in midair** (cf. 8:13; 19:17). In particular, this first of a triad of angels proclaims **the eternal gospel . . . to those who live on the earth**. John uses the technical word for **gospel** only here in Revelation; its use is made more striking since the angel intends it for the lost inhabitants of **earth** rather than for the saints who have trusted its claims and have been redeemed from the earth. More specifically, the audience for this angelic proclamation of "good news" are those on earth who worship the beast (cf. 13:8); they are the enemies of God. This surprising point is further sharpened by John who distinguishes the 144,000, "who have been redeemed *from the earth*" (14:3; *apo tēs gēs*), from these unredeemed who dwell **on the earth** (*epi tēs gēs*).

The question forced by the seer at this point is this: how can the **eternal gospel** be "good news" for God's enemies? Our response to this important question is threefold. First, the eternality of the gospel reminds the reader that its content is theocentric; it is rooted in the truth of the eternal God, "who was, and is, and is to come" (4:8). This point is underscored if, as Ford and others contend, Rome's imperial cultus and its Caesar worship lie behind John's use of the term (*Revelation*, p. 247). While neither the Roman Empire nor its Caesar have eternality, God has created all things and all things have their being in their Lord (cf. 4:11). Every creature, redeemed or unredeemed, is made in God's image and for God's purposes; logically, even the unredeemed creature must finally admit that the evil intentions of the anti-Christian kingdom are ultimately against humanity's well-being. In this sense, the **eternal gospel** heralds what every creature must acknowledge: the course of human history is undermined by the beast's evil intentions.

Second, these intentions not only corrupt human existence, they are "forced" upon everyone by the very structures of human society. While every creature is made in the image of the creator, the social order in which every creature lives has been re-made in the image of the Evil One (cf. 13:15–17). According to apocalypticism, human society corrupts human souls. From a sociological perspective, people tend to view themselves as powerless in the face of the beast's corrosive and coercive powers. Simply to survive, they find it necessary to enlist in the beast's war against the saints. Thus, for those lost, trapped, and held powerless by the anti-Christian elite, the gospel issues a liberating word and an opportunity to escape the very evils that war against humanity's well-being. God's "first" word is always a redeeming one.

Third, not only is the gospel a liberating word from God, it is an inclusive word as well. In light of the "new song" just sung (cf. 14:3), the reader is reminded that God's redemption is for everyone from "every tribe and language and people and nation" (5:9). It is apropos that the first angel proclaims God's good news **to every nation, tribe, language and people** because they are the very ones who are redeemed from evil for God by the blood of the slain Lamb.

The proper response to the **eternal gospel** is to **fear God . . . give** God **glory . . .** and **worship** God. The call to repentance is not made in a vacuum; it is issued in the light of God's vindication of the exalted Christ. Further, it is issued in the confidence that the positive yield of responding to the gospel is salvation from those evils that undermine the creator's good intentions for all creation. The **worship** of God, to whom **glory** is given rather than to the beast (cf. 13:8, 15; cf. Rom. 1:18–23), is "the fruit in keeping with repentance." Repentance envisions an eschatological decision simply because it recognizes that eternal life is granted to those who believe, and wrath to those who do not (cf. John 3:16–21; Rom. 1:16–32).

14:8 / **A second angel** continues the evangelical message of the first with another element of the "word of God." The position and repetition of the aorist verb, **fallen**, place keen emphasis on the certain and complete destruction of **Babylon the Great**—the center of the Evil One's earthly power. This is the first mention of **Babylon** in Revelation, here echoing Isaiah's oracle of the city's eventual destruction and the discrediting of its false religions (cf. Isa. 21:8–10). Yet, the prophet's prediction was focused not by the fall of Babylon but by the restoration of God's exiled people which would be signaled by the demise of their oppressors (cf. Jer. 51:6–10). John has not altered the theological intention of the OT prophets: God's gospel announces not only the end of evil's reign, but the renewal of Israel's worship of God through the exalted Christ (cf. Jer. 51:11).

The difficult phrase, **all the nations drink the maddening wine of** Babylon's **adulteries**, has been variously understood by Revelation's commentators. All agree that the phrase in some way explains why Babylon will fail; what is not as clear is the relationship between the **wine of** Babylon's **adulteries** (cf. 17:2) and the "wine of God's fury" which brings the city to its knees (14:10).

The NIV does not help matters by translating the Greek noun, *thymos*, as an adjective, **maddening**, obscuring its natural meaning, "anger," and its more substantive function within the sentence. Indeed, the weight of this phrase falls upon *thymos* which links together **wine** and **adulteries**. We would argue that *thymos* describes the oppressive effect of Babylon's bullying (**Babylon . . . made all the nations drink**) and therefore the liberating effect of the eternal gospel for all those who believe. Freedom from the dragon's anger (12:12), now mediated through the two beasts within the city, is freedom from its sociopolitical oppression of all those who live on the margins of Babylon (cf. James 5:6). For John, it simply is illogical for any person to make a *free* choice to follow the Evil One; it contradicts human experience of the dragon's corrupting influence and the abiding truth of the eternal gospel. Those who belong to the beast, therefore, do so because of its coercive power, resulting in idolatry for want of material survival (cf. 13:17). The prophetic vision of God's shalom includes a reversal in the economic conditions of the poor because to redeem one from grinding poverty is to set one free from the necessity to submit to the very social structures that impoverish.

14:9–11 / The **third angel** speaks with **a loud voice**, suggesting that its words mark the end of a series of announcements that grow in intensity as well as in volume (Beasley-Murray, *Revelation*, p. 227). The three messages taken together envision the "liberating logic" of divine grace: the first proclaims the gospel to everyone on earth; the second announces the defeat of the evil reign with its furious opposition to the goodness of God; and now the third clarifies the harsh consequences of rejecting the gospel: the one who rejects the eternal gospel that liberates from the dragon's fury **will drink of the wine of God's fury** (i.e., of God's *thymos*). This message of God's wrath, the "dark side" of divine righteousness, is another element of the eternal gospel.

The measure of **God's fury** is subsequently described in horrific terms: those who **worship the beast** will **be tormented with burning sulfur . . . and the smoke of their torment rises for ever and ever**, without any experience of God's heavenly **rest** from their trials (14:13; cf. Heb. 4:1–13). More than an objective description of God's future punishment of unbelievers, these violent images symbolize the absence of God's eternal shalom that belongs to those "redeemed from the earth." For John, the consequences of embracing or rejecting the eternal gospel are eternal; for him, the vivid images of his vision intend to call those "who live on the earth" to repentance and into God's grace and peace.

John's "aside," which asserts that the unbelievers' torment will take place **in the presence of the holy angels and the Lamb**, is not an element of John's vindication motif. The torment of the people who followed the beast does not bring satisfaction or some sort of demented delight to the angels and the Lamb. Rather, the phrase seems to insist on the certainty of God's punishment of evil because of the satisfactory completion of the Lamb's ministry and because of the ongoing presence of the holy angels who enforce God's judgments.

14:12–13 / John reflects back on his vision of the three angels and offers a twofold commentary on its implications for Christian discipleship, especially in light of his vision of the 144,000. The first part of his commentary is for those who still live in Babylon and who **obey God's commandments and remain faithful to Jesus**: their call is for **patient endurance**. According to Revelation, the singular identity of the **saints** on earth is to walk "wherever the Lamb goes" (14:4)—since the historical **Jesus** was utterly **faithful** to **God's commandments** (cf. 1 John 2:3–6). This devotion is of course challenged by the dragon's fury; and the language of **patient endurance** implies temporary hardship and heartache. It also implies the condition of God's eschatological salvation: while the disciple's devotion to Jesus is constantly challenged by the experience of social injustice and human suffering, it is required from all who hope to participate in God's final triumph over the dragon (cf. Matt. 24:13; James 1:12).

This eschatological condition frames the following promise of eschatological blessing that John is commissioned to **write**: **"Blessed are the dead who die in the Lord from now on."** The beatitude and the Spirit's subsequent confirmation form together the second half of John's interpretation of the eternal gospel, which is proclaimed by the triad of angels. The relationship of verse 13 to verse 12 is clear: "faithfulness to Christ issues in martyrdom, but the faithful dead are blessed in that they have entered victoriously into their rest" (Mounce, *Revelation*, p. 277).

The exact meaning of **from now on** is debated. Most insist that John intends a logical (rather than temporal) transition from the beatitude's promise of future blessing to the Spirit's promise of heavenly **rest**. Thus, the saints who remain faithful unto martyrdom can expect entrance into heavenly bliss. We prefer, however, to understand the phrase in a more time-specific fashion. In this instance, John is writing for those believers who face the growing prospect of martyrdom; salvation's history has kicked into a new period of intensified suffering immediately after the Evil One has been defeated by God and banished from heaven to earth. This is the **now** to which John refers. And those saints in his audience, who will be martyred during this period of increased tribulation, can expect special blessing from God, for **their deeds** (i.e., martyrdom) will follow them into heaven.

14:14 / Caird argues that this section of John's vision functions ironically, so that traditional, apocalyptic images of divine retribution are imaginatively transformed into a portrait of God's salvation of the church's martyrs (cf. *Revelation*, pp. 189–95). While one may disagree with aspects of Caird's treatment, he has correctly called our attention to the language of salvation embedded in John's description of "the great winepress of God's wrath." In this sense, John's vision continues the angelic proclamation of the eternal gospel. He constantly keeps the concluding events of salvation's history before the reader by recycling the judgment motif; accordingly, emphasis is properly placed on God's coming triumph over an already defeated foe.

The vision of three additional angels begins when John again sees **one "like a son of man,"** whom he earlier identified as the exalted Christ (cf. 1:13; Dan. 7:13). This identification is confirmed by the additional metaphors of **cloud** (cf. Acts 1:9–11) and **crown**, both of which refer of Christ's exalted status in heaven (cf. Rev. 5:13). In context, the presence of the exalted Christ confirms the truth of the eternal gospel and the importance of the triad of messages brought by the angels. John does sound a harsher note by placing **a sharp sickle in** Christ's **hand**—an OT image that symbolizes God's judgment of the unrighteous (cf. Isa. 63:3). According to Revelation, the "good news" of God's salvation includes two interrelated messages: one of the prospects for God's glorious transformation of creation, which follows God's abolition of evil and death from creation.

14:15–16 / If the one **who was sitting on the cloud** is the exalted Christ, it may strike some as strange, even presumptuous, that an angel should make a demand of him: **take your sickle and reap**. Yet, this angel **came out of the temple** where God dwells (cf. 7:15; Dan. 7:14b) with a message that **the time to reap has come**. It is God and not God's angel who makes the demand. Moreover, the message it carries from God seems fitting since the Risen Jesus had taught his apostles that knowledge about the timing of salvation's history belongs only to God (cf. Acts 1:7).

We are not told about the people who are ready for harvesting. On the one hand, the image of a **sickle** commends the interpretation that John has God's judgment of unbelievers in view; on the other hand, the image of the **harvest** is used by Jesus of gathering believers into God's kingdom (cf. John 4:35–38). Both in the OT and in rabbinical teaching, however, the harvest also refers to the gathering of unbelievers for judgment.

We have little doubt that John understood his vision of the eschatological harvest in terms of Joel 3:13, where the images depict God's eschatological war against the nations. When this war is coupled with the identification of the one **who was seated on the cloud** as a kingly "son of man" from Daniel's dream, the interpreter understands the intent of the angel's demand of the exalted Christ is to clarify God's ultimate verdict against those who have rejected the gospel—a verdict disclosed at the "coming of the Son of Man" of Gospel tradition. Also, the brevity of verse 16 has the rhetorical effect of underscoring the certainty of this conclusion to the cosmic struggle between God and the Evil One.

14:17 / There appears **another angel**, who also **came out of the temple in heaven . . .** with **a sharp sickle** (cf. 14:14). Its harvest, presumably ordained by God since it came from God's presence, will be the grapes from earth's vine, ripe for the "winepress of God's wrath." These are metaphors for God's crushing defeat of the anti-Christian kingdom. Because they repeat the images of the previous vision, they emphasize the imminence of God's coming victory over evil, which can only engender hope among the suffering saints. For them, this vision is good news because it implies the conclusion of suffering and the beginning of shalom.

14:18–20 / The final angelic messenger, **who . . . came from the altar** of God (cf. 8:3–5; 6:9), issues God's instructions to its angelic colleague to "gather the clusters of grapes" **from the earth's vine**. Although we do not know why John adds that this angel **had charge of the fire**, he perhaps uses yet another symbol for divine judgment for emphasis (cf. 2 Thess. 1:7; John 15:6). Or John may be alluding to the Gospel tradition where unbelievers on **the earth's vine** who are gathered for judgment are contrasted with faithful disciples on Christ's "vine" who are gathered for eternal life (John 15:5–8; cf. Matt. 13:24–30). Another purpose of this contrast is to interpret divine judgment as the vindication of the exalted Lamb (who is the "true vine," John 15:1) and the vilification of Satan and his Babylon.

The vision ends with a blood bath, **rising as high as the horses' bridles for a distance of 1,600 stadia**. As a multiple of the number four, which is symbolic of the whole (i.e., four corners) world, this hyperbole symbolizes the global scope of God's judgment (cf. 7:1; 8:1). Beasley-Murray suggests that it should rather be understood as a multiple of forty, which symbolizes a traditional period of punishment for Jews (e.g., the wilderness, Num. 14:33; or Jesus' post-Easter sojourn, Acts 1:3; Beasley-Murray, *Revelation*, p. 230). This would be a more plausible explanation of the **1,600** if God's judgment were against the unfaithful within the believing community.

The location of the winepress **outside the city** is curious. John does not identify the city by name, whether Babylon or Jerusalem. The surrounding context makes it clear, however, that Babylon itself is not excluded from God's judgment. Thus, the consensus of scholarship recommends Jerusalem. Mounce suggests that the phrase alludes to Christ's death "outside the city gate" (Heb. 13:12) and envisions a theology of the cross by which every person is measured by God (*Revelation*, p. 282). But surely the focal point of the vision is the **blood** that **flowed out of the press** and not the Lamb. This **blood** is the "death-blood" of God's judgment and not the "life-blood" of God's Lamb. In fact, because the notion of "life-blood" is linked by tradition and scripture to Jerusalem's temple and specifically to its altar, the kind of **blood** that is shed **outside the city** of Jerusalem indicates death and judgment rather than life and salvation.

Additional Notes §15

14:6 / We disagree with Schüssler Fiorenza who views the **angel** as a herald of judgment rather than of glad tidings. For her, this angel proclaims a gospel of "God's judgment and justice to all the world" (*Revelation*, p. 181). Our exegesis of this passage recovers a God who desires that all people repent and come to redemption. To "fear God," is to fear the tragic consequences of rejecting the **eternal gospel** of a good God whose chief desire is that no one perish, and that everyone come to repentance.

14:8 / For the more literal meaning of **maddening**, see F. Büchsel, *thymos, TDNT*, vol. 3, pp. 167–68.

§16 The Third Sign in Heaven: Bowls of Eschatological Plagues Poured Out on Babylon (Rev. 15:1–16:16)

According to the apocalyptic view of history, the spiritual and societal conditions of human existence will continue to deteriorate, and there is nothing any sociopolitical institution can do to reverse them. Salvation comes from outside of history, from God's heavenly abode. In returning to the theme of divine judgment, already so vividly drawn in his visions of seven seals and trumpets, John is making this same point more keenly: salvation is from God and not from Babylon's rulers. John's is an imperialistic politic that champions the sovereign rule of God, and there is no room for compromise.

Perhaps this is why he begins this particular vision with echoes of the Exodus (cf. Boring, *Revelation*, p. 173): the bowls from which the wine of God's wrath is poured bear a "family resemblance" to the plagues of Egypt. In John's vision of the bowl-plagues, the true Israel stands protected by God on the other side of the Sea, made "Red" with fire. The remnant plays its harps rather than Miriam's tambourine; but nonetheless it sings the song of Moses like the victorious Israelites of old, while the beast and its worshipers—the visionary equivalents of Pharaoh and his evil Egypt (cf. Ezek. 29:3–6a)—lie broken in the wake of God's wrath. But it is the covenantal logic of the exodus event which controls any rehearsal of it, including here in John's vision. Especially in the prophetic uses of the tradition, the exodus typology reminds the people of God's faithfulness toward Israel and the Lord's sovereignty over evil. The prophet's intent was to solicit repentance and a renewal of faithfulness from Israel, to restore its relationship with God in expectation of God's promised blessing.

John's own situation is similar to the prophets; the crisis facing the church is analogous to the one that faced Israel. Thus, the "theo-logic" that makes sense of this vision is provided by the old story of Israel's exodus from Egypt. For John the plagues of Egypt are "re-visioned" as bowls of wrath. They are divine judgments of human evil, which demonstrate not only the sovereignty of God's rule but God's unconditional faithfulness to the promise to liberate and bless Israel. Yet, as the biblical setting of the exodus narrative makes clear, the terrifying reality is this: God's punishment of Egypt is indicative of what God's punishment of Israel will be if Israel fails to "pay attention to" God's commands and keep all "the Lord's decrees" (Exod. 15:26; Rev. 14:12). For those believers who wish to return to "Egypt" (or Babylon) and who are inclined to disregard God's "eternal gospel," John's vision of the bowl-plagues is also a warning to repent in order to escape a similar destiny.

15:1–2 / John sees **another . . . sign**, introducing the final celestial "sign" in a triadic sequence that began with the visions of the woman with child (12:1) and the great red dragon (12:3). As before, the seer locates the vision **in heaven**, even though it "points beyond itself and discloses the theological meaning of history" (Mounce, *Revelation*, p. 285). Even as the earlier two signs interpreted the human misery and historical ambiguity of the current period in terms of the conflict between the woman and the dragon, this third sign initiates the bowl-plagues through which the purposes of God for human history are **completed**.

John emphasizes that this third sign constitutes the **last** disclosure of **God's wrath** and, in our view, brings to conclusion the "third woe" mentioned earlier in Revelation (cf. 11:14). Since God has responded to evil in a consistent manner throughout salvation's history, the reader of Revelation assumes that the eschatological revelation of divine wrath will be similar to God's past response to Egypt's oppression of Israel, to Rome's oppression of the earliest church, and to every Babylon's oppression of each generation of God's people. *John views his vision as proleptic because the envisioned future is analogous to the enscriptured past*: the God who acted through Moses and who acted again through the exalted Lamb is the same God who will act yet again through the returning Lamb. Thus, the eschatological community can sing "the songs of Moses and the Lamb" together as two hymns with a theocentric focus of praise.

In sharp contrast to the vision of the seven bowl-plagues that follows, John describes the celebration of **those who had been**

victorious over the beast and his image (cf. 13:8). In our view, even though John does seem to have a special interest in the status of those believers who are killed for refusing to worship the beast (cf. 13:15), this community includes all who belong to the Lamb (cf. 14:4). Membership in the eschatological community does not require martyrdom, only fidelity.

15:3–4 / The phrase, **song of Moses . . . and the song of the Lamb**, prepares the reader for the hymn of praise which follows. Even though the hymn's content derives from the biblical psalter, John's reference to the **song of Moses** frames its theological importance. It is not immediately clear to the reader, however, to which version of Moses' song John refers—whether to Exodus 15 or Deuteronomy 32. Because of John's dependence upon the exodus typology, scholars have generally assumed that John has the Exodus version of the song in mind. Accordingly, the theology of this hymn is interpreted by Exodus 15: God is praised for the mighty act of Christ which once again has liberated the true Israel from their evil enemy.

However appropriate this consensus is for understanding the passage, three critical elements echo the Deuteronomist's song of Moses that may suggest John had the deuteronomistic version of the song in mind as well. First, the **great and marvelous** actions of God are called **just and true**—a phrase echoing the central theme of the deuteronomistic song (cf. Deut. 32:3–4). John's hymn, located at the conclusion of salvation's history, praises God for keeping the promise of Israel's redemption: a **just** God is **true** to the biblical promise of eschatological salvation, already hidden in the exodus event. Second, the Deuteronomist's song of Moses is set in a context of Israel's predicted unfaithfulness (cf. Deut. 31:14–29). God's own fidelity to the promise of Israel's ultimate salvation is unconditional. There will always be disparity between God's loyalty to the covenant with Israel and Israel's accommodations to pagan idolatries and immoralities. God's gracious salvation of Israel is all the more surprising, then, and even shocking given this disparity. Finally, John's hymn speaks of universal outcomes: **all nations will come and worship before you**. While the Exodus version of Moses' song also speaks of God's conquest of the nations, the setting of the song in Deuteronomy takes this one step beyond conquest (cf. Deut. 32:38) to the eschatological subjection of all nations to God (cf. Deut. 31:1–8;

32:44–33:29). This hope is repeated in John's hymn, which also looks ahead to a day when the fortunes of God's people will be reversed for the good and when the fortunes of the Lord's former enemies, now under God' curse, will be brought down. These apocalyptic themes of reversal and universal redemption, set in bold relief by the deuteronomistic song of Moses, express the extraordinary measure of God's beneficence about which the eschatological community praises in song.

15:5–8 / The agents of the devastating bowl-plagues are the **seven angels** who hold the **seven plagues** in **the temple**, where God commissions those sacred tasks which complete the promised salvation. John qualifies the importance of the temple as the site of the angelic commissioning with the appositional phrase, **the tabernacle of the Testimony**. This phrase would seem to suggest that John continues to use the Exodus narrative as a template to arrange the events of his vision. Accordingly, after crossing the Reed Sea, Israel received the Decalogue (Exod. 19–20) and preserved a copy in the ark of the covenant, which they then placed inside the **tabernacle of the Testimony** (Exod. 25–26). The two tablets of the Decalogue were a permanent reminder that God's relationship with Israel was covenantal and that Israel's ongoing history was the location where that relationship was worked out. From a covenantal perspective, Israel was obliged to respond to the gracious God of the exodus in obedience to God's Torah, written down on the two tablets (Exod. 24:8–12). All subsequent judgments by the prophets concerning Israel's fitness to receive divine blessing were based on its observance of Torah. Perhaps John has this OT pattern in mind: those who do not obey God's demand (cf. Rev. 14:12) and instead worship the beast (14:11) are justly condemned for the day of God's wrath. They have not met the covenantal obligation to honor their sovereign creator God (cf. Rom. 1:18–21).

Symbolic of their status as heavenly instruments of the creator's universal covenant with all creatures, the angels are dressed in priestly vestments—**in clean, shining linen and . . . golden sashes around their chests**. Rather than the mediation of covenantal blessing for the saints, their task will be the mediation of **the wrath of God** for those who reject God and follow the Evil One. God's destruction of the anti-Christian kingdom is not arbitrary; it is justified by divine revelation in creation, in Torah, and finally in Christ.

The **four living creatures** are also a part of John's vision. They had minor parts in John's earlier drama of the Lamb's coronation: they held the golden bowls containing the saints' prayers (5:8). The contrast between that drama and this one, where they again have custody of **seven golden bowls**, is implicit and important. In this vision, the bowls are **filled with the wrath of God** rather than the prayers of the saints as before, and the bowls are given to avenging angels rather than to the exalted Lamb. Yet, the presence of the **four living creatures**, who hold the **golden bowls** in both scenes, may well establish an integral whole: the bowl-plagues answer the prayers of the saints for God's vindication (cf. Rev. 8:3–5; Morris, *Revelation*, p. 185), which will make it possible for them to enter the promised land (15:1–4).

The final piece of noteworthy "furniture" in John's vision is the **smoke** that filled the temple. From his reading of the OT prophets, John recognizes its twofold significance. First, **smoke** symbolizes the shekinah **glory of God** (cf. Ezek. 44:4)—the demonstration of God's **power** to rule which is fully disclosed at the consummation of history (cf. Rev. 21). The presence of **smoke** is yet another visionary cue that the bowl-plagues mark the concluding chapter in the story of God's wrath (cf. 15:1).

This point is underscored in John's second observation concerning the **smoke**: it had made the only entrance into the temple impassable **until the seven plagues of the seven angels were completed**. The establishment of God's glory in the new Jerusalem will follow the destruction of the old order. By locating the commissioning of these terrible plagues in the temple, amidst this furniture of heavenly doxology, John makes a significant statement about the purpose of divine retribution. Superficial criticism of a "just and true" God, whose harsh retribution against the nations seems a contradiction in character, fails to understand that God's overarching intention is redemptive. God's judgment of a fallen world is a means to restoring a lasting covenant between creator and creation.

16:1 / Scholars have long pointed out the similarities between the first six trumpet judgments (Rev. 8:6–9:21) and the first six bowl judgments (16:1–14; cf. Beasley-Murray, *Revelation*, pp. 238–39); and we have called attention to the "hailstorm" that links the seventh trumpet to the seventh bowl. In one sense, John's vision of bowl-plagues repeats and emphasizes the previous point: divine judgment intends to bring the nations to repent and to confess God as sovereign creator and ruling Lord. Their refusal to repent, then, justifies God's condemnation of them and their anti-Christian kingdom. There is another sense, however, that John's newest vision expands and deepens the significance of this theme. On the face of it, the bowl judgments extend the scope of God's wrath. Earlier only a "third" of the created order was affected; in this vision, however, the bowls of God's wrath are poured out onto the entire earth and its unbelieving population. In fact, unlike before when the martyrs experienced a portion of God's judgment of the world order, the bowl-plagues are more discriminating and "pass over" the believing community. These differences suggest a spiral of severity, finally reaching its climax with the collapse of the world order. This is not to say that the bowl-plagues follow the completion of the trumpet-plagues according to some chronological scheme. But they do denote together a particular theological conviction that John now views through his apocalyptic lens from a different "moment" of salvation's history. The exaltation of Christ began a period of increased tribulation, envisioned by the trumpet-plagues, that will intensify in severity until the complete collapse of the fallen creation eventuates, envisioned by the bowl-plagues. The inevitability of complete chaos and the utter inability of any social institution to do anything about it points to the ultimate hope of Christ's return, when he comes from outside of history in order to transform history. Against this field of vision, then, the bowl judgments represent the conclusion of the "third woe" (cf. 11:14), the demise of evil dominion, and the preparation for the new social order characterized by God's shalom and grace.

We also find here a second prophetic typology, this one of Job, employed by John to help focus his "meta-theological" concern: why does a good God pave the path to salvation with violence and vengeance, chaos and collapse? The plague of "ugly and painful sores" poured from the first bowl on those who "had the mark of the beast" is of decisive importance for establishing a proper context for understanding the totality of the bowl judgments. And its general importance for John's vision is determined in turn by its particular allusions to the OT story of Job.

The allusive link between the two is unmistakable. (1) In both cases, the plague is "ugly and painful sores" (cf. Job 2:1–

10). (2) The purpose of the plague is similar in both cases: both plagues provoke actual responses to God which are useful in measuring humanity's relationship with God. Thus, even Job's plague is unjustly demanded by Satan as a test of Job's fidelity. John employs the same image to depict the just consequence (Rev. 16:5–7) of a response quite the opposite of Job's. Whereas Job glorified God, the world "refused to repent and glorify" God (Rev. 16:9). In that John seems to assume the logical relationship between repentance and plagues, this contrast between the two stories is vital to his theological purpose. What explains the opposite responses to God is that Job is a prophetic exemplar of true piety (cf. James 5:10–11); he glorifies God, even though plagued by horrific sores, because he enjoys a right relationship with God. The world, on the other hand, remains obdurate; it refuses to glorify God because it does not have a relationship with the Lord.

By employing the Job typology, John continues to address the problem of theodicy—a problem which comes to its climax in this vision of bowl-plagues (cf. Beasley-Murray, *Revelation*, pp. 239–41). Human misery actually occasions a test of faith in God, where one's relationship with God is clarified. In the case of Job, whose faith in God is firm, the response is to glorify God. In the case of "people who had the mark of the beast," who "cursed the name of God," the response is to refuse "to repent and glorify" God. Here, then, is John's solution to the problem of theodicy: divine judgment is just when viewed in terms of humanity's response to it, for only in humanity's misery is the true nature of their relationship with God concretely disclosed (cf. 1 Pet. 1:3–12).

The vision returns John to the heavenly **temple** and to the **seven angels** he had met earlier in the vision (cf. 15:1). Again he hears an unidentified **loud voice**, presumably the Lord's (cf. Isa. 66:6), which instructs the angels to **pour out the seven bowls of God's wrath on the earth** (cf. 14:10).

16:2–4 / The first three bowl plagues parallel the natural calamities that issued earlier from the blasts of the first three trumpets and echo certain Egyptian plagues of the exodus tradition. The difference is that this cycle of plagues attacks **people who had the mark of the beast** from its onset. The word **sores** is used in the OT in reference to leprosy. Ford believes that John meant his readers to think of leprosy and its association with idolatry and apostasy—i.e., with religiously unacceptable people (*Revelation*, p. 270). The bowl judgments concentrate the readers' attention on the unbelieving world, but from a particular perspective that justifies God's eschatological indictment of them.

The second and third bowls of wrath are poured out to destroy the sources of water and so of human life (Exod. 7:17–21). According to the trumpet judgments, only one third of the water was destroyed; now, the devastation is total. The sense John conveys is one of intensified urgency, even of a fatalism that the world's rejection of Christ has made its salvation a real impossibility. The **blood**, which has polluted the waters, carries an ironical meaning: on the one hand, Christ's blood purchases a people for God (cf. 5:9–10); yet, on the other hand, his atoning blood is rejected by the **people who had the mark of the beast**. The blood-plague envisions God's righteous judgment of a people who have rejected the blood of the Lamb.

16:5–7 / This very point is taken up again and pressed home by **the angel in charge of the waters**, whose hymn of praise echoes the earlier hymn sung by God's people in 15:3–4 (Mounce, *Revelation*, p. 295). Both acknowledge that both salvation and judgment stem from the same **Holy One . . . Lord God Almighty**, whose decisions are never capricious (unlike pagan deities) and always **true and just**. Penalties, however harsh, are not arbitrary but always **deserve**d. Because Revelation ties the temple's **altar** to God's vindication of the suffering saints (cf. 16:6; 8:3–5; 14:18), the finality of God's judgment against a fallen world is decided not only by its rejection of God who reigns from heaven but by its rejection of God's people who reign on earth (5:10).

16:8–9 / **The fourth angel poured out his bowl on the sun** (cf. Exod. 10:23). The immediate result is different than before when the loss of sunlight resulted in darkness (cf. 6:12; 8:12). This time the **sun . . . scorch**ed **people with fire . . . seared by the intense heat** (contra 7:16). Incredibly, the people's response to God is precisely the same as before: **they cursed the name of God . . .** and **refused to repent and glorify him** (cf. 9:21).

While this vision has unbelievers in view, this refrain of unbelief echoes the earlier condemnation of the Thyatiran congregation, which tolerates the false prophetess, "Jezebel," even though she is unwilling to repent of her heresies (cf. 2:21). In light of Christ's condemnation of the Thyatira church, the reader of this passage can sense John's pastoral interest in unfaithful believers, whose eschatological salvation is imperiled by their unfaithfulness and who must also repent and give God glory. Only then will they belong to the true Israel and be preserved from the scorching sun (cf. 7:16).

16:10–11 / **Darkness** is now confined to **the throne of the beast and his kingdom,** the result of the fifth bowl (cf. Exod. 10:21–29). In biblical literature, **darkness** is a metaphor for evil. In this vision of **darkness,** the creator of light (cf. Gen. 1:3) defeats evil. Among the terrors of evil is ignorance of God, also symbolized by **darkness.** Thus, pagans are characterized by their futility of mind, which separates them from God's transforming grace (cf. Eph. 4:17–18). Those who are linked with a darkened throne do not know God to give God glory; their obduracy is logical and tragic: **they refused to repent of what they had done.**

16:12–14 / The close parallelism between the sixth bowl and the sixth trumpet (cf. 9:13–19) judgments is surely intentional and warrants our close attention. In our view, the parallelism forms a complete picture of God's growing wrath against evil, and prepares the reader for the conclusion to the third woe of God's righteous retribution (Beasley-Murray, *Revelation,* pp. 243–44). As mentioned in the introductory chapter, the apocalyptic idea of history is characterized by fatalism—the unabated progress of misery and evil toward complete spiritual and social chaos. Appropriately, only one third of humanity was initially affected (cf. 9:15); here **the whole world** encounters God's wrath, indicating the devolution of earth toward its destruction. Interpreted christologically, Christ's past death and exaltation result in God's defeat of evil and death, and Christ's future return results in God's destruction of evil and death.

The central image in this parallelism is **the great river Euphrates,** a symbol of Rome's vulnerability and of the promised land (cf. 9:14). Whereas before the river was linked to angels who destroyed one third of the human population, in this new vision, **its water was dried up to prepare the way for the kings from the East,** coming from beyond the Euphrates with a demonic army under the aegis of Babylon's unholy trinity—**the dragon . . . beast . . . and false prophet**.

The phrase echoes two different typologies of redemption. The first half of the phrase echoes the exodus tradition, where God dries the bed of the Reed Sea so that God's people could escape evil Egypt. This prophetic typology continues with references to the **three evil spirits that look like frogs**—no doubt an allusion to the Egyptian plague of frogs (Exod. 8:1–15). The second half echoes the Matthean tradition of Jesus' birth, where kings come from the East to prepare the way of the Messiah, who will lead eschatological Israel on a new exodus into the promised land. What is used here as a metaphor for evil is used elsewhere as a metaphor for divine blessing. Once again, John uses irony to evoke a sense of anticipation: what currently appears to be a foreboding and mounting evil will turn into an occasion of divine blessing. The reader understands that while the army gathers **for the battle on the great day of God Almighty** to exercise its **miraculous** power with evil intent, the outcome has already been decided in favor of **God Almighty** because of the Lamb's death.

16:15–16 / This brief interlude functions as a footnote to the sixth bowl plague. As is true with each interlude found within the three judgment septets, this passage confirms the faithfulness of God as a response to the crisis of faith within John's audience. Interpreted by the point John's interludes make, the well-known caveat, **Behold! I come like a thief!** (cf. 1 Thess. 5:2–5; 2 Pet. 3:10; Matt. 24:43–44; Acts 1:6–7; Rev. 3:3), is an exhortation to repent in order to receive divine blessing. The following beatitude envisions the promise of God's faithfulness to those who are themselves faithful to God: **Blessed is he who stays awake . . . so that he may not . . . be shamefully exposed** (cf. 1 Thess. 5:6–7; 2 Cor. 5:2).

The **place** of the "battle on the great day" is identified as **Armageddon**. Attempts to locate Armageddon geographically are futile; in fact, no such place exists to the best of our knowledge (Boring, *Revelation*, p. 176). The cities of Revelation are typically locations of theological significance and should be interpreted as such. Beasley-Murray suggests the theological meaning located at **Armageddon** is prophetic and stands "for the last resistance of anti-god forces prior to the kingdom of Christ" (*Revelation*, p. 246). In any case, John is not engaged in speculation about the actual location or date of some future battle; neither is he predicting a specific event of history when evil will be completely destroyed in military combat (Ladd, *Revelation*, p. 216). John's prophetic concern is to characterize the suddenness (like being surprised by **a thief**) and the surety of God's eventual victory over the forces of evil. His pastoral concern utilizes dramatic images to evoke the impression that there is an urgent need to repent and glorify God before the consummation of salvation's history.

Additional Notes §16

15:3–4 / E. Werner says that the Easter liturgies of earliest Christianity included the reading/singing of the Exodus version of the **song of Moses** (Exod. 15). Messianic Judaism had come to read the "song" as a promise for national restoration, fulfilled by God through the Messiah, a "new" Moses. In fact, the prophetic reading (*Haftorah*) which often accompanied the "song" was Isa. 26:1, which also speaks of Israel's restoration. Cf. *The Sacred Bridge: Liturgical Parallels in Synagogue and the Early Church* (N.Y.: Schocken Books, 1970), pp. 141–44. No doubt, John and other Jewish Christians in his audience would have imported this theological meaning into this song of triumph.

16:4–6 / Morris notes another side in the irony of the **blood**. This plague well suits the crime of those who were so quick to shed the martyrs' blood; they now have only their blood to drink (*Revelation*, p. 188).

16:13 / Jews considered **frogs** "unclean" (Lev. 11:10); the plague of **frogs** confirms the "unclean" relationship between God and the people of the beast.

16:16 / J. Paulien has argued for the Palestinian locale of **Armageddon**, while stressing the cosmic character and spiritual significance of the "battle at Armageddon" in Revelation, in "The Battle Over the Battle of Armageddon," unpublished paper presented at the annual meeting of the Society of Biblical Literature, 1989. If Paulien's paper is a fair response to this problem, we can only wonder about the "cash value" of locating Armageddon on the map of the ancient Near East when its real importance according to Paulien transcends space and time. Perhaps it is best for the interpreter to understand that Armageddon belongs to John's visionary world, whose import is theological rather than historical or geographical.

§17 *The Seventh Bowl: The Final Destruction of Babylon (Rev. 16:17–17:18)*

The horrors of the seventh bowl plague share in the symbolic significance of Revelation's number seven: they represent in some sense the conclusion or completion of God's judgment against evil in accord with God's plan of salvation. The extended narrative of God's wrath poured from the seventh bowl not only indicates that God's battle against evil is at long last completed—**It is done**! It also spells out more fully the character of the anti-Christian kingdom that God has overcome.

The setting of this scene is the mythic city-state, Babylon. While a map of ancient Rome may help us recognize the city John envisions, Babylon is actually the "global village" of godless power, which determines daily life for every person at any time in human history. The description of Babylon and its punishment is an impression of social evil and its destiny. As such, Babylon is the counterpart of the new Jerusalem, the symbol of the eschatological community where divine blessing is finally found.

Several features of Babylon's fall are of significance in Revelation's understanding of the anti-Christian kingdom. While we will take each feature up in turn for analysis, two are most striking and deserve special mention. First, it is clear that Babylon's ruler, the beast, is responsible for his and Babylon's demise (cf. 17:8–16). Whether or not this vision predicts Rome's fall is unimportant; its critical purpose is to transmit timeless truth about the structures and ruling elite of the social order in any age. Secular power always corrupts the powerful and any who submit to anti-Christian norms and values. While injustice and even suffering are sometimes the result of rejecting the secular for the sacred, and while suffering heaped upon injustice may wear down the faithful and open them to compromise, the ultimate reality is this: secular power brings destruction upon itself. To lose one's life by resisting the norms and values of the anti-Christian kingdom and its rulers is actually to gain life; and the "real world" is the kingdom of God since it is the kingdom left standing at the end of the age.

Second, the dehumanizing values that characterize the evil empire are more clearly in view in this narrative than anywhere else in John's vision. The grief of those who lament the fall of Babylon (18:9–19) is centered not upon the loss of human life but upon the loss of the city and its great wealth. According to Revelation, at the foundation of evil's self-destruction is its love and concern for Mammon and self rather than for God and neighbor. Perhaps implicit in this narrative is this conviction: if the people of God abandon the gospel for the seductions of worldliness, then the global village itself is lost to the self-corrupting influences of its own rulers and social institutions. Of course, John's apocalyptic view of society is rather fatalistic: without the presence of God's people, who now stand outside the city (cf. 15:2), Babylon the Great is doomed to destruction.

16:17–21 / Prologues introduce stories; they provide readers with clues that guide them to intended meanings found within the story world. Thus, when **the seventh angel** pours **out his bowl into the air**, the resulting apocalyptic storm provides a perspective on the collapse of Babylon, the story of which is told in 17:1–19:10.

Everything John writes down describes finality, beginning with the **loud voice** that announces **"It is done!"** Of various natural phenomena that confirm God's edict on earth, the most devastating is the **severe earthquake** unlike any that **has ever occurred since man has been on earth**. The **earthquake** carries symbolic significance as an eschatological clue: in OT and intertestamental writings, earthquakes signal the apocalypse of God's final judgment (cf. Isa. 13:9–13; 24:17–20; Hag. 2:6–7; T. Levi 3:9). Further, this hailstorm suggests that God's judgment concludes what the first great hailstorm helped to announce (Rev. 11:19): God has triumphed through the exalted lamb.

In this case, God's eschatological judgment is exacted especially on **the great city . . . Babylon the Great**, the center of secular power. The city is destroyed—**split into three parts**—as the recipient of a **cup filled with the . . . fury of** God's **wrath** (cf. 14:8). It is the contents of this eschatological **cup** that John is now prepared to describe in detail.

John provides two additional clues that help measure the totality of the city's destruction. First, the earthquake has devastated the very ground on which Babylon is built; **islands . . . and mountains**, a complete geophysical reality, are leveled into a plain. Second, the people of Babylon **curse God, because the plague** of hail **was so terrible**. Without the protection provided by Babylon's buildings or nature, its citizens are exposed to God's horrific wrath, symbolized by the **huge hailstones of about a hundred pounds each** (cf. Rev. 11:19; Josh. 10:11; Ezek. 38:18–22). The impression left by John's description of the devastating earthquake concerns not so much the completeness of God's triumph over evil as its inevitability. At this point, then, the obdurate people can only **curse God**—a final act of resignation to the Lord's sovereignty and God's certain punishment of them.

17:1–2 / Within the framework of Revelation, the vision of Babylon's prostitute and her punishment functions as part of an extended footnote (17:1–19:10) that describes the contents of "the cup filled with the wine of the fury" of God's wrath (16:19b). Its complexity and even confusion have led some to question John's sources (cf. Beasley-Murray, *Revelation*, pp. 249–50). However, this betrays a failure to read the story as a wonderfully crafted "mystery," in agreement with the clue provided by the angelic interlocutor (17:7). Thus, John's "astonishment" upon seeing the gaudy whore (17:6b), followed by the astonishment expressed by "the inhabitants of the earth" at the reappearance of the beast (17:8) are actually proper responses to this vision that every competent reader, insider or outsider, should share.

Indeed, John's conversation with **one of the seven angels** concerning **the punishment of the great prostitute** (17:1) evokes a considerable degree of suspense in the reader as the angel reveals one clue after another, until finally it provides John with the shocking conclusion: "the beast and the ten horns . . . will bring her to ruin . . . and burn her with fire" (17:16).

What is so shocking about the story's climax is that the powers of the anti-Christian kingdom engage each other in a self-defeating civil war! One suspects the readers are more familiar with the prior picture of the demise of evil that John draws: "the Lamb will overcome them because he is Lord of lords and King of kings" (17:14). That is, evil's demise comes from outside of the social order—from heaven where truth and righteousness have already triumphed. In the punishment of the prostitute, however, evil turns upon itself in order to "accomplish God's purpose" (17:17). For all its short-term intoxications, society's seduction by the idols of secular materialism will lead to the destruction of the **inhabitants of the earth.**

An angelic messenger, identified only as **one of the seven . . . who had the seven bowls,** bids John to **Come** into the visionary world to witness the **punishment of the great prostitute.** The opening formula, **Come, I will show you,** is used again in 21:9 to introduce John to "the bride, the wife of the Lamb." This common formula suggests that John sees a contrast between the prostitute and the bride. We found this same contrast implicit in 14:1–5, where John sets forth the conditions of Christian discipleship. There is a sense in which this vision about the prostitute prepares the reader for the vision of the Bride, the new Jerusalem, which will conclude Revelation. John's pastoral perspective is made clearer in arranging his visions in this way; he is concerned that the believer not be **intoxicated with the wine of** the prostitute's **adulteries** (cf. 14:4a) and therefore be disqualified from the 144,000, who constitute the faithful Bride of the Lamb (cf. 14:3b).

The angel also locates the prostitute in a specific place, **on many waters,** keeping company with **the kings . . . and the inhabitants of the earth.** The precise identification of the vision's various participants is delayed until the conclusion, when we discover the harlot is actually Babylon and the company she keeps actually hates her and will help destroy her. The **waters** on which they have convened their orgy no doubt allude to the geographical location of ancient Babylon (cf. Jer 51:13), even though the "spin" John gives his description of mythic Babylon derives from ancient Rome and its ruling elite (Boring, *Revelation,* pp. 179–83).

It would be a mistake in our view to take **adulteries** literally as "sexual impurity" (contra Morris, *Revelation,* p. 198). Rather, John uses a prophetic typology to cast religious apostasy as sexual infidelity (cf. Hos. 2:5; Nah. 3:4; Isa. 23:16–17; Jer. 2:20–31; 13:27; Ezek. 16:15–19; Caird, *Revelation,* pp. 212–13). What disqualifies Babylon's citizens from the eschatological community is their refusal to acknowledge God as sovereign creator (16:9, 11, 21; cf. Rom. 1:19–21).

17:3–6a / Having accepted the angel's invitation to witness the prostitute's punishment, John is transported into the visionary world of Babylon by **the Spirit** (cf. 1:10; 4:2; 21:10). Rather

than viewing the prostitute from close by "on many waters," John
is **carried . . . into a desert**, where he is better able to scrutinize
her from a distance and where he lives in solidarity with the messianic community (cf. 12:6, 14). Unlike the desert region where
the faithful were protected by God (12:6, 14), however, this stark
and isolated place is "an appropriate setting for a vision of judgment" (Mounce, *Revelation*, p. 308). The evils of the prostitute will
not distort or interrupt his view of her from there.

John first sees the evil **woman sitting on a scarlet beast**,
clothed in garments of imperial **purple and scarlet** in contrast to
the bride's simple apparel of "fine linen, bright and clean" (19:8a).
Because the bride's linen symbolizes "the righteous acts of the
saints" (19:8b), the prostitute's contrasting clothes no doubt symbolize her contrasting deeds of unrighteousness. She is also be-
jewelled **with gold, precious stones and pearls** in contrast to the
even greater riches that adorn the heavenly Jerusalem, the Bride
of the Lamb (cf. 21:19–21). While the harlot personifies wealth
and power, the seat of her splendor, the **scarlet beast**, is linked
by its red color to the "enormous red dragon" (12:3), Satan (cf.
Morris, *Revelation*, p. 202). Her influence is unquestionably
demonic. Thus, the **golden cup in her hand** (cf. Jer. 51:7) contains **abominable things** (cf. 18:6) and **filth** (cf. Caird, *Revelation*,
p. 214), which intoxicated her **with the blood of the** martyred
saints. The contents of her **golden cup** are thereby contrasted with
the heavenly golden bowls which hold "the prayers of the saints"
(cf. 5:8). These various contrasts portend another ultimate contrast: for all the brilliance of her appearance, the prostitute's destiny is destruction rather than salvation. Indeed, we know already
that the third woe culminates with God's vindication of the martyred saints (cf. 16:5–6).

17:6b–8 / John's astonishment at the spectacle of the evil
woman causes the **angel** to query him: **Why are you astonished?**
The question is rhetorical, and the angel proceeds to explain **the
mystery of the woman and of the beast she rides**, adding mystery to mystery. The angel speaks initially only of **the beast, . . .**
which **once was, now is not, and yet will come**—a riddle whose
language reflects the well-known "Nero *redivivus*" legend that the
infamous Nero would be resurrected by the Evil One and return
to earth as Anti-Christ (cf. 13:3–4; Caird, *Revelation*, pp. 215–19;
Charles, *Revelation*, vol. 2, pp. 67–72). The phrase is also similar

in structure to the creedal formula John earlier used for God (cf. 1:4). By this, some have argued that John intends to contrast the beast's identity, whose power is satanic and temporary, with God, whose power is redemptive and eternal. In any case, the angel delays giving its cipher for the riddle until 17:9–11.

The angel speaks first of two stages that comprise the beast's future: **the beast . . . will come out of the Abyss and go to his destruction** (cf. 9:1; 11:7). Its source is evil; whenever the beast arises from its home, it comes to destroy. Ironically, however, the way of the beast, which intends to corrupt and destroy others, ends in self-destruction rather than in "grace and shalom" which is the way of Christ (cf. 1:4). Perhaps the greater irony is that the **inhabitants of earth**, whose sinfulness refuses God's grace and shalom, continue to be fascinated by evil power, which will ultimately destroy them.

17:9–11 / The appeal to **wisdom** was used before in 13:18 to solve the political significance of another cryptogram for Roman rule, the number "666." Most would argue that the angel makes it rather easy for any reader to solve this riddle. Rome was well-known as the city built on **seven hills**; thus, most would recognize the seven-headed beast the woman rides as Rome. Yet, surely John's shift to a more literal image of secular power does not intend to deny its symbolic power. In fact, the number **seven** might carry symbolic meaning for completeness, and **hills** might draw upon the OT where it stands for political power (cf. Jer. 51:25). Thus, rather than referring to Rome, John may well intend to speak of all political kingdoms—a general reference which calls for **wisdom** (Mounce, *Revelation*, p. 314).

In any case, John is not engaging in a polemic against ancient Rome; rather, Rome is the current and best example of mythic Babylon, of secular power that characterizes every other place of human existence. Moreover, the Caesars—past, present and future—are simply the recent exemplars of those ruling elite that have continued to conduct Satan's business in the sociopolitical order. In this sense, while the angel's second interpretation of the beast's **seven heads** as meaning **seven kings** may well have the reign of first-century Caesars in mind from Tiberius to Domitian as many have speculated (cf. Schüssler Fiorenza, *Revelation*, pp. 41–42), it is our preference to take the angel's cipher as a timeless metaphor for secular rule. Any historical construction of John's comment is fraught with enormous difficulty; and he has consistently employed **seven** as a symbol of totality or completion. The addition of an **eighth king** would seem to indicate that there will always be a ruling elite, bent on evil, governing Babylon—at least **for a little while**. In that the meaning of the beast in verse 8 seems to refer to ruling elite of the anti-Christian kingdom, John's purpose is not to confuse but to collapse king and kingdom as equal parts of a common reality.

It is significant in our view that there is a *terminus ad quem*. Eternality belongs to God, and thus to "grace and shalom." The beast's reign of terror has limited duration and can not continue beyond that final moment of **his destruction**, which is ordained by God "from the creation of the world."

17:12–14 / The angel's interpretation of the beast's **ten horns** continues the essential thrust of the previous cipher. Like "mountain," the animal's horn is a familiar OT symbol for authority or power (cf. Dan. 7:7, 24) and in Revelation for satanic power (cf. 12:3). The **ten kings who have not yet received a kingdom** may refer back, as Beasley-Murray recommends, to the "kings from the East" who exercise their authority outside the borders of Babylon (16:12, 16; *Revelation*, p. 258). If this is correct, then we understand why it is that "the beast and the ten horns" (17:16) will finally turn against Babylon's whore, whose only influence lies within the city's borders.

Although **they have one purpose and will give their . . . authority to the beast**, the authority of the beast's confederacy lasts only **one hour** (cf. 18:10, 17, 19) "for the Antichrist himself speedily goes to perdition" (17:11; Beasley-Murray, *Revelation*, p. 258). While these clues do not add much to John's understanding of the mystery, the angel does provide a compressed definition of the beast's *terminus ad quem*: the beast and ten kings **will make war against the Lamb**, which the Lamb quickly wins **because he is Lord of lords and King of kings** (cf. 19:11–21). The **faithful followers** who accompany the Lamb do so not to fight but to witness his destruction of the beast and its royal liege. Because only true disciples follow the Lamb "wherever he goes" (14:4), they share in his triumph as well as in his suffering.

17:15–18 / The angel is now prepared to show John what it promised to him at the outset: the **prostitute**'s identity as well as her punishment. With these last clues the mystery is solved. The final clue provides the identity of the **woman**: she is **the great city**, Babylon, which **rules over the kings of the earth.** This should startle the reader, since she is brought **to ruin**, left **naked, her flesh** eaten, and burned **with fire** by those very kings over which she now rules! They have deceived her, for they really belong to **the beast** (cf. 17:13). *The destiny of the anti-God kingdom is self-destruction.*

The vocabulary used to describe the prostitute's punishment in verse 16 alludes to the OT story of two whoring sisters, Oholah and Oholibah, found in Ezekiel 23. John draws upon this typology to interpret and write down the climax of his vision for his readers. Ezekiel employs the story as a typology of Israel's idolatry (Ezek. 23:48–49); accordingly, the two sisters represent Israel. They become prostitutes in Egypt, giving themselves with increasing lewdness to the ruling elite of Israel's various enemies (Ezek. 23:1–21). In disgust, the Lord first provoked their lovers and ex-lovers to disfigure them (Ezek. 23:22–27), and then the Lord handed them over to their hated enemies to leave them "naked," to kill their sons and daughters, and to "burn down" their houses with fire (Ezek. 23:28–47).

For John, Ezekiel's oracle comprises **God's words**, which **are fulfilled** in the new situation inaugurated by the slain Lamb. In this sense, it provides a theological frame to understand the angel's vision of the prostitute and evil's self-destruction. John states it sharply: evil destroys evil, so that **God** can **accomplish his purpose**. The dualism of Christian apocalypticism is theocentric and ironical. Even as the sisters' illicit lovers became agents of God's punishment, so also the great prostitute's satanic lovers turn on her, performing on God's behalf what God had promised: the destruction of the evil dominion she represents.

But there is a caveat behind John's use of Ezekiel 23: recall that the two whoring sisters represent apostate Israel, who is punished because of idolatry. By way of analogy, the story of the prostitute could be the story of an unfaithful church, whose destiny is destruction if it fails to repent and keep itself pure (cf. Rev. 2:20–23), and to follow the Lamb wherever he goes.

Additional Notes §17

Schüssler Fiorenza admits to the difficulty of locating 17:1–19:10 within Revelation, whether to place it with the visions of Christ's parousia which begin at 19:11 or with the bowl septet that precedes it. She finally settles for neither and understands its role as an extended parenthesis or "intercalation" between the bowl-plagues, which end God's judgment, and Christ's parousia, which ushers in God's salvation (*Revelation*, pp. 172–73).

16:21 / The weight of the **huge hailstones** is literally one "talent" each, or between 50 and 100 pounds.

17:3 / Morris views the wilderness image as a deliberate negation of the evil city; thus, John is taken there in solidarity with the believing community, which was also taken there earlier in its flight from the dragon (*Revelation*, p. 199).

17:4 / Boring suggests that John's description of the woman's attire intends to evoke images of the new Jerusalem, envisioned in Revelation 21 (*Revelation*, p. 179). In this sense, then, when John views the woman, he actually sees a city—not the new Jerusalem but Babylon. The equation of the woman with the evil city Babylon becomes clear by the end of the chapter, when John finally solves the "mystery" and writes that "the woman you saw is the great city" (17:18). That John intends to contrast Babylon and the new Jerusalem in concluding Revelation is made even more certain by the equation of both cities with contrasting women: Babylon is a whore and the new Jerusalem is the Bride of the Lamb.

17:5 / The difficult punctuation of the **title**, written on the woman's forehead, is only one (although perhaps minor) ingredient of the confusion surrounding this vision. The NIV has included **mystery** in the title rather than in the formula which introduces it; either way is grammatically possible. If it is true that for an ancient people the significance of a name is that it predicts one's destiny, the NIV's decision to include **mystery** in the woman's name is important for the telling of her story. Indeed, John narrates her story as a "mystery story."

17:8 / Schüssler Fiorenza argues that the riddle of the beast is cast in a prophetic form by John, and we concur with her that it predicts an archetype fulfilled in every age, and not a particular city, Rome, fulfilled only in John's day (*Revelation*, pp. 164–65, 185–86). Many scholars, however, have understood this riddle in terms of actual Roman rulers, who **once was, now is not, and yet will come**. This smacks of historicist reductionism and fails to appreciate fully the transhistorical thrust of symbolic representation. John is not engaged in a polemic against the Ro-

man Empire per se; rather, his polemic is against the anti-Christian kingdom of which Rome is but the best current example.

17:15–18 / Beasley-Murray's unsuccessful efforts to apologize for
John's incorrect prediction of Rome's demise (*Revelation*, pp. 261–62) stem
from the incorrect presumption that **the great city** must refer to historical Rome. If one is forced to equate Babylon with Rome, Beasley-Murray's
concern is justified. We think his assumption, however, is mistaken.
Babylon's setting may well have been patterned after Rome, even as the
beast may have been patterned after Nero. In John's visionary world, however, such corollaries to the "real world" continue beyond Rome and Nero
to those worlds and rulers familiar to each reader of Revelation.

§18 The Aftermath of Babylon's Destruction (Rev. 18:1–19:10)

In chapter 18, John describes a variety of responses, from heaven (18:1–8, 20) and on earth (18:9–19), to the shocking news of Babylon's destruction. These responses constitute the climactic scene of the seventh trumpet-plague and the "third woe" that precede the inbreaking of God's reign on earth. Drawing upon biblical "doom-songs" and laments that were written of other city-states (cf. Beasley-Murray, *Revelation*, p. 262), John composes a dirge about Babylon's destruction which deepens the significance of his prior message about the evils of the secular order and God's triumph over them. It is incorrect in our view to interpret Babylon's fall as a "celebration," an occasion for vengefulness of the oppressed against former oppressors; the tone is much too somber for this. Neither does this portrait comprise an unconnected collection of "taunt-songs"; the evocative images (more than the themes) are too coherent in their final form. The reader is invited to enter into the considerable pathos that attends this material to consider the final responses of a failed people, who have refused to turn and give glory to God, and their fallen institutions.

Boring is correct to call attention to the importance of the pastiche of prophetic passages to which John alludes in this chapter (*Revelation*, pp. 185–86). For John, this eschatological event is the fulfillment of God's promised vindication of the Christian gospel. Further, there is a pattern by which God executes justice against the enemies of God's people within their ongoing history. In this sense, the destruction of Babylon is consistent with prophecies leveled against other evil city-states—such as the biblical Tyre (Ezek. 26–28; Isa. 23:1–18), Babylon (Isa. 13:19–22; 47:7–9; Jer. 50–51), and Nineveh (Zeph. 2:14–15; Nah. 3). John's audience can readily find hope (or reason to repent) in their own difficult situation from the prophetic oracles found in their Bible.

The chapter is divided into three parts, each with a particular function. (1) The angelic annunciation of Babylon's doom is reported as a dirge over the city (18:1–3). Included in this dirge are the two fundamental reasons for God's indictment of the city— political self-interest and materialism (18:3). Both idolatrous dispositions result in antagonism toward God's reign and to its witness in God's people. (2) The heavenly speech that follows (18:4–20) is bracketed by the two imperatives which inform the church's response to Babylon's evils in light of God's call to holiness. The church should "come out of her . . . (and) not share in her sins" (18:4), and the church should "rejoice" in God's vindication (18:20). The various laments in between indicate the values of the social order which the faithful are to renounce in that they lead a people away from God's salvation and toward God's judgment. It is striking that the imperative is not for engagement against but for separation from the sociopolitical order. (3) The concluding action performed by the "mighty angel" (18:21–24) repeats in reverse order the two reasons for condemning Babylon, announced earlier by the "angel with great authority" (18:1): "Your merchants were the world's great men./By your magic spell all the nations were led astray" (18:23). These concluding words repeat the central theme of this chapter that describes responses from "people-on-the street" to Babylon's demise: secular power, conceived of in political or economic terms, is self-corrupting because it forms a functional atheism that denies the sovereign rule of God.

18:1 / John envisions yet **another angel coming down from heaven**, bearing God's indictment of earthly Babylon. The importance of his message is expressed by its visage, for this angel **had great authority, and the earth was illuminated by his splendor**. The glory of the angel's coming is in stark contrast with the gloom of its message. Yet, John's most critical theological point is embedded within this contrast: the yield of Babylon's gloom is God's glory. The gospel is that the Lord has triumphed over the likes of Babylon and that God has liberated the Lamb's faithful from Babylon's evils to serve God forever.

18:2–3 / The great angel's dirge begins by an ironical summary of the great event: **Fallen! Fallen is Babylon the Great!** (cf. 16:19). That Babylon lies in ruins is indicated by its occupation

by **demons . . . every evil spirit . . . every unclean and detestable bird**—all symbols of death and desertion (cf. Isa. 13: 20–22;
34:11–15; Jer. 51:37; Luke 11:24–26).

The reasons for its fall suggest its former greatness. It brok-
ered political power with **nations . . .** and **the kings of the earth**.
Yet, its relationship with them was profane and illicit in that Babylon demands submission to its secular agenda and interests rather
than to God's reign. The image of **adultery** to characterize this
relationship is an allusion to the familiar prophetic typology of
Israel's idolatry. John's point, however, is a political one: it is idolatry whenever political values are legitimized by claims of national
sovereignty. Only God is sovereign over the affairs of nations. In
John's world, Rome's political greatness led to its arrogant refusal
to submit its aims and purposes to the will of God and to its
choosing instead the emperor cultus as the true and approved
religion of God.

Babylon's functional atheism is detected in the economic
sphere as well. There **the merchants of the earth** profited from
excessive luxuries. The word for **excessive** (*strenos*) occurs only
here in the NT and lacks any precise equivalent elsewhere. Beckwith understands it as "self-indulgence with accompanying arro-
gance and wanton exercise of strength" (*Revelation*, p. 713), which
seems true to the immediate context. The will of the social order
and its ruling elite dominates in a world where "might makes
right." Merchants value economic profit, even as kings value national security. Such is the nature of idolatry, which results in self-
destruction and divine judgment. Moreover, since God's judgment is due in part to Babylon's treatment of God's people (18:24),
John's point interprets the church's experience of powerlessness
and poverty as well. The eschaton is for those who are now marginalized, whose political and economic conditions will be reversed in revelation of God's righteousness (cf. Luke 1:51–53).

18:4–5 / The second major section of the dirge is spoken
by **another voice from heaven**, presumably angelic, which first
addresses God's people (18:4–5) and God's executioners (18:6–
8), before rehearsing the laments of Babylon's friends (18:9–19)
and finally concluding with an exhortation for God's people to
rejoice in God's vindication (18:20).

The opening citation of a familiar divine command, **Come
out of her, my people** (cf. Gen. 12:1; Num. 16:23; Jer. 50:8; 51:6,

45; Isa. 48:20; 52:11; Zech. 2:6–7), may very well reflect the sectarian tendencies of the Johannine community. Not only is there an ideological imperative to resist the secular materialistic values and convictions of the surrounding social order, John may well have intended to call his audience to remove itself physically from society in order to live in a segregated community, consecrated to God and to one another.

The command to form a consecrated community is issued for two reasons: (1) so that the community **will not share** Babylon's **sins**, and therefore, (2) not **receive any of her plagues** from God who **has remembered her crimes** (cf. 16:19). Some scholars (e.g., Charles) criticize John for confusing his readers, since here he speaks of Babylon's future destruction when he has just spoken of its past destruction in verse 2. Yet, the form of John's composition is a poetic dirge-song of Babylon's destruction and not a discursive narrative about it. We should be able to give John a poet's (or seer's) license!

18:6–8 / The heavenly voice turns from God's people to Babylon's executioners, already identified as the evil beast and its liege of ten kings (17:16–17), with the demand to **Give back to her as she has given**. In light of the accusations leveled against Babylon in verse 3, the retributive justice of God is framed by the OT, which stipulates double (or capital) punishment for the sins of political and economic exploitation (cf. Isa. 40:2).

The **plagues** that will destroy the city are then enumerated: **death, mourning and famine . . .** and **fire**, which is a paraphrase of the oracle against Babylon found in Isaiah 47:7–9. However, the oracle of plagues is centered by the reversal of Babylon, which can boast, **"I sit as queen; I am not a widow, and I will never mourn"** (cf. Rev. 3:17). But **in one day** it will be destroyed by plagues. Such is the frailty of secular power. Such is the greater power of God, **for mighty is the Lord God who judges her**.

18:9–10 / With this third subunit of the second section of the dirge John gathers together a series of three laments from Babylon's friends. As with every lament, there is considerable ambivalence expressed by **the kings of the earth**. On the one hand, **they . . . weep and mourn over** Babylon; yet, on the other hand, they helped to bring about the city's end because they **committed adultery with her and shared her luxury**.

These **kings** are not those of 17:16 who participate in Babylon's destruction; they keep their distance. Thus, while their distress seems genuine, they do not help save the city but rather announce its judgment. Perhaps they are political realists. While recognizing Babylon as a **great city** . . . a **city of power**, they view its **doom** as inevitable. The phrase, **in one hour**, is repeated throughout the lament to indicate the obvious: God's power will quickly overwhelm the evil city to judge it justly for its "one hour of authority" (17:12) during which its ruling elite persecuted the Lamb (17:13–14). Fair is fair!

18:11–17a / Like the kings of the earth, **the merchants of the earth will weep and mourn over** Babylon (cf. 18:9). The class of **merchants** (cf. 18:3) appears in John's vision for the first time. In part this reflects John's dependency on Ezekiel's dirge-song against Tyre, which also catalogues the wares of merchants (Ezek. 27:12–24; cf. Isa. 23). Yet, it also reflects the current situation of John's audience, which apparently has been either marginalized (cf. 2:9) or compromised (cf. 3:17) by the economic structures of the Roman world. At the very least, believers faced enormous economic pressures to participate in the Roman culture and its values in order to enjoy its material benefits. These values, however, are anti-Christian. While the distress of "kings of the earth" was over the city's torment, the merchants mourn because they are losing profits and customers as the city burns. As Beasley-Murray says, "The merchants . . . are concerned neither for the miseries of the innocent nor for the sufferings of the city, but solely for the loss of trade" (*Revelation*, p. 267). Their disregard for human life reflects the values of their choice for materialism over theism (cf. Luke 12:1–34; 14:1–6).

Most of the **cargoes** listed belong to the middle class. The concluding reference to **bodies and souls of men** is important because it resists the gnosticizing bifurcation of material from spiritual. Rather than referring only to slave trade (cf. Ezek. 27:13; 1 Tim. 1:10), John adds to the expression **souls of men** which implies that middle-class materialism corrupts and enslaves human beings from inside out.

The shifts of person from second to third and of tense from present to past (aorist) in verse 14 cue the reader away from the announcement of loss of business by the merchants to the continuation of the lament for the city. The speakers are unspecified but probably are the merchants who **stand far off** with the kings of the earth and comment in a profoundly self-interested way about the loss of Babylon's wealth. The similar structure of their lament with that of the kings would suggest agreement about the city's inevitable and imminent fate.

18:17b–19 / **Every sea captain . . .** and **the sailors** constitute the final group of dependents, who weep and mourn for their city. Because their interest is the maritime industry, they lament the loss of **ships on the sea** and the **wealth** they brought to the city. Their poignant question, **Was there ever a city like this great city?** echoes Ezekiel 27:32. Ezekiel asks this question about Tyre, thought at that time to be an invincible naval power in the ancient world. The prophet's point is rhetorical and intends to contrast the apparent power of Tyre with that of a sovereign God who could destroy the city with ease and with reason.

The apparent invincibility of secular power and human ingenuity, whether Tyrean, Roman, or North American, poses a threat to the believer. The compromise of faith is often viewed as expedient, given the very real evidence of secular power which surrounds the church. Given Rome's obvious powers and seductions, sometimes at odds with the gospel, John is naturally concerned that the believing community will want membership in Rome's middle class instead of in God's kingdom. The Laodicean congregation seems already to have made that decision.

Perhaps John concludes the mariners' lament in the present (18:19) rather than the future tense (18:9–10, 15–17a) to make God's judgment of Babylon's materialism seem "more real, more immediate to the reader" (Collins, *Crisis & Catharsis*, p. 119). In this sense, the whole dirge makes a more descriptive and less poetic statement and forces the readers to deal with their situation in a more realistic manner. The optimism of nationalism (kings), of middle class affluence (merchants), and of secular humanism (mariners), wherever it exists, is exposed as lies and fictions. Human efforts to build a great world or a lasting peace will only self-destruct.

18:20 / The somber tone of the laments over Babylon quickly changes to celebration as the angel concludes its speech by moving John's attention back to **heaven**, where God's victory has already been secured for Babylon's **saints and apostles and prophets**. The language of the angel's final commentary on

Babylon's fate is terse and forensic, typical of a sentence issued in a Roman courtroom. Its meaning, however, is ambiguous and contested. At the very least, it intends to justify God's verdict against Babylon (cf. Caird, *Revelation*, pp. 228–30). Further, God's judgment of Babylon vindicates the church's devotion to the norms and values of God's reign, especially the devotion of those martyred for their faithfulness.

18:21–24 / The preceding imperative to **rejoice** over Babylon's tragedy is a rather disturbing one. It is made more so by the action and speech of the **mighty angel** who contrasts heavenly delight with earthly gloom. The act of casting the **millstone . . . into the sea**, the home of evil powers, is similar to that of the angel who hurled the fiery censer toward earth in answer to the church's prayer that God begin the time of vindication (cf. 8:4–5). This new action, then, marks the completion of that period in salvation's history.

The heroic deed of the **mighty angel** (cf. Rev. 5:2; 10:1) also reminds one of Jeremiah, who also tied his prophecies against Babylon to a stone which he threw into the Euphrates (cf. Jer. 51:63). This enacted parable was subsequently interpreted as confirming the certainty and finality of "the disaster (God) will bring upon her" (Jer. 51:64). In this new context, the angel's pronouncement brackets, together with the opening stanza (18:2–3), the declaration of mythic Babylon's demise. Babylon, once filled with the music and crafts of its creative citizens, has become a haunt for "demons and detestable birds." Even its best citizens, the musicians and artisans, will be silenced because of its evil.

The couplet that declares **music . . . will never be heard in you again/No workman of any trade will be found in you again** captures a profound theological sentiment. The stilling of the creative arts tells of God's absence (cf. Isa. 5:12; 24:8). The creator God's presence has always been felt and acknowledged through the creative arts of God's creatures in testimony of the Lord's rule over creation (cf. Rev. 4:11).

Since Babylon has become a "home for demons," **the light of a lamp will never shine**. And marriage, a symbol of continuity, is no longer relevant since **the great city Babylon will be thrown down, never to be found again**.

The relationship between the last two sentences and the rest of the song is not apparent, except to repeat and therefore to emphasize the two great evils of John's Babylon: the **merchants'** economics of exploitation and the kings' politics of deception, which have resulted in the destruction of **all who have been killed on the earth**. Indeed, the myths of national security and economic contentment form the false gods which cast **the magic spell** not only on John's Roman world but on every other society of human history.

19:1–3 / Now that the third woe is completed, the reader is ready to hear God's concluding word that speaks of salvation rather than of judgment. These doxologies describe the logical response of worship to the angel's earlier demand for the heavenly community to "Rejoice . . . O heaven/Rejoice, saints and apostles and prophets!" (18:20). They also form part of the heavenly liturgy of joy that is marked by the repeated acclamations of **Hallelujah!** (19:1, 3, 4, 6)—found only here in the NT but often in the OT Psalter where it means "Praise the Lord!" In the Psalter this invocation typically summoned the worshiping community to acknowledge God's salvation, often from those situations characterized by their difficulty and evil—that is, from the very places represented by Babylon in Revelation.

The collocation of heavenly hymns that introduce chapter 19 concludes John's extended description of the seventh bowl-plague. These hymns parallel those that commenced with the blast of the seventh trumpet in Revelation 11:15–18. In both instances, the heavenly chorus consists of a multitude of loud voices (11:15; 19:1, 6) and is led by the twenty-four elders (11:16; 19:4). Their praise and worship is theocentric, acknowledging the power (11:17; 19:1) and reign (11:15, 17; 19:6) of the eternal (11:15; 19:3) God. Further, in both visions, doxology is the proper response of "both small and great" (11:18; 19:5) because God's righteous wrath is executed against unrighteous nations/Babylon (11:18; 19:2) on behalf of the righteous community of faith.

The parallelism between the seventh trumpet and bowl judgments reflects obvious theological and rhetorical importance. Recall that the seventh trumpet concludes a vision of the beginning of God's victory over evil through the slaughtered yet exalted Paschal Lamb. Indeed, God's reign over the "kingdom of the world" (11:15) has begun in great power (11:17) because of the Lamb's blood (cf. 5:9–10). Yet, the focus of this earlier doxology looks *backward* in salvation's history to its penultimate moment when the messianic kingdom was established (11:15) in heaven (11:19). At the moment of Christ's coronation in heaven, God's struggle against the evil foe ended in heaven where the biblical promise of salvation was fulfilled. That the war in heaven between God and the Evil One must conclude on earth in precisely the same way it concluded in heaven is disclosed by the opening of the heavenly temple (11:19). Moreover, it is from this profoundly hopeful perspective that the faithful community now addresses the trials and tribulations of the present evil age, envisioned in chapters 12 and 13. This present passage points back to that central section of Revelation, once again with a note on God's triumph over the "kingdom of the world." In this case, however, God's triumph is total and the evil kingdom is utterly demolished from earth. God's reign over the world, which had already begun in heaven with the Christ event, is now complete on earth. In this way, John transports the reader out of the present to the end of the age, "for the wedding of the Lamb has come/and his bride has made herself ready" (19:7).

Finally, the intratextual conversation between the concluding doxologies sounded by the seventh trumpet and those poured out from the seventh bowl form an *inclusio* and complete the foundation of John's exhortation to his audience: the community of believers confronts the evils of the present age not only with the confidence that the risen Lamb's death has *already* "purchased (a people) for God . . . and has made them to be a kingdom and priests" (5:9-10); but with the hope that in the imminent future the returning Lamb will dispense eschatological blessings to those invited to his wedding feast (19:9).

The first heavenly chorus sounds like **the roar of a great multitude**, no doubt angelic (contra Mounce, *Revelation*, p. 337). Their concluding praise echoes the doxology which opened this section of the vision in 12:10a: "Now have come the salvation and the power and the kingdom of our God." The claim made by both doxologies puts a particular "spin" on the current period of salvation's history, described especially in chapters 12 and 13. Despite the pretensions of secular power and its claim to rule over the "real world," the eschatological events which continue to unfold from Christ's exaltation assert a different reality: **Salvation and glory and power belong to our God**. The self-destruction of Babylon, when coupled with God's judgment over it, further clarifies what the doxology celebrates: truth and justice prevail because the **power belongs to our God** rather than to "the great prostitute," Babylon.

The unmistakable irony reflected in the phrase, **smoke from her goes up for ever and ever**, recalls Babylon's fires (17:16, 18; 18:8, 9, 18; Isa. 34:9–10) but also the incense of heavenly worship (8:3–4; cf. 14:11). Such is the dynamic of worship and praise. The reality of God's reign, which centers all Christian devotion, forms a dialectic between God's judgment of evil and the triumph of good through Christ. As Caird puts it, "the reality (John) is expressing is the victory of love over all that stands in love's way" (*Revelation*, p. 232).

19:4–5 / The second doxology offered in the exchange between those closest to God, **the twenty-four elders and the four living creatures**, and the voice from God's throne is significant for two reasons. First, the significance of the doxology derives from the significance of the choral members who sing it. All the songs of the twenty-four elders (4:8, 11; 5:9–10; 11:17–18) rehearse Revelation's central themes, now implicit in their **Amen, Hallelujah!** (cf. Ps. 104:35). Second, the significance of the liturgist's response derives from the setting, the **throne** of God. All of Revelation's great themes are really about the one theological axiom of John's faith: because of the slain Lamb, God's reign has triumphed over evil. The invitation to praise God is given to God's people, **both small and great**, who recognize the victory of God in the ashes of Babylon and so **fear him** in recognition of God's sovereignty.

19:6–8 / The fourth voice John hears is likened to a **great multitude** and to **the roar of rushing waters and . . . loud peals of thunder**. Its detailed description and the images of overwhelming noise suggest that the third doxology has dramatic and eschatological importance similar to that expressed at the blast of the seventh trumpet (cf. 11:15–19). This parallelism is structurally significant as well, since both this third doxology and the seventh trumpet function as transitional episodes within John's composition.

This multitude, however, is not angelic; it comprises God's servants (cf. 5:10; 19:4–5). The boundaries separating the angelic community in heaven from the human one on earth have now become less discrete: both communities shout **Hallelujah!** in mutual confirmation that **our Lord God Almighty reigns** (cf. 19:1). This exhortation for the eschatological community to **rejoice and be glad** plays off of the earlier command to "rejoice" (cf. 18:20)—although that imperative obliges the eschatological community to find joy in a condemned Babylon, while here it rejoices because **the wedding of the Lamb has come**. The former joy evokes not a sense of delight but of pathos for a people who refused God's goodness. The current prospect of a wedding celebration allows the "saints and apostles and prophets" to **be glad**. Given the dynamic movement of John's salvation from judgment to final justification, this seems logical. With evil judged, the messianic banquet can begin.

The prospect of a happy marriage is an important prophetic typology (Beasley-Murray, *Revelation*, pp. 273-74). However, according to the OT, in almost every case, such a prospect goes unfulfilled because of Israel's faithlessness. Thus, the prophets of God look to the future and even to the Messiah as the time of fulfillment, when Israel will be God's faithful bride. Behind the prophetic use of this marriage-typology are the ideals of the covenantal relationship between God and Israel. The experiences of intimacy and mutual support which nurture a good marriage ought also to characterize the relationship between God and God's people. Such a relationship constitutes the OT promise which has now been fulfilled because of the **Lamb**-groom (cf. Eph. 5:21-32). Indeed, the true Israel of God is the **bride**, the church.

John's own commentary on the last line of the doxology, which interprets the **fine linen . . .** as **the righteous acts of the saints**, is important in this context for two reasons. First, John repeats the condition whereby **the bride has made herself ready** for redemption: **righteous acts**. Because the **fine linen . . . was given to her to wear** by God, some have understood *dikaiōmata*, "righteous acts," as a forensic rather than an existential reality (e.g., Morris, *Revelation*, pp. 220-21). For John, however, eschatological fitness demands righteous acts in keeping with the Lamb. The church is given the garment to wear, but it must still put it on! Perhaps John describes the linen as "clean" instead of "white" as he did earlier (7:14) in order to distinguish between God's saving response, which "washed their robes and made them white in the blood of the Lamb," and the community's proper response to God, in which case the "clean" linen "stands for the righteous acts of the saints." Hence, in John's final instance, "white and clean" are found together in reference to the trimphant community (19:14). Second, this righteousness constitutes a life apart from the way of Babylon. Earlier in 14:4, John provided his readers with the two conditions of Christian discipleship: (1) follow the Lamb, which would yield righteous acts; and (2) do not commit adultery with the prostitute, Babylon. The wedding dress symbolizes chastity; the true disciple is not one of Babylon's "johns" (cf. 17:1–2) and lives a "pure life" which reflects the norms and values of God's kingdom.

19:9–10 / Many scholars have commented on the confusion John causes by retaining the marriage-typology while changing the church's status at the wedding feast from bride to guest (cf. Matt. 22:1–14). But such shifts in Revelation are rhetorical and serve to attract the reader's attention to transitions in John's composition. In this case, John prepares his readers for the final, climactic vision of God's triumph beginning at 19:11.

Moreover, the importance of this transitional episode to what follows is noted by the repetition of John's commission to **write** down (cf. 1:19; 14:13; 21:5) the beatitude, **Blessed are those who are invited to the wedding supper of the Lamb!** This is the fourth of seven beatitudes in Revelation (1:3; 14:13; 16:15; 20:6; 22:7, 14), and seems to help explain the significance of the preceding doxology. Its importance for John is made even more emphatic by the angel's remark that the beatitude comprises **the true words of God** (cf. 21:5; 22:6) and by John's response of **worship** at the angel's **feet**—in response to the message and *not* to the angelic messenger.

What should we make of all this? Perhaps it is best not to put too fine a point on any difference between bride and guest; the wedding's the thing, because it is the Lamb's wedding. Even the **supper** motif is incidental to the text's meaning, as 19:17–18 seems to suggest. What is important in this passage is the question evoked by the statement about eschatological blessings dispensed to those **who are invited to the wedding supper**. The language of "invitation" was used to speak of the divine election of a true Israel. Jesus used this motif to correct official Judaism's exclusivist definition of election (cf. Luke 14:15–24). John's point

is in continuity with **the testimony of Jesus**: divine blessing comes
to "both small and great" if "you fear God" (19:5). It is this point
that establishes the criterion by which the community of faith
must "test the spirits to see whether they are from God" (cf.
1 John 4:1–6). According to the author of 1 John, fear of the world
yields to the love of God (4:18) when God's children realize that
their destiny is not the day of judgment of the world (4:17) but
victory over the world (5:4).

Additional Notes   §18

18:1–3 / A. Y. Collins, in fact, complains that many believers appeal to Babylon's destruction as an outlet for envy, hatred, resentment,
vengefulness, and aggression of the weak against the strong—emotions
which themselves are anti-Christian! In her mind, however, the intended
response is a social radicalism which withdraws from the social order
rather than mourning for it or celebrating its overthrow (*Crisis & Catharsis*, pp. 121–38). Further, she argues that the very form into which John
has shaped his vision of Babylon's destruction suggests such a social function; see "Revelation 18: Taunt-Song or Dirge?," in *L'Apocalypse Johannique et l'apocalyptique dans le Nouveau Testament*, BETL 53, ed. J. Lambrecht
(Gembloux: Duculot, 1980), pp. 185–204.

18:4–5 / For a treatment of the sociological sectarianism of John's
idea of church, which is reflected by the exhortation to **come out of** Babylon, **my people**, see Raymond E. Brown, *The Community of the Beloved
Disciple* (N.Y.: Paulist Press, 1979).

18:11 / The NIV incorrectly translates the phrase, *klaiousin kai
penthousin*, in the future tense, **will weep and mourn**, presumably to
maintain its parallelism with the future tense of the preceding phrase,
klausousin kai kopsontai, found in 18:9. However, the present tense in this
verse should be maintained, rendering the phrase, "The merchants of
the earth weep and mourn." The present tense intensifies the merchants'
greed and callousness, which I think John wants to portray here. Corrupted by economic values of the social order, the merchants do not
mourn the city or its citizens; rather, they lament the loss of their own
markets and profits!

18:14 / Charles places verse 14 after verse 21 because it seems
to him to break the natural flow of the passage (*Revelation*, vol. 2, pp.
107–8). In our view, it does no better to re-locate it where Charles does;
to do so not only orphans the verse, but obscures its rhetorical function
within the final form of Revelation 18.

18:20 / Those commentators who excuse the difficulty of this verse by simply citing the justice of God's execution of unbelievers are far too facile in their analysis, if not also chauvinistic in their spirituality. The severe contrast between the mourning spectators and the rejoicing believers is *not* about our longing that justice is done (as Morris insists, *Revelation*, p. 215); rather, it should evoke a profound longing for Babylon's conversion.

19:1 / The NIV translation, **a great multitude**, incorrectly places emphasis on number of voices rather than on the dramatic volume of what John heard.

19:10 / Some scholars contend that the angel's exhortation, **Worship God!** intends to end angel worship among John's readers. This conjecture is without foundation. If anything, the angel only reminds John (and his audience) that the mark of true religion is to **Worship God!** The **testimony of Jesus** is for this theocentric end; and in continuity with the messianic mission, the **spirit of prophecy** now inspires John to write Revelation (cf. Caird, *Revelation*, pp. 237–38). Cf. J. M. Ford, " 'For the Testimony of Jesus is the Spirit of Prophecy' (Rev. 19:10)," *ITQ* 42 (1975), pp. 284–91, who interprets the phrase, **testimony of Jesus**, in a "subjective" sense so that the testimony conveyed by the **spirit of prophecy** concerns a private confirmation of the vision from Jesus to John.

§19 The Return of the Exalted Lamb: The Ultimate Event of Salvation's History (Rev. 19:11–20:15)

Viewed in a macroscopic way, the main body of John's book of visions narrates the three decisive moments of salvation's history. Sharply put, John's message to the seven churches is this: what has already transpired (5:1–11:19) together with what has not yet taken place (14:1–19:10; 19:11–22:6a) must inform the believing community's response both to God and to its present tribulation (12:1–13:18). This section of Revelation, then, clarifies the community's eschatological point of reference toward the present world order. In doing so, John completes his all-encompassing perspective from which the faithful disciple can view good and evil in order to "follow the Lamb wherever he goes."

John does not introduce the reader to anything new in this section of his composition; indeed, the new covenant has already been established for God by the slain Lamb, and the "kingdom of the world" has already been defeated and replaced by the reign of God and God's Christ. The reader will find, therefore, thematic continuity between this and previous sections of John's vision (esp. Rev. 2–3; 7; 12–13). The essential difference, besides a temporal one, is spatial. This final section of Revelation tells the story of the future apocalyptic eruption of God's salvation within human history; therefore, what has already been realized within the heavenly realm at Christ's exaltation and what has been constantly predicted by the seer in Revelation are now envisioned as a concrete reality. The conclusion to God's judgment of the anti-Christian kingdom and its ruling elite yields to God's final and full redemption of the Christian kingdom and its ruling priesthood, which has been created for *earth* by Christ (cf. 5:10). John's theological point resists any teaching that spiritualizes the revelation of God's salvation within human experience. In fact, the Christian gospel proclaims the opposite: the triumph of God is a public and cosmic event, because the power of God reverses every social and spiritual dimension of human existence into conformity with the creator's good intentions for it.

We have argued that current social pressures in John's world threatened to corrupt the witness of those under his care. One evidence of such a compromise, expressed best by the gnostic teaching of the Nicolaitans at Ephesus and Pergamum and by the prophecies of "Jezebel" at Thyatira, is to differentiate between the "spiritual" and the "material." That is, Christian spirituality is reduced to an exclusive concern for the personal and internal, or for the intellectual and religious aspects of human existence. Definitions of Christian discipleship exclude the sociopolitical (e.g., how one views the state and its public policy) or socioeconomic (e.g., how one spends money and views property) realities of life. In its most perverted forms, the church views its worship of God as a private affair; in its public life, the community of believers conforms to the secular norms and materialistic values of the surrounding society. The prophetic impulse of the Lord Jesus and earliest Christianity are thus silenced altogether. The unbelieving nations, who can see no real difference between the cultural myths and the church's gospel, remain ignorant of God's horrible judgment or of the prospect of peace under God's transforming grace. In this way, therefore, the shift of venue from heaven to earth serves John's pastoral purposes. His is yet another effort to make clear that humanity's decisions, personal and public, have real and eternal consequences.

This section of John's book of visions describes a single event, Christ's return to earth, and its various results, concluding with the establishment of the eschatological community in the garden of the city of God. The composition is a collocation of seven different visions (19:11–16, 17–18, 19–21; 20:1–3, 4–10, 11–15; 21:1–22:6a), each introduced by the apocalyptic formula, "and I saw" (*kai eidon*). The sequence of these visions is not chronological, at least in a historical sense. John's vision concerns the complexity of a single event, the second coming of Christ, and does not chart a series of events over an extended period of time. Each vision of the whole portrays a distinct and critical aspect of God's coming victory in Christ. Together the seven visions comprise "a tour through an eschatological art gallery in which the theme of God's victory at the end of history is treated in seven different pictures, each complete in itself with its own message and with little concern for chronology" (Boring, *Revelation*, p. 195). In this important sense, then, this material is not about eschatological timetables, but is a re-conceptualization of Christ's second coming as the ultimate and concluding event of God's vindication within history.

John first narrates the second coming as an eschatological war, predicted earlier (17:14). Jesus is first the warrior, who eats at the grisly "supper of God" (19:17–18), and only later is he the groom, who participates in the joyful "wedding of the Lamb" (cf. 21:9). Each successive scene portrays the Lamb conquering the ruling elite of the evil dominion, first the beast with its earthly followers (19:17–21) and then Satan (20:1–10), who has been consigned to earth following Christ's coronation in heaven (12:7–17). With God's reign firmly established on earth, God is now prepared to judge the "great and small" (20:11–15; cf. 19:5) in accord with biblical prophecy (Dan. 7:9–10). With the passing of the symbols of fallen creation, "death and Hades" (20:13–14), John invites the readers into a new creation and to the wedding of a restored Israel and God's Lamb who live with God forever (21:1–22:6a). When the eschatological community receives the promised inheritance from God, of course, the readers have reached the high point of the whole book. John's concern for the vitality of his audience's witness is finally addressed by referring not to his readers' history but to God's future.

Finally, while John's use of the formula, "and I saw," is important as an organizing device, his startling negation of the formula in 21:22, "and I did *not* see a temple in the city," cues the reader to recall 11:19's grand opening of the temple in heaven. The reader now understands the full import of the vision of the seventh trumpet in the overall context of Revelation: God's triumph over the Evil One in heaven that took place at Christ's exaltation foreshadows God's triumph over the Evil on earth that will take place at Christ's parousia. The first heaven (and its temple) will pass away (cf. 21:1) and a new Jerusalem (without a temple) will be the dwelling place where God lives with redeemed humanity forever (cf. 21:3). This development reflects Revelation's portrait of salvation's history—from exaltation to parousia, from heaven to earth.

19:11 / In his first vision of Christ's parousia, John again draws from the font of Jewish tradition, which sometimes cast its anticipation for a Messiah in militaristic images (cf. Ps. Sol. 17:23–27). It is Messiah, after all, who will rule the nations with an iron scepter (cf. Ps. 2:9; Rev. 19:15) and who alone can rightly claim Caesar's title, "King of kings and Lord of lords."

Some have complained that this violent imagery is out of keeping with other NT portraits of Christ's return. Moreover, they say, it is out of keeping with NT Christology that depicts Jesus as a "Prince of Peace" and not as a mighty warrior. These are legitimate concerns. If we limit our discussion to Revelation, however, we should first understand the images of this future "war on earth" and of the earlier "war in heaven" (12:7–12) as belonging to the same symbol system. The interpreter's second concern is to make theological meaning of this symbol system: what do these symbols of war tell us about God and about God's gospel? Sharply put, the theological issue at stake is God's decisive vindication of Christ and God's certain triumph over evil through him. If this is also the essential point of our present text, then John's apocalyptic portrait of Christ's return is consistent with NT Christology, which instructs the reader that the Lord's parousia is God's cosmic (and so final) vindication of Christ and also of his disciples (Ladd, *Revelation*, p. 252). The dramatic character of the war-images intends this rhetorical effect: it helps focus on a *person* (more than an event) in whom the entire community of faith finds its life's meaning and direction.

A final note: when the prophet speaks of the second coming of Christ, he is not claiming that Christ has been absent from us since his ascension. In the Fourth Gospel, this concern is first expressed by Thomas, who wondered how he could find his way to God (John 14:5), after the "One Way" to God predicted his imminent departure from the disciples (John 14:1–4). Jesus responds to their fear by promising them the Paraclete, who will continue to convey his comfort and instruction to them (John 14:15–31). According to Johannine teaching, then, the purpose of the parousia is not to resume the messianic work, since it continues through the Paraclete. Rather, the Paschal Lamb returns to earth in order to usher in on earth what is already a reality in heaven.

Once before John **saw heaven standing open** (cf. 4:1), and he was ushered into the transcendent realm. In that case, a "door" into the heavenly throne room of God was opened to him. In this case, however, John finds **a white horse** and its **rider** coming out from the heavenly throne room toward earth. The color, **white**, is an eschatological symbol; and the **white horse** is a symbol of victory (cf. 6:2). Thus, John recognizes that the vision he is about to see concerns the coming triumph of God's salvation on earth, which has now been completed through the one who rides on the **white horse**.

Because God is **faithful and true** (cf. Isa. 66:16), and because God makes judgments **with justice** (cf. Rev. 19:2; 16:5), these are appropriate characteristics for the messianic **rider** (cf. Rev. 1:5; 3:14; Isa. 11:4; Ps. 96:13), who comes to earth from God's throne and **makes war** against God's enemies. On this eschatological battleground, the faithfulness, truth, and justice of God's reign will be revealed for all to see.

19:12–13 / With the disclosure of the rider's identity, the battle's outcome is apparent even before it is waged. The reader knows the rider's identity by looking into **his eyes** which **are like blazing fire**. He is the coming Son of Man (cf. 1:13–14; 2:18; Matt. 24:26–31, par.), whose justice derives from his vigilant care of his people (cf. Caird, *Revelation*, p. 241) and from his ability to penetrate the pretense and deceptions of the Evil One (cf. 19:20; 20:8; cf. Beasley-Murray, *Revelation*, p. 279). Further, he has the status as God's anointed Messiah and appointed Lord over the cosmos. As symbolic of his singular authority, vividly expressed by his name "King of kings and Lord of lords" (19:16), he wears **many crowns**.

The precise meaning of the rider's unknown **name** is contested and insoluble. The interpreter's essential problem is to understand this name in relationship to his public names, "Faithful and True" (19:11), "Word of God" (19:13), and "King of kings and Lord of lords" (19:16). John has already used the secrecy motif to legitimize his authority as seer (10:4): having knowledge, especially revealed knowledge, to which others have no access is a form or symbol of one's "power" over them. In this same sense, perhaps John has included this identifying mark as a symbol not only of Christ's authority but of his own.

Additionally, the interpreter should understand the rider's publicized names as related to his messianic mission as **Word of God** (cf. John 1:1–18), in which he is "Faithful and True" to God, and after which he is exalted to his current status as "Lord of lords" (cf. John 20:28; Phil. 2:9–11). In this sequence, the unknown name would be made public only after his eschatological mission is completed. Significantly, in Revelation's benediction, Jesus does "name" himself "the Alpha and the Omega" (22:13)— the Lord God's name (1:8). Perhaps this is the unknown name, disclosed only after the "Day of the Lord" is completed and Christ's full equality with God is disclosed in the new Jerusalem.

The rider **is dressed in a robe dipped in blood**. Since the eschatological battle has not yet begun, the **blood** on the rider's robe can not be that of God's enemies; it must be his own. Rather than consider this a midrash on Isaiah 63:1–6, where the stained robe symbolizes God's just retribution against God's enemies (Mounce, *Revelation*, p. 345), we prefer the patristic advice that recommends this image be understood by Revelation 5:5–6. The essential christological theme of Revelation demands that we view the conquering Lion first as the slaughtered Lamb (cf. Caird, *Revelation*, pp. 242–44). On his robe are the stains of his passion, because of which he is called the "Faithful and True" to God's love and by which a people has been purchased for God. This is why the rider is also named **the Word of God**. Although interpreting the significance of Jesus as the incarnate Word of God carries a variety of meanings, that this conviction is central to John's understanding means that through Jesus' messianic mission "God fulfilled his divine purpose" (Mounce, *Revelation*, p. 346). According to John, in the passion of God's incarnate Word an eternal age was set into motion, when God's promise of a restored Israel would be fulfilled. In this sense, the supreme manifestation of Messiah's glory is not political power but self-sacrificial passion (cf. John 12:23–43). Ironically, it is at the parousia of the Word expressed as slain Lamb that the age will come to its conclusion.

19:14–16 / **The armies of heaven** may consist of angels as most scholars contend. This association agrees with the Jewish apocalyptic tradition (cf. T. Levi 3:3) and would have been understood by John and his audience; however, their eschatological dress of **fine linen, white and clean**, together with their **white horses** calls to mind the eschatological community (cf. Rev. 7:9–17; 14:4; 19:8; 22:14). Further, unlike angelic armies in other apocalyptic portrayals, which actually participate in the eschatological battle, these armies **were following him** as a community of disciples (cf. 14:4) and do not wage war with Messiah. In our view, the image intends to convey an important theological point: God's promised salvation is fulfilled by Christ alone; however, its blessing belongs to all those who "follow the Lamb wherever he goes."

Like most narratives of war in Scripture, Christ's conquest of God's enemies is unconventional. The point of biblical battles is not to defend militarism; the point is to defend the faithfulness of God. Thus, Christ destroys the evil nations not with a literal **sharp sword** but with the proclaimed word that comes **out of his mouth** (cf. 1:16; Isa. 11:3–5). But what words come from Messiah's mouth? The Christian proclamation of the slain Lamb, who is named "Faithful and True" (cf. Eph. 6:17). That is, by the preaching of the gospel about Christ's faithfulness to God, the claims of the anti-Christian kingdom and its rulers are exposed as lies and deceptions; and by its message, God's condemnation of the nations is found to be true (cf. Heb. 4:11–12).

The other two images which John draws from the OT—the one of **an iron scepter** (Ps. 2:9) and the other of **the winepress of the fury of the wrath of God Almighty** (cf. 14:20; Isa. 63:3)— are also used of the justice of divine judgment against evil. They are symbols of real power, but power consistent with the incarnate Word of God, the slain Lamb. They are used here to underscore his right to rule as KINGS OF KINGS AND LORDS OF LORDS (cf. 17:14) and thus the power of proclaiming a gospel centered by him. Who can possibly stand against its claims or deny the surety of its promises? Christ's vindication as Lord over earth and the realization of the gospel's promises within history simply bear testimony to what heaven has already confirmed.

This third name for Jesus is written **on his robe and on his thigh**. Many have wondered why John would report how Christ will publicize his name; all assume the name carries theological significance in relationship to itself. Both within the ancient world (cf. Beasley-Murray, *Revelation*, pp. 281–82) and within Revelation (13:16–17; 14:1; 17:3), the social function of marks indelibly tattooed into human flesh was to indicate a person's community. A name on a robe, like names on company coats or team jackets today, may also have identified a person's group; and its quality typically indicated one's standing within it (cf. James 2:2). The rider's identity is already known; what this third name, tattooed on his thigh and emblazoned on his robe, indicates is his status as Lord over God's eschatological community.

19:17-21 / John's second (vv. 17–18) and third (vv. 19–21) visions are of the eschatological war, already predicted in 16:16 and 17:12–14. Of course, there are many mythological and biblical antecedents of a final, cosmic battle, which John undeniably draws upon (esp. Ezek. 38–39), for he follows a similar plot. The forces of good are pitted against the forces of evil, including actual enemies, for one last show-down, when good triumphs and evil is destroyed. In John's version, the reign of God is represented by God's Messiah and his community of disciples; they are opposed by armies consisting of **all people . . . small and great**, who have refused to repent and give glory to God, and those evil powers who lead them, the **beast and the kings of the earth**.

However, "no battle is described; there could be none in John's theology" (Boring, *Revelation*, p. 199). The outcome of the eschatological war has already been decided by the cross and the empty tomb; the second coming only makes God's victory manifest. Thus, John first sees **an angel standing in the sun**, where **all the birds flying in midair** can see and hear its announcement about **the great supper of God** (cf. Ezek. 39:17). The angel has invited vultures to this feast, even though its purpose is not unlike the Lamb's wedding feast, in which the faithful are invited: both beasts and disciples are convened together to eat a supper which celebrates their creator's triumph. Yet, in stark contrast to the Lamb's feast, which celebrates the victory of God for the Lord's people, this grim and grisly supper for vultures commemorates the victory of God over those who have rejected the Lord (cf. Caird, *Revelation*, pp. 247–48).

John then envisions the battle's end; however, there is no actual fighting, since Christ's armies are really not soldiers but disciples, and his weapon is the preached gospel of Jesus Christ rather than conventional military arms. Indeed, **the beast and the kings of the earth and their armies . . . and . . . the false prophet** are those who reject the truth of the gospel and by so doing **make war against the rider on the horse and his army**. While the beast, kings, and false prophet are symbolic of the powers of the evil kingdom, **their armies** are not then demonic—any more than the Lamb's army is angelic. The beast musters his troops from among the unbelieving world. While they **were killed with the sword** that comes from the mouth of the Lord (19:15; cf. Isa. 11:4), their fate is "postponed" until after the millennium (cf. 20:8).

This is not the case of the first beast and false prophet (cf. 13:13–17). These two members of the unholy trinity are the first two to be **thrown alive into the fiery lake of burning sulfur.** Satan (20:10), along with death and Hades (20:14) and all unbelievers (20:15), will follow. The place of their eternal torment is identified only in Revelation in the NT, even though the association of eternal punishment with "fire" and "water" motifs is common. The source for John's image could have been the volcanic sites in the Dead Sea region, where burning sulfur caused an offensive stench. This seems an appropriate image for the fate of the rebellious, idolatrous anti-Christian kingdom.

20:1–3 / The next two consequences of Christ's parousia envision the destiny of the final and most powerful member of the evil trinity, **Satan.** Because Christ's first advent resulted in Satan's banishment from heaven (cf. 12:9), the reader assumes that Christ's second advent will have a similar effect on earth— and so it does, as we will soon find out. At first, John sees not the dragon, but rather **an angel coming down out of heaven** to earth where the Evil One now lives. This angel comes as Satan's jailer. In the one hand, it holds **the key to the Abyss** to lock and seal it over the devil, and in the other **a great chain** to bind him **for a thousand years.** His evil influence, which stems from **deceiving the nations**, has ceased altogether until the close of the thousand-year period when **he must be set free for a short time**.

In keeping with our treatment of Revelation, this fourth vision should not to be understood as the next in a sequence of historical events that follow Christ's parousia. This seems clear from the context, since John has already envisioned the destruction of the nations (19:15, 21), even though here he speaks of their deception by Satan as though they still existed. Nor should we assume that **a thousand years** refers to chronological years, since John has consistently employed the numbers and dates of God's reign for theological purposes.

Indeed, one's interpretation of this difficult passage is largely determined by how one understands the idiom, **a thousand years** or millennium. In doing so, the interpreter must resist determining the text's meaning ahead on time in light of certain theological assumptions, whether premillennial, postmillennial, or amillennial. The interpreter should also be careful not to force a particular idea of the millennium to function as a testing ground for one's hermeneutics or the litmus test of one's orthodoxy. Such ideological or apologetic interests tend only to obscure the profound theological freight the idea carries within Revelation.

The idea of a limited messianic reign on earth of specified duration, falling immediately prior to the inauguration of the eternal reign of God on earth, is not found in the OT or in any Jewish writing of John's day. What one does find, however, in both the OT and intertestamental writings, is a firm hope in the eternal reign of God on earth *that begins with the triumph and reign of God's messiah*. Revelation's idea of a millennial reign provides a depth of meaning to John's conviction that Christ's second coming legitimizes his lordship upon earth.

In order to illuminate this point, the interpreter must first reconstruct the kind of millennium that was known to John and his readers (cf. Boring, *Revelation*, pp. 206–8). The idea of a messianic reign was fashioned in the context of a rabbinical debate over biblical eschatology (cf. Ford, *Revelation*, p. 352). One prominent voice in this debate was "prophetic" and viewed God's salvation as the coming transformation of human history. According to this view, the messianic reign (i.e., a "millennium"), the "trigger" for God's eternal reign, would begin when world evil is overthrown by Messiah and human existence is thereby allowed to conform to God's original intentions for it. Another voice was "apocalyptic" and viewed God's salvation as the passing away of human history as we know and experience it. In this case, Messiah comes from outside of history to establish a new order which replaces the old. What is most important to note about this debate is that these differing rabbinical voices agreed that the "day of Lord Messiah" would be transitional and lead a restored Israel into God's eternal reign of shalom. Earliest Christianity, shaped within the womb of Judaism, took part in this debate and agreed with this consensus: the "day of the Lord Jesus" is transitional and will lead a true Israel into God's promised rest. Thus, in Revelation, John's idea of **a thousand years** interprets the second coming as a transitional messianic reign that will trigger the passing away of evil and usher in eternity. John uses the idea of a millennium to interpret the parousia rather than to insert it as a separate piece in a larger, more complex and temporal eschatological puzzle.

We might add that the early Christian saying found in 2 Peter 3:8, which itself is a midrash on Psalm 90:4, provides us with another important clue for interpreting John's idea of Christ's millennial reign. In 2 Peter's "little apocalypse," the author contends against those who scoff at the hope of the day of the Lord (3:3–4). The theological implication of their resistance to the "blessed hope" of Christian faith is that God will not fulfill the promise of a new creation (3:5–7). The ethical implication is that without hope there is little motivation "to live holy and godly lives" (3:11). In 2 Peter 3:8–9, the centerpiece of this passage, the author responds to the scoffers: salvation's history proceeds according to God's timetable and not according to humanity's. And God's timetable accords with God's patience, which waits on unbelieving humanity so that "no one (need) perish, but everyone (may) come to repentance" (3:9b). In context, the delay of Christ's return is interpreted by God's patience, and God's patience discloses God's own faithfulness to commitments made. Christianity's firm hope, tried in the face of scoffers, rests in a God who is a promise-giver *and* a promise-keeper.

As an expression of God's redemptive patience, 2 Peter reformulates time itself so that "with the Lord a day is like a thousand years, and a thousand years are like a day" (3:8). God's patience resists human calculation (cf. Jubilees 4:30). In this sense, the events that comprise the day of the Lord (3:10) may seem to take a millennium—especially to scoffers! In our view, then, the idea of a millennium found in 2 Peter is symbolic for the redemptive plan of a faithful God whose promises are patiently fulfilled according to a divine timetable and not one drawn up by scoffers or well-meaning prognosticators (cf. Acts 1:7; 1 Thess. 5:1–2).

John may well have known 2 Peter's idea of a millennium and utilized it here. The situation of 2 Peter is similar to the one that faces the first readers of Revelation. Further, both authors root their pastoral exhortations in a common theological conviction that God will restore a people who have truly repented and remained faithful to God's gospel. On this basis, we suspect that the phrase, **a thousand years**, functions in John's vision similar to 2 Peter as an idiom for the faithfulness of God; thus, the parousia vindicates not only the slain Lamb but his faithful God.

Within this framework, then, we are now able to locate John's millennial perspective on Christ's second coming. According to its first reference in 20:2, the millennium deals with **the**

dragon, that ancient serpent, who is the devil, or Satan and the final stage of his career as deceiver. God's faithfulness, revealed fully at Christ's parousia, concerns first of all Satan's banishment from earth, where God's people and not Satan's are destined to reign (cf. 5:10). Actually, this concluding chapter in Satan's story comprises two periods of time introduced here by John: not only the **thousand years** of Satan's exile, but a **short time** after his exile when he will be released to do what he does best—deceive the nations. We should assume that both periods of time, as God counts it, bracket the conclusion in the history of God's struggle against Satan, during which God has always had the upper hand.

More specifically, in four ways this final stage of Satan's career is much like its previous stage inaugurated at Christ's exaltation (cf. 12:7–17). First, and most essentially, it is with the advent of Christ's reign that Satan is defeated. Second, Satan is again demoted, this time from earth to the "Abyss." Clearly, this manifests God's triumph and sovereignty over the Evil One. Third, his demotion is expressed as a further constraint placed upon Satan by God, making it now impossible for him to deceive the nations. Before he could and did deceive the nations through his demonic agents, even though he could not deceive or threaten the faithful church. Finally, the dragon recognized that his time on earth was short (cf. 12:12); and Revelation itself always makes the period of Satan's activity definite in time in concert with God's ordination. This vision of Satan's banishment from earth not only confirms the limited duration of his siege; it also indicates that the final stage of his defeat is also definite and has an end. Its first period lasts for **a thousand years** and its second for **a short time**—and then what? In light of this history, the reader should assume that there is certainly another judgment awaiting Satan following this period of time. But to where is Satan demoted after the Abyss?

20:4–10 / John's next vision actually continues from the preceding one by combining an additional, more positive commentary on the millennium as a consequence of the parousia (20:4–6) with an expanded note on his earlier (and cryptic) comment that Satan **must** be released from exile in the Abyss "for a short time" (20:7–10). Together, then, these two visions (20:1–10) form two different perspectives of the final stage and status of Satan's struggle against the vastly more powerful reign of

God's Christ, who is now revealed as the "King of kings and
Lord of lords."

When Satan was bound in the Abyss for a thousand years,
the eschatological community **came to life and reigned with
Christ**. This was the community of Christ's disciples (14:1–5), **who
had been beheaded because of their testimony for Jesus and because of the word of God** during the "great tribulation," together
with those who **had not worshiped the beast**—i.e., the idols of
the social order. This resurrected body is not the martyr church
as some argue (e.g., Caird); rather, this is the whole community
of "overcomers." The eschatological community is composed of
two groups of believers, the martyred and unmartyred faithful,
all of whom have met the conditions of Christian discipleship
(14:4–5). Thus, John refers here to all those within his seven
churches who repent or endure and so overcome evil for good
(cf. Rev. 2–3). Insofar as the experiences of these seven congregations parallel those of congregations of every age, this **first resurrection** includes all believers who remain faithful to Christ.

They are seated together on **thrones** symbolic of their
earthly reign (cf. Dan. 7:9; Luke 22:30, par.; 1 Cor. 6:2–3) as
priests for God (cf. Rev. 1:6; 5:10; Heb. 9:14)—a royal priesthood on earth (Exod. 19:6). Echoes to the "new song" (5:9–10)
abound; indeed, the slain Lamb has returned with his blood on
his robe to realize in history what God has already accomplished
on the cross. The import of this picture of the millennium, then,
is that the parousia is a day of vindication for the Messiah's
community, even as it is for the Messiah. The church is triumphant too because of God's Lamb (cf. Mounce, *Revelation*, pp.
358–59).

The point can be more keenly made when the two different images of the millennium are juxtaposed. On the one hand,
John envisions an exiled Satan; and on the other, he envisions
a reigning Christ with his devoted community. In spite of current appearances and experiences, God's creation belongs not to
Satan but to God's Christ and his people, earth's true royalty. Unlike those who rule over Satan's kingdom, the faithful community will reign as priests and serve God's interests (Schüssler
Fiorenza, *Revelation*, p. 123).

Much has been made of the contrast between the **first resurrection** and the **second death** as that relates to the idea of the

millennium. Some have maintained that the idiom, **first resurrection**, implies a "second resurrection." Some would define a second resurrection in the terms of a realized eschatology (so Caird, *Revelation*, pp. 254–55), while others prefer the terms of a futuristic eschatology (so Ladd, *Revelation*, p. 268). John never speaks, however, of a second resurrection; therefore, the interpreter should understand **first resurrection** within this context as a symbol for the eschatological priority God accords to the regnant community of Christian overcomers. They are the first to experience the blessing and holiness of the eschaton when Christ returns in his glory (cf. Ford, *Revelation*, p. 350). John employs this idiom as an exhortation for those in his embattled audience to overcome evil.

The **second death**, on the other hand, is a euphemism for the fate of those who do not share in the eschatological blessing of eternal life (cf. 2:11; 20:14). They are those who have not received the transforming **power** from God that reverses death into life; they are those who have not met the conditions of Christian discipleship. What their destiny is in objective terms, however, we can only imagine, for John writes "with parables and symbols which point to ideas beyond their verbal expression" (Beasley-Murray, *Revelation*, p. 299).

John now returns his vision to Satan, who has been released from his exile "for a short time." Why does John insist on the necessity of Satan's short-term freedom? Why **must** the nations be deceived once again, since the reader already knows they will be destroyed? The essential clue to these questions lies within the passage itself, and more specifically in John's clever substitution of **Gog and Magog** for the **nations**. Jewish tradition had already recognized these rulers of Ezekiel's prophecy (Ezek. 38–39) as types of world rulers, whose evil power and cunning were directed against Israel. God will destroy them in vindication of God's faithfulness toward Israel in the eschatological battle "during the days of the Messiah" (cf. 3 Enoch 45:5). According to Ezekiel, God uses sword (38:21), fire (39:6), and burning sulfur (38:22) to execute judgment against the prince Gog and Magog. John also finds these instruments of divine judgment in his vision; so that **fire . . . devoured** Gog and Magog, and their lord Satan is cast into **the lake of burning sulfur** where he joins **the beast and the false prophet** (cf. 19:20). They will be **tormented day and**

night for ever and ever (cf. Rev. 14:10). John's rehearsal of the well-known prophetic typology of "Gog and Magog" does not predict a particular event or place, but rather imagines another result of Christ's parousia (cf. Ezek. 39:25–29).

This is, then, Satan's final demotion. Why he continues to act in character after his prison term of a thousand years had ended, and why the nations allow Satan to seduce them away from that which could give them shalom, speaks to the very nature of sin. Satan's ongoing role within salvation's history, even in defeat, is to force humanity's ultimate decisions concerning eternal life and death. The Evil One's mission is to deceive humanity so that it does not choose wisely. One's free decision to rebel against God or to worship God is the result of certain habits of mind and heart. Recall that the only force used by the rider on the white horse was the sword of his mouth; the only source of power used by his enemy is deception. The spiritual struggle is for the nations' mind! It is this which explains John's insistence on repentance—the transformation of the mind—the very thing the nations refused to do—for this is required to change rebellion into devotion. Without it, they are rather easy prey for the deceiver, even though he leads them toward their own destruction.

20:11–15 / Next the seer sees **a great white throne and him who** is **seated on it**; he witnesses there the last judgment as yet a final episode in the concluding chapter of God's triumph at Christ's parousia. What is so striking about this vision is not John's recapitulation of the universal judgment theme—that **the dead, great and small,** stood **before the throne** to be judged by God according to the **books**. Rather, it is the realization that God's judgment of all creatures and nations, and of Satan and his unholy comrades, does not yet conclude the history of evil. The final enemies are **death and Hades** (cf. 1:17–18) because they are the results of evil in the world. They too, together with the demonic **sea**, have lost their power over redeemed humanity with Satan's demise.

The **great white throne** symbolizes God's great power over evil's reign. Before the throne, **the books** kept in heaven to record **what** the dead **had done** are opened. This act does not represent God's smothering omniscience so that every person's every deed has been recorded by God to be broadcast at some later time. Rather the proper meaning of this image is to note with confidence that God's record is accurate and fair and God's judgment is "faithful and true."

The **book of life** is kept by the Lamb as the essential artifact of his reign (cf. 21:27); in it he records the names of those who overcome (cf. 3:5), his faithful disciples, and those who will reign with him. To them the promised life is given by the one who sits on the throne; they are those who have been purchased for God by the Lamb's blood and have been made into a kingdom to reign on earth and into priests to serve our God (cf. 5:9–10; 20:4–6). This book is the kingdom's register: in it are the names of those who have reserved space in the new Jerusalem because of their faith in and faithfulness toward God and God's Lamb.

Additional Notes §19

19:11–22:6a / Schüssler Fiorenza speaks of these final visions of Christ's parousia as a "mosaic" of themes, designed as the "final eschatological event" (*Revelation*, p. 47).

19:12 / Ladd prefers to see the unknown name as a symbol of mystery: the profound depth of Christ's majesty can not be fully comprehended by the human mind (*Revelation*, p. 254).

19:16 / When the dual name for Jesus, "King of kings, Lord of lords," is written into Aramaic, and when each consonant is given numerical value, the sum totals "777"—symbolic of perfection. P. Skehan finds here a cryptic contrast to the Antichrist, whose number is "666" and who does not measure up to Christ; "King of kings, Lord of lords," *CBQ* 10 (1948), p. 398. Morris further appeals to Ps. 45:3, which links "sword" and "side" together. On this basis, he suggests that the third name is actually the messianic sword which conquers God's foes (*Revelation*, p. 225).

19:20 / The NIV translates the opening *kai* as an adversative, **but**, rather than as a conjunction, "and." This decision undergirds the impression that the eschatological war is a bloodless coup: Christ's blood is the only blood shed, and by his blood God has already defeated God's evil foes who are prepared "to make war."

20:2 / The literature on the idea of a millennium is enormous and mostly conservative. Besides the standard commentaries and Bible dictionaries, the interpreter's select bibliography should include G. E. Ladd, "Revelation 20 and the Millennium," *RevExp* 57 (1960), pp. 167–75; R. Summers, "Revelation 20: An Interpretation," *RevEx* 57 (1960), pp.

176–83; M. C. Tenney, "The Importance and Exegesis of Revelation 20:1–6," in *Truth for Today*, ed. J. F. Walvoord (Chicago: Moody Press, 1963), pp. 175–86; M. Rissi, *The Future of the World: An Exegetical Study of Revelation 19:11–22:15*, SBT 2/25 (Naperville, Ill.: Allenson, 1972); D. C. Smith, "The Millennial Reign of Jesus Christ: Some Observations on Rev. 20:1–10," *RQ* 16 (1973), pp. 219–30; R. G. Clouse, *The Meaning of the Millennium: Four Views* (Downers Grove, Ill.: InterVarsity Press, 1977); M. Gourgues, "The Thousand-year Reign (Rev. 20:1–6): Terrestrial or Celestial," *CBQ* 47 (1985), pp. 676–81; J. F. Walvoord, "The Theological Significance of Revelation 20:1–6," in *Essays in Honor of J. Dwight Pentecost*, eds. S. Toussaint and C. Dyer (Chicago: Moody Press, 1986), pp. 227–38. For a complete bibliography, see J. Zens, "Rev. 20:1–10: When is the Millennium?" *Search Together* 13 (1984), pp. 31.

20:3 / W. Hendricksen locates Satan's imprisonment between the two advents of Christ, when the church is able to evangelize the nations with complete freedom (*Conquerors*, pp. 185–90). This interpretation draws upon elements of Revelation 12–13, where Satan is unable to destroy the church. Further, it corresponds well to the subsequent vision of those of the "first resurrection" who will reign with Christ. In Hendricksen's sense, 20:1–3 adds a footnote to this central section of John's vision. However, nowhere does it portray the church as evangelistic, and the nations are eventually destroyed rather than converted.

Thus, Caird argues that the nations of 20:3 are not those of 19:15; and the battle of 19:20 can not be the end of the human race because we find nations in 20:3. The nations of 20:3 must be the survivors of that eschatological battle, whose political power is now broken at the second coming, and whose status has been reversed so that they are now in subjection to the once powerless church for a millennium (cf. 20:4). This, according to Caird, fulfills the promise of the "new song" which said of the Lamb's people that they would "reign on earth" (5:10; *Revelation*, pp. 251–52). However, Caird's interpretation assumes a chronology of particular kinds of events that is not otherwise insisted upon by the vision itself.

20:5 / For competing views, see M. G. Kline, "The First Resurrection," *WTJ* 37 (1975), pp. 366–75, who contends that the **first resurrection** is the death of martyrs; N. Shepherd, "The Resurrections of Revelation 20," *WTJ* 37 (1974), pp. 34–43, who argues that the **first resurrection** is of Christ; and J. Hughes, who finds no "bodily" resurrection of any kind in the passage, "Revelation 20:4–6 and the Question of the Millennium," *WTJ* 35 (1973), pp. 281–302.

20:11 / For background on the **white throne**, see T. F. Glasson, "The Last Judgment in Rev. 20 and Related Writings," *NTS* 28 (1982), pp. 528–39.

20:13 / According to John's cosmology, the **sea** is the hostile home of God's enemies.

§20 The City of God: Entering God's Promised Shalom (Rev. 21:1–22:6a)

John's final, most detailed and most important vision of Christ's parousia is of a **new heaven and a new earth, the Holy City,** and **the new Jerusalem** where **the dwelling of God is with men** and **the old order of things has passed away**. Following the return of the Lamb, after his last battle and millennial reign, after the destruction of Satan, of his evil kingdom, and finally of death itself, the vision of the eschatological city of God "may be viewed as the climax not only of the book of Revelation, but of the whole story of salvation embodied in the Bible" (Beasley-Murray, *Revelation*, p. 305). With typical eloquence, Caird adds that "Here is the real source of John's prophetic certainty, for only in comparison with the **new Jerusalem** can the queenly splendors of Babylon be recognized as the seductive gauds of an old and raddled whore" (*Revelation*, p. 262). In short, the new order is defined in terms of the presence of God and the absence of evil.

Upon closer reading of this passage, however, the interpreter will discover that John's picture of the **new Jerusalem** is actually a metaphor for the eschatological people of God, the Lamb's bride. According to the prophet, *Christian hope is centered in the prospect not of a heavenly place but of transformed human existence.* A discussion of the chiastic patterning of both the vision's prologue and the vision's main body will illustrate our point. In particular, the vortex of both chiasms helps to focus the reader's attention on the vision's climactic point: the new Jerusalem is the Lamb's Bride, the community of overcomers. Recall that a literary chiasmus functions as a rhetorical device to aid the reader in ranking the significance of various elements in a complex picture. The items found at its vortex, where the two parallel and inverted phrases intersect, are ranked as most significant. In this way, the interpreter focuses on the most critical element in the author's climactic vision of Christ's parousia. Let's develop this point more fully.

The chiasmus that shapes the vision's prologue (21:1–5a) is composed of a series of contrasts. The first contrast begins with the confirmation of the promised new creation (A; v. 1a), which John sees. This is followed by the negation of the old creation (B; v. 1b). The second contrast is between the passing away of the sea (C; v. 1c), the symbol of uncertainty caused by tribulation, and the coming of the new Jerusalem (D; v. 2a). These two contrasts are then inverted by what John hears; a vision is followed by oracle, video by audio, typical of prophetic ecstasy (cf. 2 Pet. 1:16–18). He first hears the divine confirmation of God's eschatological dwelling (D'; v. 3) where there will be no effects of evil (C'; 4a, b). These are the very things that have passed away (B'; v. 4c) with God's transformation of old things into a new order (A'; v. 5a).

At the vortex or center of this opening chiasmus is not a city but rather **a bride beautifully dressed for her husband** (E; v. 2b). The reader is drawn to John's real concern. Even though John is rather indefinite in speaking of *a* bride, his use of the marriage typology recalls 19:6, where the eschatological community is the Lamb's bride. John repeats the type in 19:7–8 where the bride's wedding dress consists of "righteous acts" and reflects the relational (or covenantal) nature of John's idea of the church: eternal life belongs to those in right relationship with God and God's Lamb, attested by righteous deeds and in continuity with both the apostolic witness to the testimony of Jesus (cf. 21:14) and the history of Israel (cf. 21:12).

The second chiasmus (21:5b—22:6a) shapes the vision's main body, which follows from and expands upon the prologue to the vision. John is recommissioned to write (A; 21:5b) about the **water of life** (B; 21:6), which is the inheritance of the community of overcomers (C; 21:7) who are not evil doers and do not belong to the **second death** (D; 21:8). John repeats these same themes in reverse order in concluding his extended description of the new Jerusalem (E; 21:9–26). The new order belongs not to the impure (D'; 21:27a) but to those found in the **Lamb's book of life** (C'; 21:27b). They will take their place in the garden where the **water of life** is found (B'; 22:1–5). This vision of the new order, which John is commissioned to write down, is **trustworthy and true** (A'; *pistoi kai alēthinoi*, 22:6a) even as the returning Lamb is also named "Faithful and True" (*pistos kai alēthinos*, 19:11).

The vortex of the second chiasmus expands the equation of new Jerusalem with bride found in the vortex of the prologue. The vision's main body proceeds from the angel's pledge to **show** John **the bride**, who is now identified as **the wife of the Lamb**. Yet, when the angel **shows** John the bride, John gets a "Cook's tour" of **the Holy City, Jerusalem** (21:9–10). This equation underscores John's understanding of God's eternal reign as a transformed *people* rather than as a place (i.e., heaven). His vision of the new order has been carefully crafted to underscore this foundational eschatological principle: the primary result of God's coming triumph over evil is a redeemed and transformed people, who live forever with God and God's Lamb. This hope provides the church with its ultimate incentive for a faithful witness to God's gospel.

21:1–5a / The prologue to John's vision of the new Jerusalem introduces the reader to its main features. As a perspective on Christ's parousia, John's portrait of the **Holy City** symbolizes a new order of human existence. Because it comes **down out of heaven** from God to earth, the reader assumes the realization of God's promised salvation will be historical and public rather than spiritual and private. Further, the impression one receives from what John sees (21:1–2) and hears (21:3–4) is that the history of human existence under the new order is characterized both by the absence of evil and its various effects (e.g., secularism, injustice, suffering, death) and by the presence of God who "tabernacles" with the worshiping community.

The **new Jerusalem** discloses the vital essence of the **new heaven and new earth**. While surely John depends upon Ezekiel's vision of the new Jerusalem, which is the site of the eschatological temple and God's *shekinah* (cf. Ezek. 40–48; esp. 40:2 and 48:35), John's emphasis is different. His Christian perspective is not religious but interpersonal; that is, God's triumph in Jesus Christ is not about a transformed cultus but about a transformed people. For this reason, he does not subordinate a new Jerusalem to a new temple as Ezekiel does. Because of this, we understand John's interpretation of his vision as the fulfillment of Ezekiel's prophecy of the eschatological cultus (contra Morris, *Revelation*, p. 238). John's use of the Ezekiel new Jerusalem typology relocates God's transforming grace and abiding glory from the temple of a restored Jerusalem (T. Dan 5:12; 2 Esdras 7:26; 10:49; cf. Heb. 12:22) to a restored people who are the new Jerusalem of John's vision. John's creative combination of the Jerusalem and marriage typologies is appropriate to his theological program, since it speaks of restoration as an intimate relationship.

In this sense, John refers to the two eschatological cities, old Babylon and new Jerusalem, as metaphors of human existence. "Babylon" denotes the world of human actions and attitudes, which yield a manner of life at odds with God's intentions for a good creation. Finally, then, unbelief is a decision against God's good intentions for humanity; Babylon's self-destruction symbolizes sin's effect on the unbelieving world. "Jerusalem" denotes yet another world—this one of faithful actions, which results in a transformed life in harmony with the creator's will (cf. 4:11). The eschatological character of Christian discipleship is a new quality of existence when God's intentions are concretely fulfilled in a "new creation," which is the people of God (cf. 2 Cor. 5:17; Gal. 5:22; 6:15; Eph. 2:10; 4:24).

The supreme blessing God dispenses at Christ's parousia is that of an eternal relationship: **Now the dwelling of God is with men, and he will live with them**. The word translated "dwelling" (*skēnē*) is used in the LXX to translate the Hebrew word (*miškan*) for "tabernacle," and is associated with the glorious presence (*shekinah*) of God (cf. Caird, *Revelation*, pp. 263–64). There is no such "building" found in the new Jerusalem (21:22) because the tabernacle has been replaced by Jesus, the embodiment of God's *shekinah* (cf. John 1:14). The application of this christological conviction to the parousia reflects a distinctive emphasis of the Johannine community which understood itself as abiding in God and God in it because of its intimate relationship with God's Son (cf. John 14–17; 1 John 4:7–21). In this sense, the fulness of the abiding glory of God will be experienced by the community at Christ's parousia.

Moreover, the use of the marriage typology also constitutes the final vindication of the community's devotion to God during the awful suffering of the present evil age. The testing of the community's faithfulness to God, which we have discussed as a problem of theodicy, comes precisely when believers are asked to trust God during those occasions when God's loving presence seems most absent from or incongruous with the actual experience of powerlessness when **death . . . mourning . . . crying . . . pain** seem to be the norm. The passing of the old order does not alter the nature of Israel's covenantal relationship with God; rather, the very nature of history has been altered so that the quality of the church's covenantal relationship with God has also been transformed in the absence of those evil powers who once sought to undermine it.

The prologue is bracketed by the language of newness: **a new heaven and a new earth** are the work of God who is **making everything new. New** is an eschatological catchword; it tells the reader to think and hope about the future of salvation's history, and specifically about the ultimate import of Christ's return. In this sense, the **new order** does not refer to a "brand new" reality; neither does Christ's parousia mark the end of human history. Rather it consummates the renewal of the **old order.** In **making everything new**, God removes all that interferes with the formation of a covenantal relationship with the believing community (cf. Heb. 8:6–13). We may now understand the cryptic reference to the passing of **sea** which probably symbolizes the uncertainty or ambiguity of current faith caused by trials and tribulations (cf. James 1:6). With the second coming comes certainty of the gospel's truth.

21:5b–8 / This passage has the singular distinction within Revelation of quoting the words of God. In introducing the vision of the new Jerusalem as the Lamb's bride, God recommissions John to **write this** vision **down.** That it is God rather than Christ or Christ's angel who commissions John may well testify to the fundamental importance of what follows in the vision's main body. The effect is one of having the Father make formal presentation of the Son's bride as "the wife of the Lamb" (21:9) to John and the other wedding guests who are witnesses of the wedding (perhaps the readers of Revelation?). This presentation suggests movement, beginning with the bride's processional out of heaven in preparation for the wedding (21:3) and concluding with the Father's announcement that the overcomers are the bride of the groom.

What follows constitutes God's **trustworthy and true** sayings (*logoi*) about the wedding's eschatological significance. In fact, it is a summary of those theological convictions that have been verified with the final coming of the new order. In this light, the authoritative pronouncement from **the Alpha and the Omega, the Beginning and the End** (cf. Rev. 1:8), that **It is done.** confirms that the antecedent promises of the new order have now been fulfilled. The Isaianic summons to drink from the **water of life** (cf. Isa. 44:3; 55:1), rehearsed by John's Jesus at the Samaritan well (cf. John 4:10–14), is satisfied by the one **who overcomes**.

We do not find a baptismal emphasis here, although the equation of water and life in Jewish cultic rituals was quite common (cf. Life of Adam and Eve 6; *ApMos* 29:12–17). John's use of the water metaphor serves theological rather than sacramental interests. As such, he wishes to continue Isaiah's use of water as symbolizing the restored covenant between the remnant Israel, the community of overcomers, and God (cf. Rev. 7:16).

John chooses to frame his fundamental eschatological conviction by echoing the covenantal formula of the Davidic covenant, **I will be his God and he will be my son** (2 Sam. 7:14 par.). His decision to do so is striking in two ways. First, this same formula is used elsewhere in the NT of Jesus (Heb. 1:5, 12:7; Luke 1:32–33; et al.). In these instances, the Davidic formula functions as a messianic title that not only conveys something of the intimate relationship between God and Jesus—like that shared between King David and God—but also transmits the church's conviction that Jesus is God's Christ, the promised heir to David's throne. That is, the Davidic covenant became a messianic promise that Jesus then fulfilled. Both parts are claims for Jesus' uniqueness. Thus, when John transfers the messianic formula from Christ to Christ's bride, he also changes the idiom for God, from "Father" to "**God**," in order to retain his conviction that Jesus is the "only begotten Son of God" (cf. John 1:17–18; Beasley-Murray, *Revelation*, pp. 313–14).

Our second point, however, alludes to the Isaianic texts that serve as the "scripture-scape" for this vision (Isa. 44:3; 55:1). That prophecy indicates that the blessings of the Davidic covenant will finally be fulfilled not in an individual but in a remnant people. Further, they are a people consisting not only of Jews (cf. Isa. 44:3–5) but also of Gentiles (cf. Isa. 55:3–5). Membership in the eschatological community is not based upon ethnicity—perhaps the contention of some of John's Jewish opponents. Rather, it is based upon one's response to God and whether one meets the theological (orthodoxy) and ethical (orthopraxy) conditions of covenant. Thus, those who belong to the **second death** rather than "first resurrection" (cf. Rev. 20:4–6) are **the cowardly, the unbelieving . . . the idolaters and all liars** who can not belong to the messianic community because of improper responses to God. They are not dressed in the "fine linen" of righteous deeds; they have not followed the Lamb, and so they cannot drink from the **spring of the water of life**; rather they are thrown into the waters of **the fiery lake of burning sulfur** (cf. 19:20; 20:10, 14, 15).

21:9–10 / **One of the seven angels** that had previously shown John the punishment of Babylon's whore (cf. 17:1) is now commissioned by God to show John the **wife of the Lamb**. While the angel's mission is to disclose the contrast between these two women, it also makes it clear that they represent two contrasting spheres or "cities" of human relationships (cf. 17:18). This explains why the angel, who pledges to **show** John **the bride**, then **showed** him **the Holy City, Jerusalem**. This expansion of John's earlier vision of the city (in 21:2) actually reverses the order of presentation, heightening the significance of the Lamb's bride: on this occasion the angel first identifies **the bride** as **the wife of the Lamb**, and then shows John **the Holy City**. The description of the city's architecture that follows in 21:11–26 actually describes the bride; this particular city is the realization of a particular human community, the faithful church (cf. Boring, *Revelation*, pp. 219–24).

John is transported to a **mountain great and high** to view the bride. The significance of his vantage point is indicated by the prophetic formula, **in the Spirit** (cf. 1:10): what follows for John is further indication that God will fulfill the promise of redemption. According to biblical prophecy, the **mountain** is Mount Zion, the building site for the eschatological city (cf. Ezek. 40:2; 28:13–14; Isa. 2:2; Mic. 4:1; cf. Caird, *Revelation*, pp. 269–70). Its **great and high** elevation is symbolic of the city's power and influence in the age to come; for "the glory and honor of the nations will be brought into it" (21:26). In fact, John's vantage point is the very spot to which the eschatological city will descend **out of heaven from God**; thus, the angel has brought him to a place where he can easily survey the city from within its opened gates. Himself a member of the community of overcomers (cf. 1:9), the seer is now an insider to these eschatological mysteries of God and is able to be a faithful witness to "the word of God and the testimony of Jesus."

Moreover, this text recalls the "desert" region where John is earlier led "in the Spirit" to witness the judgment of the "great prostitute" (cf. 17:3a). The desert, an isolated and forboding place, is apropos to the prostitute's evil and eventual execution. By contrast, the angel now leads John to a mountain where he sees a vision of shalom and eternal life. Thus, the image of the great **mountain** cues the reader for a vision of the bride's triumph, which will be very different in tone and spirit yet similar in power and importance to the prior vision of the prostitute's defeat.

21:11–26 / Our commentary on John's vision of the new Jerusalem will try to conceive of its architecture in interpersonal terms, in keeping with our thesis that the new Jerusalem is the Lamb's bride, the community of his faithful disciples. Specifically, three landmarks on the cityscape are studied by John: (1) the city's wall (21:12–14), (2) the city's plat (21:15–17), and (3) the materials used to construct the city, especially its foundation stones (21:18–21).

Before we comment further on these three features, two additional elements must be noted because of their importance to the other three. First, John's survey of the city is bracketed by his more general observation that the city radiates with the **glory** (*shekinah*) **of God** (21:11, 23), the tangible proof of God's presence. It is the surety of God's presence that provides **light** (or truth) for **the nations** (21:24–26) and ensures that **nothing impure will ever enter** into the city (21:27). Upon even a cursory reading of the Fourth Gospel, one notes the importance of the "glory" motif to the theology of the Johannine tradition; the essence and the aim of the Word's messianic mission is his glory (John 1:14). Thus, in John's narrative of Jesus' public ministry, teaching interprets miracles as powerful "signs" that reveal the transforming nature of God's glory within history, culminating in Jesus' passion as the full revelation of God's glory (cf. John 7:39; 8:54; 11:4; 12:16, 23, 28; 13:31, 32; 14:13; 15:8; 16:14; 17:1, 4, 5, 10). By locating God's glory in Christ's death rather than in his miracles, John shows the reader that the glory of God is ultimately God's forgiveness of sin rather than the Lord's miraculous power over nature; that is, "the glory of God is manifest for the salvation of man in Jesus" (so D. M. Smith, *John*, p. 30). This, then, is the essence of God's Word which is the **light** of truth (cf. John 1:9; 1 John 2:8) first seen in Christ and now seen by all the **nations** (cf. 5:9) who follow after him.

The new Jerusalem is the domicile of a glorified people. Their glorification is testimony that their sins have been forgiven by the Lamb of God, and their relationship with a holy God has thereby been secured. This realization stands at the center of Christian hope: if the Lamb is glorified because of his faithfulness to God even unto death, so also will the Lamb's followers be glorified at his parousia because of their devotion to him. The failure of those who followed the beast to give glory to God (cf. 16:9), in contrast with the heavenly beings (4:9, 11; 5:12, 13; 19:1, 7) and the eschatological people (cf. 7:12), rejects the core of Christian proclamation. Because they remain in sin, their names are not written "in the Lamb's book of life"; because they remain impure, they are excluded from the new Jerusalem and the shalom of God.

Second, more important than what John finds in the city is what he does not find: **I did not see a temple in the city** (21:22). Most commentators point out that this remark differentiates John from other Jewish writers for whom the realization of Ezekiel's eschatological temple was an essential element of their idea of hope. Perhaps John himself had expected to find such a temple in his vision and this text registers his surprise. A better explanation, however, is that this passage marks the essential protest of Christian proclamation that speaks of hope in terms of relationships rather than in terms of places and things. John's comment agrees with Jesus (cf. Mark 14:57–59, par.) and Stephen (Acts 6:13; 7:48–53; cf. 21:28), who were executed in part for shifting the center of Jewish worship from the temple and its formal cultus to a dynamic, personal relationship with God as exemplified in and effected through the life and death of God's Christ. The writer of Hebrews reminds us that the Son's *relationship* to God and to God's people is priestly; and this relationship transcends the limitations of the temple cultus on earth (cf. Heb. 9:1–14). In this sense, then, even as the new Jerusalem "is" the people of God, so also its temple "is" **the Lord God Almighty and the Lamb** (cf. 11:17–19). Now we turn to the critical landmarks of the new Jerusalem for comment.

John first saw that the city had **a great, high wall** (21:12–14). There are good reasons why the seer should be attracted to the city's wall. Much like the well-known skyscrapers that define and distinguish today's great cities or the Great Wall of China, the wall surrounding an ancient city gave it a distinctive identity. John reports that the wall of the new Jerusalem was **great** and **high**, symbolic then of the city's exalted status among the nations. But the wall had a more practical function: to protect those who lived within. Indeed, all such potential threats have since been banished and "nothing impure will ever enter the city" (21:27). Those who live within the city's walls are kept secure for an eternity.

Like the eschatological Jerusalem of Ezekiel's vision (Ezek. 48:30–34), the wall of John's Jerusalem has **twelve gates**, corresponding to the **twelve tribes of Israel** (cf. Rev. 7:1–8); it has **twelve foundations** as well, corresponding to the **twelve apostles of the Lamb** (cf. 21:19–20). Rather than looking for zodiacal significance in John's description (e.g., Caird, *Revelation*, pp. 271–72), the interpreter should quest after the theological significance of the city's wall. First, the gates surround the city and symbolize the universal or inclusive character of God's salvation (cf. 5:9). The credentials of the eschatological people of God are spiritual and not ethnic; thus, any person from any nation can enter into the community of faith to find God's blessing. Second, the addition of **twelve apostles** to **twelve tribes** "maintains the continuity of the OT and the Christian Church" (Charles, *Revelation*, vol. 2, p. 162). The number twelve symbolizes the ongoing community of faith in whose history God's salvation is worked out; the history of the twelve tribes (cf. Heb. 11:10) continues in the history of twelve apostles, who represent the true church. John's vision of the new Jerusalem is the concluding chapter in that ecclesiastical history (cf. Heb. 12:22–28). Third, the apostolic witness to Jesus Christ is foundational for **all** the nations (cf. Matt. 16:17–19; Eph. 2:20), Jewish and Gentile (cf. Eph. 2:11–13), because it confirms the biblical promises of God's salvation, first entrusted to God's prophets and now fulfilled through Christ. The essential difference between God's revelation in Christ and God's revelation to Israel is not one of content but one of intent. The apostles did not bear witness to a "brand new" thing, as though God revealed one thing to Israel and another thing to the church;

God is one God. Rather, they recognized that the biblical promises given to Israel through the prophets were now fulfilled in the ministry of the Messiah. This is precisely the point John is making: the wall surrounding new Jerusalem symbolizes the fulfillment of Israel's hope for God's shalom and locates its final realization in the community of overcomers.

Secondly, the angel then **measured the city with the rod** of gold (21:15-17). In an earlier vision (11:1-2), John was given a reed to measure the "temple of God and the altar." Here, it is the angel and not John who measures the city, simply because its dimensions are beyond human computation and comprehension: each side measures **12,000 stadia**, or about 1400 miles! While Ezekiel's majestic city was a square, John's Jerusalem is cubic. Rather than a symbol of perfection, as Greek philosophy would have surmised, the city's cubical shape is probably of theological interest to John as a symbol of God's presence. Knowing that the temple's "holy of holies" was also a cube (cf. 1 Kings 6:20) although much smaller (about thirty feet per side), and that it too was the location of God's *shekinah*, John links the city's shape with the presence of God which pervades and sustains it (see above; Mounce, *Revelation*, p. 380).

The measurements also rehearse the significance John finds in the number **twelve**; every dimension is a multiple of twelve. Of the method of measurement, Caird understands the final phrase, **which the angel was using**, as a "proviso" that the **man's measurement** was really angelic (*Revelation*, pp. 273-74). His rendering argues against the NIV, which distinguishes the angelic measurer from the human measurement it employs. The text's syntax is admittedly obscure; however, Caird's interpretation (and translation) is preferred since it underscores the symbolic character of the angel's action: the angel is measuring the location where God's true Israel (i.e., "the Twelve") live in worship and praise of God who dwells there with them.

Finally, John describes the precious gems and building materials used to build the **city walls** (21:18-20) and their **gates** of pearl (21:21a; cf. Isa. 54:12; for the significance of pearl gates see Ford, *Revelation*, pp. 343-44); the main street, like the rest of the city, was paved with **pure gold, like transparent glass** (21:21b). W. Reader remains unconvinced by both ancient and modern attempts to explain these rare and valuable materials by any other known list of stones in biblical (e.g., Exod. 28:17–20; cf. Isa. 54:11–12) or pagan (e.g., zodiac signs) traditions. He rather relates John's list of stones to the gem stories found in Pseudo-Philo's *Biblical Antiquities* written about the same time as John's Revelation but within the milieu of the Palestinian Jewish synagogues. In this midrashic document, the jewel motif carries theological significance: jewels represent the purified people of God. Moreover, because the stones are emblematic of God's good creation, they were hidden during the period of Israel's sin, then to be recovered at the time of eschatological Israel's final purification and salvation (cf. *BibAnt* 26).

John's use of the jewel motif is similar, but with one important Christian interpretation. Earlier, he noted that the names of the apostles are inscribed on the foundations of the city wall (21:14), thus linking the church's spiritual and eschatological foundations to the teaching of the apostles. Reader keenly notes that the list of gems in 21:19b–20, stated in the nominative case, is *not* appositional to 21:19a, which is stated in the dative. Rather, John supposes that each foundation stone consists of one single enormous gem (so Reader), much like the wall itself that is fabricated entirely with jasper or the city that is fabricated with gold (21:18). Again, the critical theological point is that the city's foundation is apostolic; the true Israel of God is the people nurtured by the witness of the twelve apostles to the risen Jesus.

The critical pastoral point is that the eschatological community, purified and perfected at the parousia of Christ, consists of those whose faith is patterned after the apostles'. No doubt, John has in mind those Christian teachers whose instruction opposes the apostolic tradition and threatens the salvation of the believing community (cf. 2:6, 14–15, 20; 1 John 2:18–27). To overcome evil is to repudiate any teaching contrary to the apostolic "testimony of Jesus Christ."

John ends his tour on the main street, which is paved with gold. He mentioned earlier (cf. 21:18) that the entire city is made with a **gold** of high quality—**as pure as glass** (cf. Morris, *Revelation*, p. 246). In this second reference to the city's gold, he singles out for special comment its **great street**. Why? Perhaps the seer wants the reader to recall an earlier vision of yet another main street in yet another "great city" where the bodies of the "two witnesses," who represent the community of overcomers, were discarded by the beast for public inspection and ridicule (cf. 11:8–10). Yet, like the Lamb's before them, their defeat is as transitory as the beast's momentary triumph. By repeating the image of the main street in a great city, John rehearses this same point again: the street of their former shame has now been replaced by the street of their eternal glory. Such is the ironic character of Christian hope: while believers may well be objects of public ridicule during the present age, their situation will be reversed at Christ's return.

21:27 / This verse, along with the description of the "paradise of God" that follows (22:1–5), forms the chiastic bracket that concentrates John's vision of the new Jerusalem. This concluding stop on John's tour of the eschatological city combines with the earlier speech of God (21:5–8) to provide the themes proper to any interpretation of John's vision of Christian hope. Recall that God specified those **shameful or deceitful** characteristics of the **impure** (cf. the vice-list in 21:8a), who are placed in the "lake of burning sulfur . . . the second death" (21:8b) rather than in **the Lamb's book of life**. The community of overcomers exists in harmony with the character of a holy God, disclosed in the life of God's Lamb. Because of his redemptive work, the vital hope of the believing community now is for a finished transformation of character so that at his parousia they will be able to live a manner of life intended by God from creation (cf. 4:11).

God's earlier speech also indicated something of the nature of the community's inheritance of eternal life (cf. 21:7a): it is predicated on the relationship between the overcomer, a "Son," and "his God" (cf. 21:7b). The chiastic patterning of this vision guides the reader to the subsequent expansion of this point in 21:27b, where John reports that only those **whose names are written in the Lamb's book of life** will enter into their inheritance. The relationship between the eschatological community and its God depends on a commitment to the prior action of the slain Lamb (cf. 3:5; Morris, *Revelation*, p. 248); only then can the overcomer refer to the Lamb's God as "his God" (cf. 3:12) and to God's Son as "brother" (cf. Heb. 2:11, 17).

22:1–5 / The phrase, **Then the angel showed me**, seems to indicate John's decision to add a separate "paradise tradition" into his vision of the new Jerusalem. The reasons for this are clearly theological: he thereby indicates that God's redemption returns the new creation—the community of overcomers—to the Garden of Eden and to the creator's intentions for humanity (Caird, *Revelation*, p. 280; Boring, *Revelation*, p. 218). These intentions, already indicated by the "new song" at the Lamb's exaltation, are twofold (5:9–10): to create a people who can now serve God (22:3) and reign with God for ever (22:5). These intentions are fully realized at the Lamb's return.

Fitting this passage into the chiastic patterning of John's second vision of the new Jerusalem further illuminates his theological program. Before, God promised that "I will give (the one who overcomes) to drink . . . from the spring of the water of life" (21:6). John uses the paradise tradition to recall and expand upon this important biblical image of hope (Zech. 14:8; Ezek. 47:1–12), the **water of life**, in two important ways. First, John now locates the source of this water: it flows **from the throne of God and of the Lamb**. Rather than locating Christian hope in the promise of a restored city (Zech. 8; cf. Ps. 46:4) or temple (Ezek. 40–48) as the prophets did, John's Gospel proclaims a person, Christ Jesus, through whom God has already fulfilled the promise of life (cf. John 7:37–9). Second, by placing the **river** (cf. Gen. 2:9–10) with **the tree of life** (cf. Rev. 2:7; Gen. 2:9; 3:21–22) and **the crops of** monthly **fruit** (cf. Gen. 3:3), John draws the reader back into the Garden of Eden as a place of promise, this time for the **healing of the nations** rather than for their **curse** (cf. Zech 14:11). In a sense, the images suggest this "Central Park" in the city of God not only regains Eden's promise but actually improves upon it! After all, Adam and Eve were never allowed to eat the fruit on the "tree of life"; and they were dismissed from the garden, now guarded by angels, so they could not eat the tree's fruit and live forever (cf. Gen. 3:22–23). The phrases, **there will be no more night** and **the Lord God will give them light**, are additional links to the creation story (Gen. 1:3–5). In fact, the "night/light" dualism marks out God's work on the "first day" of the original creation. Perhaps here the negation of this dualism—there is **no more night . . . or sun**—functions as a final element of John's *inclusio*. Especially if **night** is also used as a metaphor for evil, as it often is in Scripture, then John's point seems to be that God's new creation is a reversal of the old, cursed creation because there is nothing in it which might prompt God's people to rebel against God and the Lamb. The new creation, then, is characterized not only by the absence of evil, but by the absence of human desire to rebel against God's reign.

Eve and then Adam's evil had been in seeking to acquire divine knowledge through illicit means. Now they bask in the presence of God; receiving God's light, the community of overcomers can now **see his face**. Although we disagree with Caird's conclusion that a community of martyrs (rather than a more inclusive community of faithful disciples; cf. 21:12, 14) occupies John's new Jerusalem, we do agree that these idioms for divine presence reflect the intimate knowledge of God as a manifestation of the new covenant: God's people "have also come to bear the impress of his nature on their lives (cf. 1 John iii.2; 2 Cor. iii. 18; 1 Cor. xv. 49)" (*Revelation*, pp. 280–81). Further, this more personal acquaintance with God reverses God's **curse** of Cain, who was banished not only from the land but from God's presence (cf. Gen. 4:10–14).

While John does not tell us from what the nations are healed, the many allusions to the former Eden lead the reader to assume that God's merciful healing which takes place in the paradise of the new Jerusalem constitutes God's restoration of all that is lost in humanity's fall. Not only immortality is regained, but a nourishing relationship with God and the Lamb as well. Moreover, in recalling that Cain's murder of Abel was the ultimate offense against a human relationship, even as Eve and Adam's rebellion was the ultimate offense against their covenant with God, the interpreter recognizes that *both* the divine and human dimensions of relationship are now restored in the paradise of God. The eschatological community of overcomers is recognized by their righted relationship with God and with each other.

In this regard, let me make a concluding point about the closing refrain in John's portrait of paradise, **And they will reign for ever and ever**. According to the creation story, the ultimate value to which God gave human life is indicated by God's decision to "let (humanity) rule . . . over all the creatures" (Gen. 1:26). In that story, of course, humanity's evil is defined in part as the corruption of their reign over God's creation. In fact, God's restoration of the covenant with Noah (cf. Gen. 9:8–17) seeks to reestablish humanity's rule over creation (cf. Gen. 9:1–7). Against this biblical backdrop, then, the interpreter of Revelation recalls that John's idea of eternal life includes the establishment of the believing community's rule over the new creation (1:6; 5:10; cf. 1 Pet. 2:5, 9–10).

22:6a / The last element of John's chiastic patterning of his vision of the new Jerusalem repeats God's justification of why John should write the vision down: **These words are trustworthy and true** (cf. 21:5b). Although the NIV indicates that these words are spoken by **the angel**, the text does not identify the speaker. Perhaps the speaker is God, who repeats the earlier verdict about John's vision in 21:5b to frame its importance for his readers. Perhaps the speaker is the Risen Christ, or his mediating angel, since the phrase does remind us that Christ is called "Faithful and True" (cf. 3:14; 19:11). At day's end, however, the exact identity of the speaker is not as important as the sentiment spoken: in a world of competing options, where Christian discipleship is challenged in a variety of ways, the believing community may fully depend upon John's account of Christian hope as **trustworthy and true**.

Additional Notes   §20

21:2, 9–10 / For a superb treatment of our point that the **new Jerusalem** is not an actual place but **the Bride** for Christ, the church, see Robert H. Gundry, "The New Jerusalem: People as Place, not Place for People," *NovT* 29 (1987), pp. 254–64. Less convincing is Peter DuBrul's, "Jerusalem in the Apocalypse of John," in *Jerusalem: Seat of Theology*, ed. D. Burrell (Jerusalem/Tantur: Ecumenical Institute for Theological Research, 1982), pp. 57–77. We noted in the Introduction that John has constructed a parallelism, vaguely chiastic, between key phrases found in Christ's exhortations to overcome, transmitted to the seven churches through their angels (Rev. 2–3), and John's vision of the new Jerusalem (see Introduction). The theological conclusion we derived from this literary construction is that for John the community of overcomers *is* the new Jerusalem.

21:2 / For a recent study of John's nuptial imagery as an expression of the final stage of God's salvation of eschatological Israel, see Jan Fekkes, III, "Revelation 19–21 and Isaian Nuptial Imagery," *JBL* 109 (1990), pp. 269–87. Fekkes contends that Isaiah's prophecy of a "new Jerusalem" in Isa. 54:11–12 lies behind John's understanding of his vision of Christ's parousia in Revelation 19–21. More specifically, the bride is a metaphor for acts of faithfulness (cf. 19:8), which prepare her for the eschatological union with the Lamb. According to Fekkes, John's equating of place with people, city with bride, intensifies his use of the promise-fulfillment motif: the bride, who prepares herself for the Lamb by deeds of right-eousness, will become Isaiah's promised "temple-city"—a place in which God and the Lamb dwell and are worshiped forever.

21:1–5a / Our outline of this vision differs somewhat from most modern scholars, who divide the vision of the new Jerusalem into the following integral units according to their literary function: (1) a prologue to the vision, typically 21:1–8; (2) followed by an extended description of the eschatological city, typically 21:9–27; and (3) concluded by the re-hearsal of a familiar "paradise tradition," found in 22:1–5. E.g., M. Rissi, *The Future of the World* (London: SCM Press, 1970); Beasley-Murray, *Reve-lation*, pp. 314–18. Our twofold division draws upon literary (i.e., chi-astic) patterning, although we agree that the first functions as prologue while the second includes a paradise tradition.

21:11, 23, 26 / John's use of **glory** no doubt alludes to the open-ing verse of Isaiah's theophany (Isa. 6:1–13) and also to his Great Ser-vant Song (52:13–53:12). Interestingly, in the larger contexts of both Isaianic passages, God's glory and then the Servant's glory are resisted or rejected by Israel (cf. Isa. 6:9–10; 52:15). In the central passage of his Gospel, the fourth evangelist picks up this tension between the revelation of God's glory in Christ Jesus and Israel's rejection of him (John 12:38–40): that is, Jewish rejection of God's glory found in Jesus Christ is the fulfillment of biblical prophecy. Christ's "hour" of glorification on the cross not only represents his vindication; it also symbolizes Jewish re-jection of Messiah that accords with God's redemptive plans as revealed within Scripture. In this same sense, the glory motif is employed here in Revelation as a "proof-from-prophecy" that God's promised triumph over evil will be fulfilled within history.

21:19–20 / For the background of this passage and its importance in John's vision of the new Jerusalem, see William Reader, "The Twelve Jewels of Revelation 21:19–20: Tradition History and Modern Interpreta-tions," *JBL* 100 (1981), pp. 433–57. Parallel texts in Pseudo-Philo are found in D. J. Harrington, "Pseudo-Philo," in *The OT Pseudepigrapha*, vol. 2, ed. J. H. Charlesworth (Garden City, N.Y.: Doubleday, 1985), pp. 297–377.

22:1–5 / The development of the idea of paradise coincided with the development of the idea of afterlife. The OT contains only vague ref-erences to the resurrection of the believing community (cf. Isa. 26; Dan. 12) and virtually nothing about the future place for the risen people of God. Increasing speculation about these matters is charted in the inter-testamental pseudepigrapha; and much of this literature includes mid-rash on the biblical description of the Garden of Eden (e.g., 1 Enoch 32; 2 Enoch 8; Life of Adam and Eve 37). John's own version of paradise clearly belongs to this Jewish tradition, although he stresses its earthly and "real" (rather than the heavenly and thus "spiritual") environs. In this way, he extends the Johannine response to the christological speculations of nascent gnosticism or docetism, echoed in 1 John and the Fourth Gospel, to eschatological concerns.

22:3a / My colleague, Frank A. Spina, has pointed out that Cain's curse is personal and more demanding than God's previous curse "of the ground" in that he was charged to till cursed ground rather than good ground. As such it marks a regression in God's relations with humanity from creation to creature. Indeed, Adam and Eve were banished from the Garden but not from God's face. It was they who hid themselves from God, not vice versa as in Cain's case (cf. Gen. 3:8–10 with 4:10–14); see F. A. Spina, "The Ground(s) (*'adamah*) of Cain's Rejection: Gen. 4 in the Context of the Primeval History," forthcoming in *ZAW*. In our view, John is here alluding to the old story of Cain's curse rather than to the Moses tradition (cf. Exod. 33:20–23; Mounce, *Revelation*, pp. 387–88; Boring, *Revelation*, p. 216), a christological tradition (cf. Matt. 5:8; Beasley-Murray, *Revelation*, pp. 332–33), or a prophetic tradition (Ezek. 48:35; Morris, *Revelation*, p. 249); in fact, the same idiom, "face" (*to prosōpon*), is used in both texts. The idioms of divine presence envisage the pervasive character of God's transformation of the redeemed community as they "backtrack" their way, past the cursed Cain, and a fallen Adam and Eve, into the paradise of God where they find they now can eat and drink unhindered from the fruit of the tree of life and the river of the water of life.

22:4 / Most commentaries contend that the antecedent of **his face** is God; thus, this phrase constitutes "perhaps the greatest of all eternity's blessings" (Mounce, *Revelation*, p. 387) and a clear reversal of earlier restrictions against this kind of direct and immediate encounter between human beings and God. A case could be made, however, that this phrase refers to the **lamb**, which would be consistent with John's earlier vision of the 144,000 (cf. Rev. 14:1) as well as with the text's grammar, since *to arnion*, "Lamb," is the most immediate predecessor to "his face" (i.e., "the throne of God and of the Lamb . . . his face").

§21 *The Epistolary Benediction (Rev. 22:6b–21)*

The concluding section of early Christian letters often contains the author's benediction, typically expressed as a prayer or doxology, but often accompanied by many other pastoral conventions as well. In his letters, for example, Paul sometimes closes his correspondence by greeting various acquaintances in a particular congregation (cf. Rom. 16), perhaps to encourage them in their faith (cf. 1 Cor. 16:19–20) or to give them instructions (cf. Col. 4:15–16). In several of his letters, he includes a list of moral and spiritual exhortations (cf. 1 Thess. 5:12–22) as well as a summary of the advice given in the letter's body (cf. Gal. 6:12–16). The letter writer also uses this concluding section to make personal requests. Sometimes with considerable import, Paul even tells his audience how the composition was transcribed (cf. Gal. 6:11; Philem. 19), or by whom it is delivered (cf. Col. 4:7-9).

While the author is likely to use familiar liturgical forms and literary conventions in bidding goodbye to his audience, he does so with an eye to the crisis that occasioned his letter. Thus, while the content and its arrangement within the benedictory might appear quite traditional and even arbitrary in application, they intend to convey pastoral advice for that particular situation. It is vital for the interpreter to remember that letters are substitutes for the absent writer. Letters are necessarily more pointed than visits, but no less personal and practical in purpose.

These general remarks about epistolary benedictions provide a context within which to understand Revelation's concluding paragraphs. Commentators often dismiss this material because it seems so haphazardly drawn and pointless. A few, like Charles, even want to reshape it to give it "proper" form in order to find meaning from it. Surely this is a mistake for both theological and literary reasons. As literature, John's final words function as his "Amen" (cf. 22:21); similar to other epistolary benedictions we find within the NT, they comprise a collection of various traditional exhortations and literary conventions, rather loosely assembled, which together intend to summarize and focus the entire composition in a profoundly pastoral manner. Hardly pointless theologically, this material provides Revelation's reader with an overarching perspective on the book's importance for Christian discipleship; it is like an epilogue that rounds out the composition and makes it whole and complete.

22:6b-7 / By employing an inverted parallelism, John summarizes the two critical themes that dominate the rest of his benediction (cf. Mounce, *Revelation*, p. 390); they are also the constitutive elements of a proper perspective by which the entire composition should be read (cf. Beasley-Murray, *Revelation*, p. 335). First, the clause, **The Lord . . . sent his angel to show his servants**, alludes to the opening words of Revelation (cf. 1:1). John reminds his readers that the source of any prophecy is **the God of the spirits** who alone inspires seers to speak words that are "trustworthy and true" (cf. 19:10). Further, by more specifically mentioning the **angel**, which brought him visions from Christ (cf. 1:1), John keeps his own inspired revelation in view. His real interest is not to offer an *apologia* for Christian prophecy, or even to argue that his God has fulfilled OT prophecy through Christ Jesus. Rather, by bracketing his entire composition off by parallel statements about his own inspiration, the seer wraps it up in a cloak of revealed certainty. His composition can be trusted as true from beginning to end because it is revealed by **the Lord, the God of the spirits**.

The parallel phrase (22:7b) repeats this same claim but expands it in the form of a personal beatitude: **Blessed is he who keeps the words of the prophecy in this book**. Not only does John write a book of inspired prophecy, but its reader is inspired by God in order to attain wisdom about the path to eschatological blessing. While beatitudes were common conventions of prophetic compositions (Schüssler Fiorenza, *Revelation*, pp. 164–65), they mirror a noteworthy element of early Christianity's notion of the divine inspiration of Scripture (cf. 2 Tim. 3:15–16). God's inspiring action, which transforms scriptural texts into conduits of information about God's Word and will, is found at both their writing *and* their reading. With respect to Revelation, John is inspired to write down the prophecy delivered to him as an apocalypse; but the one who **keeps** what John has written down is then the recipient of divine blessings at the end of the age (cf. Rev. 1:3).

John's centers his summary by asserting that the divinely inspired message of Revelation is true not only in a metaphysical sense, it is true about physical (i.e., historical) **things** as well. John, a Christian prophet, predicts the parousia of Christ **that must soon take place** in history (cf. 1:3)—a prediction of salvation history's climactic event that lies behind every vision he has written down. However, in this benediction, John does not rehearse the "content" of his prophecy. His purpose, underscored by the parallel saying from the Risen Christ, is to emphasize the imminence of its fulfillment: **Behold, I am coming soon!** (cf. Rev. 3:11). In fact, John writes with pastoral concerns for the present that will be made abundantly clear at the second coming of Christ. Significantly, the Lord's promise—repeated three times—links the community's past, present, and future in the person of the Lord Jesus.

Thus, for the interpreter to reify John's purpose into a doctrine of imminence is to lose much of its rhetorical power; the prophet is a pastor, not a systematic theologian! He is not concerned, at least in any formal or academic way, to calculate the timing of Christ's parousia. Rather he is interested to motivate his audience to respond to Christ immediately and properly in the light of his soon and sudden return. In this sense, then, the visions and images found in Revelation are determined by the expectation of an indeterminate although imminent parousia. John's perspective toward Christ's return should cause the interpreter to resist the creation of elaborate charts and timetables that promise to date the second coming; rather, Revelation's portrait of Christ's exaltation and his imminent parousia is calculated to evoke repentance from sin and faithfulness to the Lamb.

22:8–11 / The exhortations contained in benedictions often provide necessary motivations to act upon what the author has previously written. In that what John has written is true, and in that what he has predicted as the ultimate event of human history could occur at any moment, he expands his commissioning experience to describe the proper response to his prophecy.

John's autobiographical assertion that he was **the one who heard and saw** the visions contained in his book is another closing convention used by Paul (cf. Rom. 16:22; 1 Cor. 16:21; Gal. 6:11; 2 Thess. 3:17; Philem. 19; Col. 4:18). The use of this epistolary convention in the benediction indicates that the author endorses the letter's content and sends it as true and useful.

Yet, John proceeds to tell how, upon receiving the visions from the angel of the Lord (cf. 1:1), he **fell down to worship at the feet of the angel** (cf. Rev. 19:10). On the one hand, John's response to his ecstatic experience is logical and even proper: John recognizes the divine source of his visions and worships God in the presence of the angelic mediator. The interpreter should take note that John does not say that he intended to worship the angel; neither is there is anything in Revelation that suggests that John is nervous about any incidence of angel worship within his audience. It is inconceivable that John himself would fall prey to this idolatry; to do so would be to exhibit the sort of confusion expected of a pagan convert (cf. Acts 10:25–26), or of a gnostic Christian (cf. Col. 2:18), or of a convert from hellenistic Judaism, but not of someone like John who stood so firmly within the apostolic tradition. In this light, then, John's report of the angel's response to his worship serves a rhetorical role: John wishes to clarify that the proper response to his composition is not to worship the book itself or the one who wrote it but to **Worship God!**

The angelic command, **do not seal up the words** (cf. Rev. 10:4), repeats the earlier saying of the Risen Christ (22:7). Daniel's prophecy was "sealed" for an extended period of time (cf. Dan. 12:4, 9); John's exhortation is precisely the opposite: his audience is to "publish" his composition, for it consists of **words of prophecy** whose fulfillment **is near**. Without doubt, John has Daniel's exhortation in mind and reverses its force to underscore his confidence that Daniel's prophecy has now been fulfilled by Christ. John's reinterpretation of Daniel's apocalyptic formula is thoroughly "Christian" and conveys both a theological conviction and a more literal, temporal claim central for Christian formation. Theologically, since God's kingdom was brought near by Christ (cf. Mark 1:15), the promise of its judgment and of its salvation is always at hand in the gospel (Ladd, *Revelation*, p. 291). Temporally, the historic realization of these two promises is at hand in the parousia of Christ.

The meaning of the angelic exhortation, **Let him who does wrong continue to do wrong . . . and let him who is holy continue to be holy**, is unclear and remains contested. Internal evidence (cf. 22:17) suggests that the interpreter should not construe these words as promoting the kind of religious determinism that makes conversion or repentance impossible for some people

(Beasley-Murray, *Revelation*, p. 337). In our view, this phrase refers to the inviolate nature of John's prophecy such that any response to it, whether obdurate or obedient, does not change its message. In light of Daniel's concluding exhortation (12:9–13), the wise thing to do is to continue on one's way, assured that all prophecy will be fulfilled because God is both the giver and the guarantor of its truth (cf. James 5:12). From this theocentric perspective, prophecy establishes the church's rule of faith. Whether one is **wrong** and **vile** or **right** and **holy**, history will proceed to its end in absolute accord with the promise contained in the "word of God" and its fulfillment according to "the testimony of Jesus Christ." Measured by this rule, those who are **wrong** and **vile** will be judged, and those who are **right** and **holy** will certainly be redeemed.

22:12–16 / The second exhortation is given by the Risen Christ, who repeats his earlier saying (22:7) in order to emphasize that his imminent parousia is also a time for divine judgment. The connection between God's coming triumph over evil and God's universal judgment of evil derives from the prophet Isaiah (40:10); and the subsequent embellishment that God's universal judgment is based on humanity's works also derives from OT teaching (cf. Prov. 24:12; Jer. 17:10; Ps. 62:1)—a point well known in earliest Christianity (cf. Rom. 2:6–10; Luke 10:25–29; James 1:22–27; 2:8–13). Especially according to the Pauline midrash on Proverbs 24:12 found in Romans 2:6–10, God's retributive justice rewards those whose works are good and punishes those whose works are evil. If we assume that John's sense of divine justice is similar to Paul's, then the interpreter must not assume that Christ's saying refers only to the community of overcomers, whose **reward** is salvation (cf. Rev. 20:4–6); but God's coming triumph is the occasion to dispense justice to all evildoers, whose **reward** is punishment (cf. 22:11). Christ's exhortation, then, is directed to the faithful as a pastoral word of encouragement, but also to the disobedient as a prophetic word of rebuke.

Because he bears definitive testimony to the word of God, Jesus Christ now claims that the eschatological judgment of everyone's deeds lies **with me**. His authority to mediate God's coming judgment is based upon his exalted status as **Alpha and Omega** (cf. Rev. 1:8; 21:6), **the First and the Last** (cf. Rev. 1:17), the Beginning and the End (cf. Rev. 21:6). The sequence of these three titles of Christ's lordship follows their occurrence within Revelation. The addition of the first and last titles to the series is striking, however, since elsewhere they refer to God (1:8; 21:6) and not to Christ. John's concluding point seems explicit enough: in light of his eschatological vindication, Christ has authority to mediate God's universal judgment and shares perfectly all of God's purposes (Caird, *Revelation*, p. 285) as well as God's status within the worshiping community (cf. Rev. 21:22).

In keeping with the structure (and so "theo-logic") of Christ's earlier benediction (22:7), a beatitude now follows: Blessed are those who . . . go through the gates into the city. Those who respond properly to John's prophecy that Christ is coming soon, with either repentance or hope, will receive the promised blessing of a good God. In light of John's eschatology, on the one hand, the community of overcomers who wash their robes (cf. 7:14) will eat from the tree of life found in the paradise of the city, the new Jerusalem (cf. 22:1–5). On the other hand, those who practice "wrong and vile" things are unclean, like dogs (cf. Phil. 3:2; Ps. 22:16, 20), and are placed outside the city (cf. 21:8, 27). We should not suppose that those outside the city consist only of unbelievers. The immediate context insists on a universal judgment by works (rather than by faith alone), which includes believers. Further, the list of vices characterizes some believers found in the congregations who first read John's book. For example, some Christians in Thyatira have turned to the teaching of a certain "Jezebel," who has misled them into sexual immorality and idolatry (cf. 2:20). Elsewhere in the NT, James speaks of materialistic believers as murderers (cf. James 4:2; 5:6), and Paul refers to Jewish Christian opponents in Philippi as "dogs" (cf. Phil. 3:2). Thus, the rhetorical function of the vice list may well intend to bid certain believers, whose apostate tendencies imperil their salvation, to repent.

Jesus concludes his exhortation with a second triad (cf. 22:12), this one comprised of messianic titles: I am the Root (cf. 5:5; Isa. 11:1,10) and the Offspring of David, and the bright Morning Star (cf. 2:28; Num. 24:17). In this case, John's Christ uses these titles to justify his angel's mediation of John's visions (cf. 1:1). The plural you extends the influence of the angel's mediation beyond John to all those who belong to the churches, to whom this book of visions was first addressed. (From a canonical perspective the scope of the angel's work includes all readers in every age who recognize John's prophecy as part of the church's ongoing rule of faith and life.)

Finally, the two triads of titles found in Christ's exhortation, when taken together, portray the exalted Lamb as "both Lord and Christ" (cf. Acts 2:36). He is so named by God because of his faithful testimony to God. It becomes the Christian's hope, then, that God will surely exalt all those who faithfully follow the Lamb of God wherever he goes.

22:17 / The believing community, along with the **Spirit** of the Risen Christ, issues the invitation, **Come!**, but to whom? The options are essentially three: (1) to the unbelieving world as an "altar call" (Mounce, *Revelation*, p. 395); (2) to Christ as a petition (Beasley-Murray, *Revelation*, pp. 343–44); or (3) to those believers whose intended response to Revelation is greater devotion to Christ. The second option makes best sense of the immediate context, which is focused by the oracle from the Risen Christ, "I am coming soon" (22:7, 12, 20). The **bride** is the embattled church, whose petition logically arises from a context of social repression and spiritual struggle: Come back here, Christ, and the sooner the better! The **Spirit** participates in this request as the church's Paraclete, given by God to bring comfort in Christ's absence (cf. John 14:18). However, this option does not explain the concluding invitation directed toward those who need grace, not comfort.

While we have argued that John's composition does not intend to conceal the gospel from the unbelieving world and at points even purposes its conversion, his audience is the church. In this light, then, the first option does not make sense of Revelation's epistolary setting: John's benediction is given to an audience of Christian congregations. Further, the Johannine idea of the Spirit limits its realm to the believing community (cf. John 14:16–17); it is not clear, then, why John would have the Spirit invite Christ to return as part of an evangelistic program.

The concluding invitation, **whoever is thirsty . . . take the free gift of the water of life**, is not to introduce the unbeliever to God's justifying grace (contra Beasley-Murray, *Revelation*, p. 345), but rather is meant for those readers who are in need of

God's sanctifying grace. It is for the rededication of believers rather than for the conversion of the lost.

This interplay between the invitation for Christ to return to earth and for the immature believer to return to God is similar to what we find in the NT book of James. The imminence of the Lord's parousia (James 5:7–9) provides incentive to bring back those believers who "wander from the truth" (James 5:19), since they will be saved from the eschatological consequences of "a multitude of sins" (James 5:20). Likewise, John's invitation envisions a promise, especially for those immature believers who have given in to the temptations and fictions of the anti-Christian kingdom: the waters of eternal life, the gift of a gracious God, will flow over those believers who return to God.

22:18–20a / The warning against "adding to or taking away from" the **words . . . of the prophecy** is a rather common literary convention in the ancient world. Most commentators contend that the passage warns scribes to take care when transcribing the manuscript for other audiences. The author's exhortation, then, guards against sloppiness, but also against embellishing the author's composition or even "correcting" it, which would then distort his intended meaning.

John's warning, however, includes **everyone who hears the words . . . of this book**; and he again refers to these words as a **prophecy**—a rule for faith and life (cf. 22:10–11). The force and scope of this warning suggest a theological intention. That is, John is concerned not with scribes who may well copy his composition for other readers in the future, but with his first readers. His concern is not that the Apocalypse will be corrupted during its transmission but that it will be dismissed as unimportant for the faith of its readers. In this sense, John's use of the adding/subtracting motif is parallel to the binding/loosing motif found in Matthew (16:19; 18:18–19). In both contexts, the issue at stake is the continuing authority of divine revelation. Whether we take the penalty literally or as part of John's symbolic world (cf. Mounce, *Revelation*, p. 396), the point of its peril seems clear enough: those who read Revelation are obliged to obey its words to ensure for themselves **the tree of life in the holy city** (cf. Rev. 22:1–5). Not to do so will result in the **plagues described in this book**. In light of the ultimacy of the decision the believer must make upon hearing Revelation's message, the affirmation, **Yes, I am coming soon.**

Amen. is repeated, this third and final time with a sense of heightened urgency: the parousia is imminent and a decision must be immediate.

22:20b–21 / Revelation's last word to its readers is a prayer; it is the normal way in which NT writers end their letters. Even though they are often overlooked by interpreters, closing prayers are not incidental to the author's overarching purposes. While they typically include liturgical conventions, well-known and practiced forms of Christian worship, they typically correspond to and help concentrate the message of the whole composition. Thus, on the one hand, we can speak about the petition, **Come, Lord Jesus** (which translates the traditional benediction, "Marana-tha"; cf. 1 Cor. 16:22), as a significant feature of early Christian worship, especially as a eucharistic prayer. This may further remind us that Revelation was read to congregations gathered for worship (cf. Beasley-Murray, *Revelation*, pp. 348–49). Yet, on the other hand, by setting the petition into the context of Revelation, John gives it meaning that transcends its meaning for Christian liturgy. As Caird puts it, "No one who has read his book can have any illusions about what the prayer is asking. It is a prayer that Christ will come again to win the victory which is both Calvary and Armageddon. It is a prayer that the Christian, confronted by the great ordeal, may 'endure as one who sees the invisible' (Heb. xi. 27), and may hear above the harsh sentence of a Roman judge the triumph song of heaven" (*Revelation*, p. 288).

The same can be said of the second part of John's benediction, which asks that God's **grace** be given to **God's people**. On the one hand, the prayer reflects a theology of grace: God redeems God's people from sin and death and restores them to wholeness by the work of God's unconditional grace, which is made manifest in and conveyed through Jesus Christ and the power of his Spirit. However, when we posit this idea within John's apocalyptic composition, it is given a certain weight, a more specific application that is all important to the readers. Indeed, all of what John sees and hears and then writes down touches on dimensions of God's transforming grace. We are reminded, most especially by the climactic visions of Christ's parousia, that the exercise of divine grace empowers salvation through the Lamb; and we are also reminded that it empowers a response of faithfulness to the Lamb. Both Christian faith and Christian life are gifts of God's grace. Yet, in no other book of Scripture is another, darker side to grace so vividly described as in the visions of God's judgment. God's judging wrath is also an expression of grace (cf. Rom. 1:18). By God's grace the Evil One is defeated and his kingdom is brought down in ruins; and by God's grace, human sin, social evil, Hades, and death are all destroyed. The petition, "Marana-tha!" invites Christ to return both to tear down evil and to build up salvation so that God's grace will fully triumph and God's people will be transformed to live with God and the Lamb forever.

Additional Notes   §21

For a still useful analysis of epistolary benedictions, see Robert Jewett, "The Form and Function of the Homiletic Benediction," *ATR* 51 (1969), pp. 18–34; also Doty, *Letters*, pp. 39–42. The rather general exhortations found in the benedictions of NT letters are not uniquely "Christian" but are usually taken from the pool of moral literature (paranaesis) common to various religious or social movements of the day. What makes them Christian is their adaptation to the situation of a Christian congregation as discussed in the body of the letter. Thus, the author's intentions for his closing advice are consistent with and understood by his purposes for the entire book.

22:6b / The particle **must** (*dei*) is pregnant with meaning. John uses it here as an idiom of prophecy: because God is ultimately committed to the restoration of all things good and the abolition of all things evil, and because God has predicted the full realization of this redemptive program at the Lord's parousia, it **must soon take place**. John's intention, therefore, is to evoke not speculation about the "when" of the "then," but confidence in the "who" of the "then."

22:7b / The present participle, *terōn*, which the NIV translates **keeps**, indicates that the continual observance of the **words of the prophecy in this book** is required. John is not interested in a quick and easy response to his prediction of Christ's soon return; his pastoral ambition is that his audience forge a consistent and persistent response of obedience to the gospel in light of the certain hope of Christ's parousia.

22:12 / The Greek word for **reward**, *misthos*, is used in the NT for those wages justly due a worker. For the worker of evil, the reward is punishment (cf. 2 Pet. 2:13, 15) and for the worker of good, blessing (cf. Matt. 10:41; Luke 6:35).

22:13 / Jesus' self-ascription, **the Alpha and the Omega**, is critical since it refers elsewhere to God (1:8). After maintaining a hierarchy between God and the Risen Jesus (e.g., Father-Son, Sovereign-Lamb), John brings the two together as cosmic equals in his benediction. In his forthcoming monograph, *The Past of Jesus in the Gospels*, SNTSMS 68 (Cambridge: University Press), E. E. Lemcio argues that God's resurrection of Jesus marked a substantive change in his status, and that this change is indicated in the gospel narratives by the contrast between pre-Easter and post-Easter portraits of Jesus. Perhaps a similar contrast can be found in Revelation's description of pre-parousia and post-parousia portraits of the Risen Jesus. If so, then I would suggest that one effect of the parousia will be another substantive change in how the faith community perceives the status of Christ: he is now God's equal—equal parts of the eschatological temple (21:22).

22:14–15 / The use of **dogs** to describe the evildoers is especially harsh. According to Beasley-Murray, to refer to someone as a dog is to express "utmost contempt for him" (*Revelation*, p. 341). I suspect, however, that the term is employed here with cultic rather than sociological emphasis. Those who are evil are ritually unclean like dogs (cf. Deut. 23:18–19), are removed from the **city** of God, and are not allowed to re-enter until purified (cf. Deut. 23:9–11). When reinterpreted by this deuteronomic text and by our interpretation of John's vision of the holy city, Christ's exhortation becomes clearer: those who practice evil are excluded from the eschatological community which has been purified and now enjoys a lasting relationship with God and God's Lamb—the relationship envisioned by the new Jerusalem.

22:16 / In the intertestamental literature, especially reflected by the Dead Sea writings (CD 7.18; 1QPs J 9–18; 1QM 9.6; 4QPBless 5.27), the midrashim on Numbers 24:17 interpret "Jacob's star" as predicting a Davidic messiah. Typically, these commentaries depict a period of release from suffering following the advent of this eschatological "star" (T. Levi 18:3–14; T. Jud. 24:1–6). Against this background, John's reference to a **Morning Star** reflects the Jewish tradition of a Davidic Messiah, who is **Jesus**.

D. Aune has recently argued that the pronoun **you** refers to "the prophetic circle of John of Patmos," which is responsible for the distribution and presentation of John's Revelation to the seven Asian **churches**; cf. "The Prophetic Circle of John of Patmos," *JSNT* 37 (1989), pp. 103–16.

22:17–18 / The word "wander" appears frequently in the OT and NT and in the writings of Second Temple Judaism and earliest Christianity. Typically it refers to moral error which is the result of submitting to the Evil One rather than to God (cf. James 4:7). In this sense, "the Truth" consists not in a creed of theological convictions but in a life of devotion to God. This is precisely what John has in mind. The **water of life** is a metaphor for divine grace which empowers a people to act upon the **words . . . of this book**, because it proclaims the gospel of God by which all people, including believers, will be judged. Thus, the

Lord's soon return as judge (cf. James 5:9) motivates obedience to the truth and demand of God's gospel.

22:18–20 / Notice that John assumes his audience **hears** rather than "reads" his composition. While ancient scribes often transcribed texts which were read to them, it is more likely that John has in mind those congregations to whom the composition is sent and for whom it will be read at a public meeting. The closing prayer, which includes the traditional liturgical response, *Marana-tha,* **Come, Lord Jesus,** suggests that such gatherings were occasions for public worship. In fact, this setting for the reading and hearing of John's Revelation was apropos for the sort of spiritual benefaction that the Pastor-seer intended.

No doubt, John has the vision of bowl-**plagues** in mind, described in 15:1–19:20, since they are directed at those who "refused to repent and glorify God" (16:9, 11; cf. 2:21).

22:21 / The final sentence contains a number of textual problems, and the NIV has decided against the critical text at one point. The Greek text of NA[26] has the concluding phrase as, *meta pantōn,* "with all," opting for the shortest of seven possible readings of this phrase that we find in the textual history of Revelation; cf. Metzger, *TCGNT,* pp. 766–67. Boring translates this phrase, "with all people," arguing that John's theology of grace requires a universal salvation (*Revelation,* pp. 226–31). The NIV, however, has decided in favor of a minority reading, *meta tōn hagiōn,* "with God's people," because of superior internal evidence. Twelve times in Revelation *hagiōn* is used in reference to God's people; (and in 8:3 *hagiōn* is used with *pantōn,* "all of God's people"). This is an important textual decision because of its theological implications. If we follow NA[26], John's benediction at the very least universalizes the book's address: even as God's grace is bestowed first upon the seven Asian congregations in his greeting (1:4), now at book's end God's grace is extended to all those congregations who might read it. Ford may be correct that this prayer is added by a later editor whose concern is no longer the seven congregations who first read John's original composition but the whole church which now reads Revelation as its "scripture" (*Revelation,* p. 424).

For Further Reading

Except for a list of important commentaries on Revelation and another list of helpful background studies, the bibliography follows the major divisions of the outline included in the commentary's Introduction.

Commentaries

Beasley-Murray, G. R. *The Book of Revelation.* NCB. Grand Rapids: Eerdmans, 1974.

Beckwith, I. T. *The Apocalypse of John.* Grand Rapids: Baker, reprint, 1919.

Blevins, J. L. *Revelation.* KPG. Atlanta: John Knox, 1988.

Boring, M. E. *Revelation.* Interpretation. Atlanta: John Knox Press, 1989.

Bowman, J. W. *The Drama of the Book of Revelation.* Philadelphia: Westminster Press, 1955.

Bousset, W. *Die Offenbarung Johannis.* MeyerK. Göttingen: Vandenhoeck & Ruprecht, 1906.

Caird, G. B. *The Revelation of St. John the Divine.* HNTC. New York: Harper & Row, 1966.

Charles, R. H. *A Critical and Exegetical Commentary on the Revelation of St. John.* 2 vols. ICC. Edinburgh: T. & T. Clark, 1920.

Collins, A. Y. *The Apocalypse.* NTM. Wilmington, Del.: Glazier, 1979.

_____. *Crisis & Catharsis: The Power of the Apocalypse.* Philadelphia: Westminster Press, 1984.

Eller, V. *The Most Revealing Book of the Bible.* Grand Rapids: Eerdmans, 1974.

Ellul, J. *Apocalypse: The Book of Revelation.* New York: Seabury, 1977.

Farrer, A. M. *The Revelation of St. John the Divine.* Oxford: University Press, 1964.

Ford, J. M. *Revelation.* AB. Garden City, N.Y.: Doubleday, 1975.

Glasson, T. F. *The Revelation of John.* CBC. Cambridge: University Press, 1965.

Hadorn, W. *Die Offenbarung des Johannes.* THKNT. Leipzig: Deichert, 1928.

Hendricksen, W. *More than Conquerors: an Interpretation of the Book of Revelation*. Grand Rapids: Baker, 1940.

Kiddle, M. *The Revelation of St. John*. MNTC. London: Hodder & Stoughton, 1940.

Kraft, H. *Die Offenbarung des Johannes*. HNT. Tübingen: J. C. B. Mohr, 1974.

Krodel, G. A. *Revelation*. ACNT. Minneapolis: Augsburg, 1989.

Ladd, G. E. *A Commentary on the Revelation of John*. Grand Rapids: Eerdmans, 1972.

Lohmeyer, E. *Die Offenbarung Johannes*. HNT. Tübingen: J. C. B. Mohr, 1953.

Lohse, E. *Die Offenbarung des Johannes*, 12th ed. NTD. Göttingen: Vandenhoeck & Ruprecht, 1979.

Morris, L. *The Revelation of St. John*. TNTC. Grand Rapids: Eerdmans, 1969.

Mounce, R. H. *The Book of Revelation*. NICNT. Grand Rapids: Eerdmans, 1977.

Müller, U. *Die Offenbarung des Johannes*. Wurzburg: Echter-Verlag, 1984.

Rissi, M. *Time and History: a Study on the Revelation*. ET. Richmond, Va.: John Knox Press, 1966.

Schüssler Fiorenza, E. *The Book of Revelation: Justice and Judgment*. Philadelphia: Fortress Press, 1985.

Sweet, J. P. M. *Revelation*. WPC. Philadelphia: Westminster Press, 1979.

Swete, H. B. *The Apocalypse of St. John*. Grand Rapids: Eerdmans, 1906.

Tenney, M. C. *Interpreting Revelation*. Grand Rapids: Eerdmans, 1957.

Walvoord, J. F. *The Revelation of Jesus Christ*. Chicago: Moody Press, 1966.

Zahn, T. *Die Offenbarung des Johannes*, 2 vols. KNT. Leipzig/Erlangen: Diechert, 1924–26.

Other Studies: Theological, Historical and Literary Background

Aune, D. E. *The New Testament in its Literary Environment*. Philadelphia: Westminster Press, 1987.

_____. "The Apocalypse of John and Graeco-Roman Revelatory Magic." *NTS* 33 (1986), pp. 481–501.

Barr, D. L. "The Apocalypse as a Symbolic Transformation of the World." *Interp* 38 (1984), pp. 39–50.

_____. "The Apocalypse of John as Oral Enactment." *Interp* 40 (1986), pp. 243–56.

Barrett, C. K. "The Lamb of God." *NTS* 1 (1954–55), pp. 210–18.

Bauckham, R. J. "Eschatological Earthquake in the Apocalypse of John." *NovT* 19 (1977), pp. 224–33.

_____. "The Role of the Spirit in the Apocalypse." *EQ* 52 (1980), pp. 66–83.

_____. "The Worship of Jesus in Apocalyptic Christianity." *NTS* 27 (1981), pp. 322–341.

Beale, G. K. *The Use of Daniel in Jewish Apocalyptic Literature and in the Revelation of St. John.* Lanham, Md.: University Press of America, 1984.

Beardslee, W. "New Testament Apocalyptic in Recent Interpretation." *Interp* 25 (1971), pp. 419–35.

Beasley-Murray, G. R. "The Contribution of the Book of Revelation to the Christian Belief in Immorality." *SJT* 27 (1974), pp. 76–93.

Beker, J. C. *Paul's Apocalyptic Gospel.* Philadelphia: Fortress Press, 1982.

Bowman, J. W. "The Revelation to John: Its Dramatic Structure and Message." *Interp* 9 (1955), pp. 436–53.

Braaten, C. E. "The Significance of Apocalypticism for Systematic Theology." *Interp* 25 (1971), pp. 480–99.

Brownlee, W. H. "The Priestly Character of the Church in the Apocalypse." *NTS* 5 (1958), pp. 224–25.

Bruce, F. F. "The Spirit in the Apocalypse." In *Christ and Spirit in the New Testament. Essays in Honour of C. D. F. Moule.* Edited by B. Lindars and S. S. Smalley. Pages 333–44. Cambridge: University Press, 1973.

Cambier, J. "Les images de l'Ancien Testament dans l'Apocalypse de Saint Jean." *NRT* 77 (1955), pp. 113–22.

Charles, R. H. *Eschatology.* New York: Schocken, reprint, 1963.

Charlesworth, J. H. *The Old Testament Pseudepigrapha*, 2 vols. Garden City, N.Y.: Doubleday, 1983–85.

Collins, A. Y. "The Revelation of John: An Apocalyptic Response to a Social Crisis." *CurrTM* 8 (1981), pp. 4–12.

_____. "Reading the Book of Revelation in the 20th Century." *Interp* 40 (1986), pp. 229–42.

_____. "Women's History and the Book of Revelation," *SBLSemPap* 26 (1987), pp. 80–91.

Collins, J. J., ed. *Apocalypse: The Morphology of a Genre.* Semeia 14. Missoula, Mont.: Scholars Press, 1979.

_____. *The Apocalyptic Imagination: An Introduction to the Jewish Matrix of Christianity.* New York: Crossroad, 1984.

Court, J. M. *Myth and History in the Book of Revelation.* London: SPCK, 1979.

Farrer, A. *A Rebirth of Images.* London: Dacre, 1949.

Ford, J. M. "*Shalom* in the Johannine Corpus." *HorBT* 6 (1984), pp. 67–89.

Geyser, A. "The Twelve Tribes of Israel: Judean and Judeo-Christian Apocalypticism." *NTS* 28 (1982), pp. 388–99.

Goulder, M. D. "The Apocalypse as an Annual Cycle of Prophecies." *NTS* 27 (1981), pp. 342–67.

Hamerton-Kelly, R. G. "The Temple and the Origins of Jewish Apocalyptic." *VT* 20 (1970), pp. 1–15.

Hanson, A. T. *The Wrath of the Lamb.* London: SPCK, 1957.

Hennecke, E. and W. Schneemelcher. *New Testament Apocrypha.* 2 vols. Philadelphia: Westminster Press, 1963–64, esp. 2:581–641.

Holtz, T. *Die Christologie der Apokalypse des Johannes.* 2nd ed. TU 85. Berlin: Akademie-Verlag, 1971.

Hooker, M. D. *Continuity and Discontinuity: Christianity in its Jewish Setting.* London: Epworth Press, 1986.

Hopkins, M. "The Historical Perspective of Apocalypse 1–11." *CBQ* 27 (1965), pp. 42–47.

Jenkins, F. *The Old Testament in the Book of Revelation.* Grand Rapids: Eerdmans, 1976.

Johnson, S. E. "Early Christianity in Asia Minor." *JBL* 77 (1958), pp. 1–17.

Klassen, W. "Vengeance in the Apocalypse of John." *CBQ* 28 (1966), pp. 300–11.

Koch, K. *The Rediscovery of Apocalyptic.* SBT 2/22. Naperville, Ill.: Allenson, 1972.

Ladd, G. E. "New Testament Apocalyptic." *RevEx* 78 (1981), pp. 205–09.

_____. "The Theology of the Apocalypse." *GorR* 7 (1963), pp. 73–86.

Lindsey, H. *The Late Great Planet Earth.* Grand Rapids: Zondervan, 1970.

_____. *There's a New World Coming*. Ventura, Calif.: Vision House, 1973.

Lohse, E. "Apokalyptik und Christologie." *ZNW* 62 (1971), pp. 48–67.

MacRae, G. W. "Gnosticism and the Church of John's Gospel." In *Nag Hammadi: Gnosticism and Early Christianity*. Edited by C. W. Hedrick and R. Hodgson, Jr. Pages 89–96. Peabody, Mass.: Hendrickson, 1986.

Marshall, I. H. "Martyrdom and the Parousia in the Revelation of John." In *Studia Evangelica*, vol. IV, 333–39. Berlin: Akademie-Verlag, 1968.

Megivern, J. "Wrestling with Revelation." *BTB* 8 (1978), pp. 147–54.

Michaels, J. R. "Jewish and Christian Apocalyptic Letters: 1 Peter, Revelation and 2 Baruch." *SBLSemPap* 26 (1987), pp. 268–75.

Minear, P. S. "Eschatology and History." *Interp* 5 (1951), pp. 27–39.

_____. "The Cosmology of the Apocalypse." In *Current Issues in New Testament Interpretation. Essays in Honor of O. Piper*. Edited by W. Klassen, 23–37. New York: Harper & Row, 1962.

_____. "Some Archetypal Origins of Apocalyptic Prediction." *HorBT* 1 (1980), pp. 105–35.

_____. *New Testament Apocalyptic*. IBT. Nashville: Abingdon, 1981.

O'Donovan, O. "The Political Thought of the Book of Revelation." *TynB* 37 (1986), pp. 61–94.

O'Rourke, J. J. "The Hymns of the Apocalypse." *CBQ* 30 (1969), pp. 399–409.

Parker, H. M. "The Scriptures of the Author of the Revelation of John." *IliffR* 37 (1980), pp. 35–51.

Peterson, E. "The Apocalyptic Pastor." *RefJ* 38 (1988), pp. 16–20.

Rissi, M. "The Kerygma of the Revelation to John." *Interp* 22 (1968), pp. 3–17.

Roberts, J. W. "The Interpretation of the Apocalypse." *RQ* 8 (1965), pp. 154–62.

Robinson, J. A. T. *Redating the New Testament*. Philadelphia: Westminster Press, 1976.

Russell, D. S. *The Method and Message of Jewish Apocalyptic, 200 B.C.–A.D. 100*. OTL. Philadelphia: Westminster Press, 1964.

Schmithals, W. *The Apocalyptic Movement*. Nashville: Abingdon, 1975.

Shepherd, M. H. *The Paschal Liturgy and the Apocalypse*. Richmond: John Knox Press, 1960.

Smalley, S. S. "John's Revelation and John's Community." *BJRL* 69 (1987), pp. 549–71.

Stauffer, E. *Christ and the Caesars.* Philadelphia: Westminster Press, 1955.

Stendahl, K. "Apocalypse of John and the Epistles of Paul in the Muratorian Fragment." In *Current Issues in New Testament Interpretation. Essays in Honor of O. Piper.* Edited by W. Klassen. Pages 239–45. New York: Harper & Row, 1962.

Strand, K. A. "The Book of Revelation: A Review Article on Some Recent Literature." *AUSS* 11 (1973), pp. 181–93.

Thompson, L. "Cult and Eschatology in the Apocalypse of John." *JR* 49 (1969), pp. 330–50.

_____. "A Sociological Analysis of Tribulation in the Apocalypse of John." *Semeia* 36 (1986), pp. 147–74.

Trites, A. A. "*Martys* and Martyrdom in the Apocalypse: a Semantic Study." *NovT* 15 (1973), pp. 72–80.

Trudinger, P. "The Apocalypse and the Palestinian Targum." *BTB* 16 (1986), pp. 78–9.

Vanhoye, A. "L'utilisation du livre d'Ezechiel dans l'Apocalypse." *Bib* 43 (1962), pp. 436–67.

Wilder, A. N. "The Rhetoric of Ancient and Modern Apocalyptic." *Interp* 25 (1971), pp. 436–53.

Wolff, C. "Die Gemeinde des Christus in der Apokalypse des Johannes." *NTS* 27 (1981), pp. 186–97.

Other Studies: The Greeting (Rev. 1–3)

Aune, D. E. "St. John's Portrait of the Church in the Apocalypse." *EQ* 38 (1966), pp. 131–49.

Barrett. C. K. "Gnosis and the Apocalypse of John." In *The New Testament and Gnosis.* Edited by A. Logan. Edinburgh: T. & T. Clark, 1983.

Buchanan, G. W. "The Word of God and the Apocalyptic Vision." *SBLSemPap* 14 (1978), pp. 183–92.

Charlesworth, J. "The Jewish Roots of Christology." *SJT* 39 (1986), pp. 19–41.

Jeske, R. L. "Spirit and Community in the Johannine Apocalypse." *NTS* 31 (1985), pp. 452–66.

Kirby, J. T. "The Rhetorical Situations of Revelation 1–3." *NTS* 34 (1988), pp. 197–207.

Mackay, W. M. "Another Look at the Nicolaitans." *EQ* 45 (1973), pp. 111–15.

Morrice, W. G. "John the seer." *ExpT* 97 (1985), pp. 43–46.

Muse, R. "Revelation 2–3: A Critical Analysis of Seven Prophetic Messages." *JETS* 29 (1986), pp. 147–61.

Osten S., P. von. "Christologie, Taufe, Homologie: Ein Beitrag zu Apok Joh 1,5f." *ZNW* 58 (1967), pp. 255–66.

Pesch, R. "Offenbarung Jesu Christi: Eine Auslegung von Apk 1,1–3." *BibLeb* 11 (1970), pp. 15–29.

Popkes, W. "Die Funktion der Sendschreiben in der Apokalypse: Zugleich ein Beitrag zur Spatgeschichte der neutestamentlichen Gleichnisse (Apk 2–3)." *ZNW* 74 (1983), pp. 90–107.

Rife, J. M. "The Literary Background of Revelation II–III." *JBL* 60 (1941), pp. 179–82.

Rowland, C. "The Vision of the Risen Christ in Rev. 1:13ff.: the Debt of an Early Christology to an Aspect of Jewish Angelology." *JTS* 31 (1980), pp. 1–11.

Sanders, J. N. "St. John on Patmos." *NTS* 9 (1962–63), pp. 75–85.

Sweet, J. P. M. "Maintaining the Testimony of Jesus: The Suffering of Christians in the Revelation of John." In *Suffering and Martyrdom in the New Testament*. Edited by W. Horbury. Pages 101–17. Cambridge: University Press, 1980.

Thomas, R. L. "John's Apocalyptic Outline (Rev. 1:19)." *BibSac* 123 (1966), pp. 334–41.

Other Studies: Thanksgiving (Rev. 4)

Boring, E. "The Theology of Revelation: 'the Lord our God the Almighty Reigns'." *Interp* 40 (1986), pp. 257–69.

Hammerton, H. J. "Unity of Creation in the Apocalypse." *CQR* 168 (1967), pp. 20–33.

Hurtado, L. W. "Revelation 4–5 in the Light of Jewish Apocalyptic Analogies." *JSNT* 25 (1985), pp. 105–24.

Mowry, L. "Revelation 4–5 and Early Christian Liturgical Usage." *JBL* 71 (1952), pp. 227–31.

Schubert, P. *Form and Function of the Pauline Thanksgivings*. Berlin, 1939.

Tenney, M. "The Theism of the Apocalypse." In *The Living and Active Word of God*. Edited by M. Inch and R. Youngblood. Winona Lake, Ind.: Eisenbrauns, 1983.

Vogtle, A. "Der Gott der Apokalypse: Wie redet die christliche Apokalypse von Gott?" In *La notion biblique de Dieu*. BETL 41. Edited by J. Coppens, 377–98. Louvain: Louvain University Press, 1976.

Other Studies: Sermon (Rev. 5:1–22:6a)

Bruns, J. E. "The Contrasted Women of Apoc. 12 and 17." *CBQ* 26 (1964), pp. 459–63.

Davis, D. R. "The Relationship Between the Seals, Trumpets, and Bowls in the Book of Revelation." *JETS* 16 (193), pp. 149–58.

Deutsch, C. "Transformation of Symbols: the New Jerusalem in Rev 21:1–22:5." *ZNW* 78 (1987), pp. 106–26.

Dyer, C. "The Identity of Babylon in Revelation 17–18." *BibSac* 144 (1987), pp. 305–16, 433–49.

Gaechter, P. "The Original Sequence of Apocalypse 20–22." *TS* 10 (1949), pp. 485–521.

Giblin, C. H. "Structural and Thematic Correlations in the Theology of Revelation 12–22." *Bib* 55 (1974), pp. 487–504.

_____. "Revelation 11:1–13: Its Form, Function, and Contextual Integration." *NTS* 30 (1984), pp. 433–59.

Longman, T. "The Divine Warrior: the New Testament Use of an Old Testament Motif." *WTJ* 44 (1982), pp. 290–307.

Prigent, P. *Apocalypse 12: Histoire de l'exegese*. BGBE-2. Tübingen: J. C. B. Mohr, 1959.

Schneemelcher, W. "Kirche und Staat im Neuen Testament." In *Kirche und Staat. Essays in Honor of H. Kunst*. Edited by K. Aland. Pages 1–18. Tübingen: J. C. B. Mohr, 1967.

Shea, W. "Revelation 5 and 19 as Literary Reciprocals." *AUSS* 22 (1984), pp. 249–57.

Staples, P. "Rev. XVI.4–6 and its Vindication Formula." *NovT* 14 (1972), pp. 280–93.

Strobel, A. "Abfassung und Geschichtstheologie der Apokalypse nach Kap. XVII. 9–12." *NTS* 10 (1964), pp. 433–45.

Unnik, W. C. van. " 'Worthy is the Lamb': The Background of Apoc 5." In *Melanges bibliques en hommage au R. P. Beda Rigaux*. Edited by A. Descamps and A. de Halleux. Pages 21–46. Gembloux: Duculot, 1970.

Other Studies: Benediction (Rev. 22:6b–21)

Beasley-Murray, G. R. "The Second Coming in the Book of Revelation." *EQ* 23 (1951), pp. 40–45.

Muller, B. "Die Epiloog van die Openbaring aan Johannes (22:6–21)." *Scriptura* 6 (1982), pp. 57–64.

Subject Index

Scripture Index